Premarital Counseling

Premarital Counseling

The Professional's Handbook

Second edition

Robert F. Stahmann
Brigham Young University

William J. Hiebert
Marriage and Family Counseling Service

Lexington Books
D.C. Heath and Company/Lexington, Massachusetts/Toronto

Library of Congress Cataloging-in-Publication Data

Stahmann, Robert F.
  Premarital counseling.

  Includes index.
  1. Marriage counseling.   I. Hiebert, William J.
II. Title.
HQ10.S7   1987   362.8'2   86–45593
ISBN 0–669–13925–4 (alk. paper)

Published simultaneously in Canada
Printed in the United States of America
International Standard Book Number: 0–669–13925–4
Library of Congress Catalog Card Number: 86–45593

The paper used in this publication meets the minimum requirements of American National
Standard for Information Sciences—Permanence of Paper for Printed Library Materials, ANSI
Z39.48–1984. ⊗™

87 88 89 90 8 7 6 5 4 3 2 1

To those who desire to strengthen premarital and marital relationships, their own or others'.

Contents

Figures

Preface

E ach year, in the United States, approximately 2,500,000 couples marry and some 1,250,000 couples divorce. Some 61 percent of adult women and 66 percent of adult men are married. And, while it is projected that 40 to 50 percent of couples may divorce at least once, the remarriage rates show that 75 to 80 percent of those persons who divorce, remarry. Marriage is big business and tremendous economic and psychological resources go into it. More and more, as people examine the strengths and shortcomings of marriage, they turn to premarital counselors in an attempt to gain assistance in strengthening or evaluating their potential for a stable and satisfactory marital relationship.

Our primary goal in writing and updating this book is to provide a definitive guide on the process and content of premarital counseling. In the seven years since the first edition, significant additions have been made in the literature on premarital counseling. We have attempted to reflect those in our text and bibliography. The expanded bibliography provides primary references and resources to enable the reader to pursue ideas or topics in their original source or in greater detail than was possible to present in a single volume.

The book has been written for those professionals who do premarital counseling, with a sensitivity to the interdisciplinary backgrounds of those persons who provide the service. We are aware that the clergy provide most of the premarital counseling that is done in the United States. Others in the fields of marriage and family therapy, social work, psychology, counseling, and medicine also provide premarital and remarital counseling. Thus, as we have written the book, we have attempted to speak to these many professionals, keeping in mind their various roles and responsibilities.

The book is appropriate for persons who are currently doing premarital counseling or who have been engaged in the process for a number of years. We believe that it will provide them with some refreshing insights and ideas about new ways to approach their counseling process. Students in marriage and family counseling practicums and academic courses will find the book useful. We are aware that there are also sophisticated lay counselors who are involved in the premarital counseling process, usually through church-affiliated programs. Undoubtedly, such persons will find the content of the book to be valuable to them.

Clergy, whether in practice or academic preparation, will find that we have attempted to specifically address their settings. Recent evidence is that perhaps 60 percent of premarital couples have at least one "counseling" session with a religious leader prior to marriage, and some percent of those have more in-depth premarital counseling.

We have divided the book into five parts which, considered together as a whole, include what we believe to be salient and complete considerations of the premarital counseling process. However, each of these parts focuses on a specific aspect of the premarital counseling process and may be read and understood separately. The intent of the book is to provide specific information and ideas and yet, to stimulate approaches to premarital counseling so that the reader adds to and creates approaches to the counseling process that are beyond those presented in the book or in the reader's previous practice.

I
Foundations of Premarital Counseling

1
An Overview: Developments in Premarital Counseling

Over thirty years ago, a marriage counselor indicated that if one were to judge by current divorce rates in the United States, it would be easy to conclude that many marriages take place with little if any serious planning or preparation for marriage and family life (Butterfield 1956). Certainly, this comment is being validated today, and reflects the attitude of many marriage and family counselors.

In talking with the general population, we would likely find that premarital counseling is a widely accepted idea. Probably most marriage counselors would acknowledge that premarital counseling in some form is valuable. There is, however, little written as to the practice of premarital counseling and even less reported about the evaluation of its effectiveness.

This book, then, is an attempt to bring together the current ideas and information related to the practice of premarital counseling. This chapter commences with a discussion of the background and history of premarital counseling. Then, characteristics of healthy and well-functioning premarital couples and interpersonal relationships are presented as a foundation for the premarital counseling process that is developed throughout the book.

Background of Premarital Counseling

Today, as in the past, there are three main groups that provide most premarital counseling (Stahmann and Barclay-Cope 1977). These groups are the clergy, physicians, and professional mental health workers.

Nationally, it is assumed that clergy provide most of the premarital counseling. It has been reported that in the United States during 1977, 79.2 percent of first marriages and 60.6 percent of remarriages were performed in religious, rather than civil, ceremonies (Albrecht, Bahr, and Goodman 1983). Olson (1983) estimated that clergy may have some premarital discussion, group education, or counseling with approximately two-thirds of couples who marry. Schonick (1975) documented that members of the clergy performed premarital counseling for a majority of a sample of California couples. In her study of 4,000 couples who applied for marriage licenses, 2,745 (68 percent) had used the clergy for premarital counseling.

Since the premarital physical examination is frequently required within thirty days of the application for a marriage license, physicians have little time for long-term premarital counseling. Even though premarital counseling has been historically associated with clergy and physicians, this brief time available prior to the marriage ceremony, after the contact and suggestion for premarital counseling have been made, means that the offered counseling is usually very brief and probably superficial. A recent noteworthy exception is a model described by Trainer (1979) for physicians to use in conjoint couple premarital and postmarital counseling.

Professionally trained mental health workers and marital and family counselors or therapists have long been identified as persons who provide premarital counseling. Usually the practice has been for these persons to work with troubled premarital cases. In recent years, however, there has been a significant increase in the number of preventive approaches to premarital counseling offered by professionals (Glendening and Wilson 1972, Hinkle and Moore 1971, Meadows and Taplin 1970, Stahmann and Hiebert 1977a,b, Van Zoost 1973).

Such diversity has not always been the case. Apparently, the first mention of premarital counseling as a significant process or a service of value in building emotional and physical health was in a 1928 article in the *American Journal of Obstetrics and Gynecology* (Dickenson 1928). From that time until the mid-1950s, the primary literature dealing with premarital counseling was focused toward the physician and the premarital physical examination (Matheson 1976). In the 1950s, the clergy began to develop a literature relating to premarital counseling (Burkhart 1950, Dicks 1950, Fairchild 1959, Foster and Laidlaw 1950, Mace 1952, Smith 1950, Tinque 1958, Wiser 1959). Concurrently, a professional literature apart from medicine and theology began to develop (Mudd 1957, Stone and Levine 1956).

Although there is little in the literature about the historical development of premarital counseling, our examination has led us to divide it into two basic segments. The primary shift in emphasis seems to have come following World War II.

Premarital Counseling before World War II

The professions that were providing premarital services of one kind or another prior to that time fall into two general categories: clergy and counseling professionals. We want to explore briefly the attitudes of these two professional groups before World War II.

Psychology. From 1900 until the beginning of World War II, psychology as a discipline and profession was coming into its own. With Freud and his contemporaries came the development of theoretical schools in the understanding of human personality. Psychology, to establish itself as its own discipline and profession, had to separate itself from medicine. But the origin of psychological thought, at least in its initial stages, was part and parcel of the medical world. In spite of the struggle between medicine and psychology over the issue of the supremacy and the validity of psychology, the context of birth for psychology was medicine. The medical framework, being essentially pathologically oriented and focusing on repairing the dysfunctional, influenced psychology and affected its orientation (Ackerman, Beatman, and Sherman 1961; Glick and Kessler 1974).

With this pathological orientation, the focus of psychology as it was translated into therapy was essentially individual and intrapsychic. This was a natural and logical progression from the medical framework into which psychology was born. There is evidence in the literature, however, that some early twentieth century theoreticians and clinicians postulated the importance of the family unit and the value of treating more than just the individual (Freud 1959; Rudin 1916; Moreno 1957; Sullivan 1927; Kasanin, Knight, and Sage 1934; Ackerman 1938; Kardiner 1939). Nonetheless, development of an interactional focus, the awareness of and concern about what transpires between people, did not seriously enter the psychological world until well into the mid-twentieth century (Jackson 1973).

Prior to World War II, given the individual, intrapsychic orientation, premarital counseling as we understand it today was hardly in evidence. The individual premarital counselor with an intrapsychic orientation, working in a psychological setting, would not have seen the couple together and would not have been essentially concerned about the nature of their interpersonal relationship. At that time, the typical theoretical orientation was such that any problem in the marital relationship was seen as a by-product of a problem within an individual. Neurotic or psychotic individuals caused problematic marriages. If a marriage had not commenced, there could hardly be a problem; the marriage would need to have commenced in order for the problem to have developed. With that understanding, then, the counselor in an exclusively psychological setting would hardly have involved himself or herself in the kind of premarital counseling we know today.

Theology. Early in the development of the Christian church, clergy became involved with premarital couples in one way or another. Although the early Christians saw marriage as a private, noninstitutionalized arrangement entered into with the consent of parents and without the need for priestly or civil authorization, the Christianization of Western Europe and the entrance of the church into the very fabric of political life changed the involvement of both the state and the church in marriage. Although initially the wedding ceremony was without benefit of clergy, by 398 A.D., the Synod of Carthage had already assumed the use of a priestly benediction in the ceremony (Christensen 1964, Walker 1959).

Running parallel to the growing involvement in marriage of the church and subsequently the state was the issue of permission. In the historical context, marriages were arranged. The power of parents to control the lives of unmarried children was unsurpassed. Since children in essence did not have any standing in terms of legal entity or power under the common law of the day, the control of parents was absolute. Permission also became an issue in regard to the clergy. Several of the early church fathers, such as Ignatius and Polycarp, began urging that permission to marry be received not only from parents, but also from the bishop.

But the issue of permission was not restricted to the concern of parents and clergy. Civil authorities also were concerned with permitting couples to wed. Not only were the familial and clerical structures hierarchical and monarchical; so was the civil structure. As Europe became increasingly feudal, overlords began to demand the right to oppose or consent to a marriage. By the Middle Ages, the concept of requiring a couple to have permission to marry from parents, clergy, and overlords was clearly established (Christensen 1964).

Another issue was the institutionalization of marriage. Although the early church was frequently negative toward marriage, seeing celibacy as the ideal, it became increasingly concerned about the nature of marriage and its relation to and connection with Christian life in general. As theological thought became more concentrated and structured on the issue of marriage itself, the church more and more involved itself with both the wedding ceremony and a concern for the nature of the couple's relationship. By the year 1164, the church had officially established marriage as a sacrament. With this movement came a special involvement of clergy with premarital couples (Cannon 1960, Christensen 1964, Nichols 1956).

What happened in regard to clergy involvement with premarital couples paralleled what happened in regard to clergy involvement with people involved in other initiatory sacraments. An example is the sacrament of baptism, a rite of initiation into the life of the church. In the beginnings of the Christian church, clergy began educating people about the nature of the rite and its meaning in Christian life. The reception of Communion was another kind of initiation, the initiation into the new status of adulthood in Christian life and in church life. A similar educational process developed in regard to Holy Communion and First Communion. Clergy soon began teaching people about the meaning of the sacrament prior to their receiving it. With these educational patterns established with regard to initiatory rites, it was natural that the clergy should follow a similar process in regard to marriage. In a theological sense, marriage also could be viewed as a kind of initiation rite. It brought a man and a woman into a new and different relationship with each other and with God. Thus, clergy began seeing couples prior to the wedding.

The prewedding sessions conducted by clergy prior to World War II followed the kind of instructional pattern that was typical of the other initiatory rites. The emphasis was on the nature and meaning of the rite itself: the Christian nature of marriage, the place of religion in the home, and the rehearsal of the wedding rite. With this brief historical overview, it can be seen that although clergy were involved in prewedding sessions with couples long before secular counseling professionals were on the scene, the nature of these sessions was considerably different from what we conceptualize today.

Premarital Counseling after World War II

Following World War II, there was a series of developments in the general field of psychology which made an impact both on theories of personality and human interaction (psychology) and on theories and models of ministry (theology).

Psychology. In the 1940s and the 1950s, a new concern developed in the field of psychology in general and in clinical practice in particular. As we indicated earlier, prior to World War II the focus was on individual and intrapsychic problems. With the 1940s and 1950s came a concern with the behavioral problems of children which brought with it a focus on the parent-child relationship. This concern had as its by-product the child guidance movement in America and the establishment of child guidance centers throughout the United States (Burgum 1942, Sherman and Kraines 1943, Richardson 1945). The expansion of the field of vision in terms of both theory and practice, moving away from the individual and expanding to the parent-child relationship, brought a new era of concern about what was transpiring *between* people as well as about what was going on *inside* people (Ackerman, Beatman, and Sherman 1961; Glick and Kessler 1974; Jackson 1973).

With the 1950s and 1960s came another concern. The focus of many of the researchers in that period was on the problem of schizophrenia. It was the unsolved problem of psychology, and there were no clear answers as to its nature and its treatment. Early in this century, the schizophrenic was examined and understood in individualistic, pathological terms. By the 1940s, researchers had begun to focus on the relationship between the schizophrenic patient and his or her mother (Fromm-Reichmann 1948). By the 1950s, researchers were focusing on the relationship between the schizophrenic and his or her father (Lidz and Lidz 1949, Lidz et al. 1958). As a result of significant work in the area of schizophrenia, a whole new understanding was gained, not only of the importance of the interactions between all family members, but also of the importance of the interactions between husband and wife. The by-product of this research became the movement that is known today as marital and family therapy (Glick and Kessler 1974, Jackson 1973).

Although significant work has been done since World War II in expanding the purview of psychology, it should be remembered that these developments have run parallel to an ongoing interest in the individual and intrapsychic problems. While exciting research was taking place in the field of human interaction, the primary emphasis has remained on the individual and intrapsychic makeup. In spite of the developments in the field of psychology in the 1950s and 1960s, psychology has maintained a pathological orientation. The medical model has been dominant in many of the schools of thought regarding theories of personality and human interaction. A repair orientation rather than a preventive orientation still dominates the field of psychology, both in general and in the practice of counseling.

As a way of summarizing the historical movement after World War II, we can say that while psychology and psychotherapy still maintained a heavy individual and intrapsychic focus, the development of the field of marital and family therapy moved the attention of psychology more toward interactional aspects. More important, however, the theory began to shift. As the research in marital and family therapy increased, it became evident that marital relationships and their health or lack of health were related to something beyond the mental health of the individuals in the marriage. It became clear that it really was possible to have an unhealthy marital relationship between two relatively healthy people.

Even more significant, with the theoretical framework now looking specifically at the nature of the interaction within the family and especially within the marital dyad, the relationship itself became an issue of focus. Furthermore, the emphasis was not only on the relationship itself, but also on the growing understanding that the marital relationship was not accidental but purposeful. There was also acknowledgment that some kind of bond maintained the relationship. Thus, marital and family therapists began to look at the relationship as having an existence prior to the wedding. All of this, of course, set the stage for the increased interest of later marital and family therapists in premarital counseling.

Nonetheless, premarital counseling conducted by professionals was still relatively uncommon in the 1960s. Because interactional theory was still in its infancy in the 1950s and 1960s, clinicians in the field still tended to conceptualize marital problems as the problem of one individual in the relationship. Premarital counseling as we understand it today, therefore, was not a regular part of professional clinical practice. In 1964, a survey of the professional members of the American Association of Marriage and Family Counselors indicated that practitioners of that association performed very little formal premarital counseling (Rutledge 1966).

Theology. With the developments in the general field of psychology in the 1940s and 1950s came a number of intrusions in the field of theology. Several pioneering members of the clergy had become interested in psychology as a way of expanding and understanding the nature of ministry. These individuals, with their interest in psychology and theology, initiated a movement that we can generally recognize by the name of pastoral counseling.

The pioneering clergy who had much to do with the initiation of the pastoral counseling movement were indebted, theoretically speaking, to psychoanalytic thought. As we indicated earlier, psychoanalytic thought had its origins in the medical model and in a pathological framework. Pastoral counseling, therefore, developed a heavy bias toward the pathological orientation and the medical model. This can be clearly seen in an address given by Robert Laidlow, a psychiatrist in the field of marital therapy. Speaking at a professional meeting in 1948, Laidlow, while discussing the role of the clergy in premarital counseling, indicated that the task was to serve as a screening agent and assess the health of the couple moving toward the wedding (Johnson 1953).

We postulate that with the development of the pastoral counseling movement came the shift in the attitude of the clergy toward ministry in general, but specifically toward situations that had a counseling context or quality. The shift was away from the educational, informational stance outlined earlier and toward a search for pathology and a more pathological orientation.

The role of the minister as a screening agent becomes more pronounced in the literature of pastoral counseling and specifically of premarital counseling in the 1950s and 1960s. Johnson (1953) indicates that he sees the pastor as being responsible for a marriage's continuing growth. Stewart (1970) sees the role of the pastor as that of examining the emotional readiness and maturity of a couple for marriage. Rutledge (1966) also sees the role of the clergy, and of the secular counselor, as that of examining the emotional readiness of a couple for marriage. Even Olson (1976) comments that premarital counseling for both clergy and nonclergy had had a repair orientation and a pathological focus up to that point in time.

The shift in seminary education and the new emphasis on pastoral counseling in general brought an entirely new dimension. Now the task was not simply to rehearse the wedding and instruct the couple about the Christian nature of marriage, but also to examine the emotional and psychological readiness of the couple for marriage. This became coupled with a parallel development: an increasing divorce rate. The implication that a couple who had been thoroughly examined would not be susceptible to divorce placed the clergy in the position of having the ultimate responsibility for determining the outcome of the marriage. This development, we suspect, has had a great deal to do with the tendency toward ambivalence and disillusionment in regard to their role in premarital counseling which ministers often demonstrate. On the one hand, pastors are asked to accept people as they are and minister to them at that level; on the other hand, pastors are asked to examine the psychological state of the couple and intervene in a marriage in which a certain lack of health is present. In addition, ministers, being representatives both of the church and of the state, are asked to perform the wedding on purely civil grounds. With that three-part mix, the minister who takes seriously all three roles at the same time is likely to have succumbed, in years of ministry, to a state of numbness or helplessness in resolving the dilemma.

Educational and Counseling Emphases

In recent years, the development of academic courses in marriage and family preparation—usually at the college level, but often now at the secondary level as well—has increased. The first such course was titled "Preparation for Marriage and Family Living" and was offered at Boston University in 1924 by Ernest R. Groves (Matheson 1976).

In 1929, a similar course was offered at Teachers College, Columbia University. Today, similar courses exist on almost every university campus.

Earlier writers saw premarital counseling as primarily an educational and informational service. Butterfield (1956) pointed out that just as persons develop skills in social life, so they must develop skills in family life and in functioning well in the marital relationship. He indicated that many young people were disappointed or developed problems in marriage because they brought to it very little in the way of useful skills or helpful attitudes.

Ellis (1961) argued that another cause of marital failure was ignorance about the nature of marriage itself. He observed that many people entering marriage do not have even the most elementary preparation for the demands that marriage makes on them. Ellis indicated that it is assumed that persons entering marriage will automatically know how to adapt themselves to it, when in fact this is often not the case.

Later, following a similar line of thought, Rutledge (1966) postulated that although marriage itself could be a maturing process, people must have obtained a reasonable amount of adult growth and responsibility in order to carry their share of the various responsibilities of marriage. Rutledge identified three basic factors in preparing for marriage: discovery of selfhood, continued growth as an individual, and possession of communication and problem-solving skills. He spoke of the premarital counseling process as that of opening up these three areas of life for the young couple and projecting the couple into the future, enabling them to foresee the kinds of problems and the many challenges awaiting them in marriage.

Rutledge argued that if all clinicians would devote one-fourth of their time to premarital counseling, they could make a greater impact on the health of the country than through all of their remaining therapeutic activities. More recently, Mace (1974) challenged marriage counselors to move out of the remedial routine and focus their energies on marriage preparation and marriage enrichment. We tend to agree in substance with these arguments and strongly support the currently small, yet growing emphasis on preventive premarital education and related educational and enrichment programs for mental health. However, it is unlikely that the typical marriage-family therapist will be able to move out of the traditional therapeutic or remedial services, because of the demands for treatment of dysfunction and because of the difficulty in making the transition from an exclusively therapeutic framework to a premarital counseling framework that combines an educational and a therapeutic emphasis.

The Healthy Premarital Couple

Premarital counseling is typically done with relatively healthy persons and is designed primarily as an experience to enhance and enrich growing relationships and secondarily to treat pathological ones. The goal of the counseling is to enhance the premarital relationship so that it might develop into a satisfactory and stable marital relationship. In this regard, the work of Burr (1973) and Lewis and Spanier (1979) in articulating the relationship between premarital factors and marital quality is of importance.

Building upon and extending Burr's work, Lewis and Spanier have identified four categories of premarital variables as crucial to later quality and stability of marriage. The first, the variable of premarital homogamy, states that the greater the premarital homogamy, or similarity in social and demographic factors, the higher the marital quality. The following emerge as predictors of marital stability or success: similarity of racial background, similarity of socioeconomic background, similarity of religious denominational affiliation, similarity of intelligence levels, similarity of age, and similarity of social status.

The second proposition concerning the relationship between premarital factors and marital quality identified by Lewis and Spanier relates to similarity of personal and emotional premarital resources and life experiences. The specific premarital resources identified as predictive of quality and stability of marriage were a high level of interpersonal skill functioning, good emotional health, a positive self-concept, high educational level, an older age at first marriage, a high social class, a high degree of acquaintance before marriage, and physical health.

A third proposition relates to positive parental models. Marital quality and stability was correlated with high marital quality in the family origin, high level of happiness in one's childhood, and positive relationships between the person and his or her parents.

The fourth premarital variable category identified by Lewis and

Spanier is that of support from significant others. Predictive variables were parental approval of the future mate, the person's liking for the future in-laws, and the support of significant friends for the proposed marriage.

In addition to the four major categories of variables, Lewis and Spanier identified the following additional variables relating to marital quality and stability. The first of these variables is that the greater the level of conventionality, the higher the marital quality. The second indicates that persons who have experienced premarital sexual behavior consistent with their personal value system will have higher marital quality than individuals who experienced premarital sexual behavior in opposition to their personal value system. A third proposition relates to premarital pregnancy and indicates that couples experiencing premarital pregnancy will have lower marital quality than couples not experiencing it. The final proposition offered by Lewis and Spanier is the most general, yet it is useful in attempting to understand the premarital relationship; they conclude that "the greater the likelihood that the motivation to marry is independent of problematic circumstantial factors, including internal or external pressures, the higher the marital quality" (Lewis and Spanier 1979, p. 278).

We have summarized the work of Lewis and Spanier because we believe that it can provide a framework for the counselor in designing the premarital counseling process. Because Lewis and Spanier's work has been systematically derived from the vast sociological research literature, the premarital counselor can add this information to the counseling process by appropriately using it in a counseling setting. It should be noted here that the very important aspects of mate selection and dysfunctional factors in premarital relationships will be dealt with extensively in later chapters in the book and thus have not been discussed here.

Research on Premarital Counseling

In comparison to other counseling areas, there are few studies reporting data that allow us carefully to evaluate the outcomes of premarital counseling. The research that has been done is often poorly designed because the focus has been service rather than research. The overall evaluation of premarital counseling must be considered tenuous (Schumm and Denton 1979). Yet there is a growing body of literature that supports the interest in and efficacy of the premarital counseling process.

The conjoint group premarital counseling process described in this book (specifically Stahmann and Hiebert 1980) was studied with premarital couples and newly married couples who had been married an average of five months (Hancock 1983). Hancock, in his research, which he described as a pilot, found that the premarital couples rated the content of the counseling process as very useful as indicated by a score of 83 percent. Specifically, he found that the group premarital couple format helped the premarital couples to understand their partner much better, helped them much more effectively deal with problems such as communication and conflict, and helped them know what to do when problems arise. It is interesting to note that he found that the premarital couples in his sample apparently benefited more from the process than the newly married couples, who also benefited from it.

Fowers and Olson (1986), in studying the validity of the PREPARE Inventory (PREmarital Personal and Relationship Evaluation) in premarital assessment, concluded not only that the instrument was useful, but that they could identify specific topics that premarital counseling programs should address. Relating their recommendations to PREPARE categories, they suggested that the following be considered: "(a) realistic expectations, (b) personality issues, (c) communication, (d) conflict resolution, (e) leisure activities, (f) financial management, (g) sexuality, (h) family and friends, (i) equalitarian roles, and (j) religion" (Fowers and Olson 1986, p. 412).

Other recent articles have reported efforts to study and refine premarital counseling programs. These findings have influenced the continuing development of our approaches to premarital counseling. Several assumptions that underly our approach are the following. First, those who benefit most from premarital counseling must voluntarily seek it rather than be forced into it (Stuckey et al. 1986). Second, as currently thought of in our society, the premarital counseling process is developmental and designed to assist the couple in enhancing their relationship, rather than as a screening process (Grover et al. 1985, Olson and Norem 1977). Third, premarital counseling is most beneficial if obtained early in the relationship, even one year prior to marriage (Fournier and Olson 1986). Fourth, persons requesting premarital counseling apparently expect to learn about themselves to some extent, but primarily to learn about their relationship and each other (Guldner 1971, Olson and Norem 1977). Fifth, couples and counselors favor conjoint sessions over individual sessions (Buckner and Salts 1985, Fournier and Olson 1986, Meadows and Taplin 1970). Sixth, the use of assessment instruments as part of the premarital counseling process is useful and contributes to it (Fournier and Olson 1986; Fowers and Olson 1986; Nickols, Fournier, and Nickols 1986). Seventh, the offering of postwedding follow-up sessions is important (Bader et al. 1980, Buckner and Salts 1985, Fournier and Olson 1986, Guldner 1971).

The reader will see that the premarital counseling process that we present in this book contains the content recommended by Fowers and Olson (1986) in addition to other content which we have derived from research and clinical sources such as those cited previously.

A word about training for the practice of premarital counseling: We are of the opinion that for a person to deal adequately with the premarital counseling process described in this book graduate study at the master's degree level is necessary and at least some graduate training in the area of relationship counseling, marital interaction, family studies, and assessment is required. We do not support the idea of paraprofessional or lay persons doing premarital counseling unless they are under the close supervision of a professional trained at the master's level.

2
Motivations for Marriage: Why Get Married?

We live in a world of rapidly expanding mechanization. The process of living enmeshes us in a complex network of dependency upon the utilization of extensive electronic and mechanical devices. Perhaps it is no wonder, then, that we tend to develop a mechanical attitude not only toward the world itself, but also toward the delivery of human services. No doubt this accounts for the fact that books, seminars, and conferences in the broad field of counseling concentrate extensively, if not exclusively, on techniques and strategies for change.

We believe that a clinician's theoretical framework directly influences his or her practice. To put it in more direct language, what we believe determines what we see; what we see determines what we do. For this reason we are directing this and the following chapters to a theoretical framework for understanding the motivations for marriage as well as a conceptual framework for understanding the dynamics of marriage.

If indeed we are going to define, understand, and explain *counseling*, then we need to articulate an understanding of the nature of *marriage*. If we are going to have some understanding and awareness of the dynamics of marriage, then we need to have some understanding of premarriage, or the premarital state. Thus, this chapter will have a twofold focus: (1) the forces at work that bring a man and a woman toward marriage; (2) the search to understand why it is that people get married.

Illusions of Marriage

People do not enter marriage without some preconceived ideas about it (Burr 1973). Men and women moving toward a wedding have many ideas about what marriage is supposed to be like. They dream about marriage, about the way their spouse will behave, about the satisfactions they will experience. These dreams and expectations in part are propagated by the society in which we live. Many of these dreams are myths, yet many couples move toward and into marriage believing these myths or false ideas. Since the premarital counselor is not separate from the culture in which he or she lives but is part of it, the failure to discriminate between the myths and the reality will have a potent effect on the counselor's attitude toward premarital counseling and its effectiveness. Thus, we turn to an exploration of some of the illusions of marriage (Whitaker 1973).

"Mate Selection and Marriage Are Accidental"

There is a popular idea that marriage and mate selection are a matter of chance. If the marriage does not work, and one or both spouses are unhappy, the fault must lie with chance. It certainly could not be the responsibility of the participants! When listening to people elaborate their belief that marriage is accidental, the authors are reminded of the midwestern college where, in the early part of this century, administrators would line the boys up in the boys' dorm by height, the girls in the girls' dorm by height, and then send them out of the dormitories in two long columns approaching each other. The person who was walking next to you when the columns joined became your date for the spring banquet. We suspect many people fantasize about marriage in this manner. From this point of view, certainly, there cannot be any logic in the choices made, or better yet, any responsibility for them.

We believe that the idea that mate selection is accidental is non-sense (Adams 1979, Lewis and Spanier 1979). Mate selection is one of the most accurate choosing processes that human beings engage in. We suspect that human beings choose exactly the mate they need at that point in time. This does not mean that there is not another person in the world who could fulfill some of the same needs as the person who is selected. It does mean that the partner chosen through the mate selection process is in many ways exactly the partner that the person at that time needs. We think Voltaire said it best when he said, "Every person gets exactly what they want. The trouble is, we did not know what we wanted until we got it." We suspect people usually do know, at least on some subconscious level. Many, however, prefer to believe the myth that mate selection is accidental. The myth relieves them of responsibility for failure and of responsibility for taking action.

"Marriage Is Dichotomous"

Another popular idea which society propagates is that marriage is a one-sided or lopsided relationship. This myth says that marriage is uneven and unfair. In the last analysis, says the myth, one person will win and the other will lose (Whitaker 1973).

The belief that marriage is dichotomous is most clearly visible when listening to people discuss a couple who are having marital problems or are going through a divorce. The discussion will often focus on the one-sidedness or unevenness of the marriage, portraying one partner as bad and the other as good, one as right and the other as wrong, one as intelligent and the other as stupid, one as strong and one as weak, one as healthy and one as sick.

Although many marriages appear on the surface to be one-sided, it is our contention that underneath, the couple are usually evenly balanced. For example, on the surface a husband may appear to have a nasty temper, whereas the wife appears to be quiet, submissive, and lacking anger. The trained eye, however, will see that she, too, has her way of being angry and of putting the knife in, but that it is a sneaky way. Thus, while couples often appear to be one-sided, with one person losing, we contend that in marriage, couples are usually balanced. Either both win or both lose.

The myth that marriage is dichotomous is an attempt on the part of society to inculcate the idea that marriage is nonsense. The biggest temptation, when thinking about marriages, is to believe that what happens between a husband and wife does not make sense, and that if indeed a marriage works, no one knows how or why (Whitaker 1973).

Myth and Premarital Counseling

We have addressed these two myths because we think that on a very basic level, one's attitude toward marriage and how couples are drawn together will affect one's attitude toward premarital counseling, how it is done, and, in fact, whether or not one does it at all. If one believes that marriage is accidental, premarital counseling will seem both a waste of time and pointless. Why spend energy trying to make sense out of something that does not basically and inherently make sense? If marriage is a cruel game of the world, if there is no point to it or plan as to how it works, if it is a matter of luck, then the premarital counselor will be cynical toward the premarital counseling process and/or toward marriage itself. Perhaps then the premarital counselor, like the King of Hearts in *Alice in Wonderland,* could lament: "If there is no meaning in it, that saves a world of trouble, you know, as we needn't try to find any."

No doubt one's attitude toward these two myths and whether or not one believes them will also be contingent on personal beliefs about one's own marriage and family of origin. If a person has been able to make sense out of his or her marriage and family of origin and if that person can see how people fit together and what it is they each do for the other, his or her attitude as a premarital counselor will be to find sense, or to make sense. If his or her family of origin and marriage do not seem to make sense and if that person cannot figure out what it was that attracted people to each other in his or her own networks, then premarital counseling will be difficult because the counselor's attitude will either by cynical or disbelieving.

By this point in the chapter, we hope that we have made our assumptions clear: that marriage does indeed make sense and that people marry for some purpose. Another way of saying this is that we believe that people marry to "get." We also believe that people marry to "give"; however, we want to underscore the idea that individuals marry in order to do something to themselves or for themselves: to grow, to leave home, to have an umbrella to shelter themselves from the world's rains, to hitch a ride piggyback toward a better future (Whitaker and Keith 1977).

Motivating Forces for Marriage

Our assumption that marriage is neither accidental nor dichotomous has been influenced by our clinical practice with the hundreds of couples we have seen both in marital counseling and in premarital counseling. In thinking about these couples and the manner in which they chose each other, we have discovered that the couples were apparently performing a task and involved in a process. It has struck us that many couples were involved in the task of finding some way to initiate growth. The growth could be in many areas. Perhaps it was in becoming more outgoing, more self-confident, more intimate, or some other dimension of their personality which they felt needed expansion. The mate they chose, therefore, from the millions of individuals available was exactly the person who could provide them with the kind of growth they needed. Some women, for example, seek out a particular man who can teach them to be tough, just as some men seek out a woman who can teach them to be soft. It almost seems to us that couples in some way find each other and choose each other on the basis of their potential to induce change. It is as if couples are in a strange way performing the task of therapy. Perhaps we could say that marriage is an amateur attempt at psychotherapy (Whitaker and Keith 1977).

All of this is a way of saying that we believe that marriage is purposeful and that couples choose each other on the basis of the ability of the other person to help them initiate growth. We think that couples are involved in a task of healing. It is as if many individuals at the point of dating and moving to marriage find themselves to be incomplete in some way. Their search for a mate is not haphazard but rather based on some kind of deeply intuitive homing device that relentlessly and purposely pursues exactly the kind of person who will provide them with the stimulation for the growth they are seeking. It is amazing how powerful that homing device can be. People can spot each other across a crowded room at a party or sense something in a person who is only barely visible across a street, and be instinctively drawn to the person and find a way to make the contact. The desire to grow, the desire to be completed in some way, is a powerful force at work in individuals. This force brings people together, binding them in a relationship. The attraction, which often is so powerful during the later stages of the dating process that it can be felt by outsiders to the relationship, owes some of its strength and energy to the potential for growth and the healing force that are present in the coupling process.

Although we believe that marriage makes sense and that the movement toward marriage is in some way a bid for health, we are aware that the forces that impel people toward each other are various. Some of the psychological forces at work are healthy, and others are not. Some of the forces that impel people toward marriage have within them the capability of moving the couples toward further growth and health, whereas other forces have within them the possibility of disruption or disappointment. We want now to take a look at some of those forces and comment on them briefly.

Emotional Immaturity

Some families have difficulty in completing the task of raising their children. They finish the task physically and see to it that the children have the proper food and shelter to enable them to become adults. But raising children is more than ensuring their physical growth. Raising children to be functioning, healthy adults requires that parents pay attention to the emotional well-being of their children. Families are required both to care for their children and at the same time to urge them to become independent. Families need to give the child enough care and attention so that the child feels wanted and loved. At the same time, parents need to begin gradually helping the child become more self-sufficient, more independent, ready to function on his or her own.

Some families enable their children to go away, to become independent, and to be responsible, functioning adults. Other families hang on, making decisions for their children, interrupting the children's decision-making process, and continuing to take responsibility for them. In the process, these families cripple the ability of children to become independent and responsible. Thus, children enter late adolescence or young adulthood physically ready and able to enter marriage but still not adult in terms of their own responsibility and decision-making ability. These families have made so many decisions for their children that even as young adults, these children still need somebody to help them live, to get them up in the morning, to see to it that they go to work, and so on. It is as if these families somehow do not successfully resolve the young persons' dependency needs.

These individuals, still feeling the need to be cared for, still needing the kind of responsibility that parents take, will move to a marital relationship seeking to fulfill those dependency needs that were somehow not resolved and completed in their family of origin. It is as if they look to the mate to be the good, loving, patient, understanding parent that they did not have or continue to need. It is almost as if the marriage becomes a kind of graduate day-care center where the young adult can continue the growing process. This is a powerful force, impelling toward marriage people who seek a sense of healing and completion from their family of origin. They may operate with some particular illusions about what marriage can do for them.

"I Will Be Different after Marriage"

There are people whose growing-up experiences during high school or following years is such that their relationships with other people have been painful. They have been bruised in some way, either in their relationship with their parents or in relationships with their peers. In either case, they enter young adulthood with a sense of being burned, feeling lonely and unwanted. This lack of satisfaction in relationships can cause them to fantasize a relationship that might be fulfilling, that might in some way heal the burns and bruises of their previous relationships. Marriage looms on the horizon as the great possibility, the solution to the hurts of previously painful relationships. It has within it the expectation of solving the pain and relieving the loneliness and the hurt. These people frequently expect that the mate will change them and that marriage will in some way provide them with the environment, the caring, and the love that will resolve their loneliness and hurt. Although marriage might exaggerate the loneliness or make it even worse through the years, it is not perceived that way during the dating process. Thus, the drive to cure loneliness by finding a mate who will make one well, whole, and no longer lonely is a powerful force impelling people toward marriage.

"Everybody Ought to Be Married"

Because human beings live not in isolation but in society, they experience pressure and models from society. Our American culture is a marrying culture. In spite of the fact that divorce statistics have been higher in the 1960s and 1970s than in previous decades, so have marriage statistics. Approximately nine out of every ten adults over the age of twenty-one are married. Our society expects people to marry, and in some subtle ways discriminates against those who do not.

There are people who move along the path of life and into marriage because they want to meet that societal expectation. Many people want to fit in, want to feel that they belong, want to feel "normal." Self-esteem is an important factor in the lives of individuals (Satir 1972). Most persons do what will enhance the way they are seen by other people. Because of our societal expectation of marriage, there are individuals who marry not so much because they wish to be with the person they have chosen, but because they want to seek society's esteem. Of course, this is both in the broad sense and in the narrow sense of the term; they seek society's esteem not only in the general sense, but in the specific sense. They seek the esteem of parents, friends, and peers who, as they move into their late twenties, think favorably about marriage and are usually married themselves. Because such people want to feel that they are worthy, they will move toward marriage.

"Marriage Makes Me an Adult"

We have already discussed families who have difficulty letting their children go. These are families that hang on to their young adult children. In families like these, marriage often becomes a rite of passage. In other words, marriage becomes an act that needs to be engaged in for the purpose of separating from one's family of origin.

In a way, marriage is one of life's "rule changers." As the birth of a child into the family changes the "rules" about how mother and father relate to each other, so marriage also changes the "rules" concerning how a child relates to parents. In families where young adults have difficulty taking charge of their own lives, in families that still try to run the lives of their young adult children, adolescents often make a move toward marriage as an attempt to change the rules of the family of origin. Marriage thus becomes a bid for adulthood.

The more enmeshed the family of origin—the more reluctant it is to let its children go—the higher the probability that the adult child will choose a prospective mate who will be seen as undesirable in some way. The more undesirable the mate, the more the adult child hopes he or she will break the parents' hold. Thus, the bid for adulthood can be a powerful force impelling people toward marriage if they are attempting to separate themselves from controlling parents.

Sexual Urge

Most of us are born into life in the context of families. In that context, we are cared for in infancy in ways that are both physically and emotionally close. As infants, we receive both physical attention and emotional attention (affection). As a child moves from infancy to childhood to adolescence, that physical and emotional closeness begins to change. About the time a boy or girl begins to enter puberty, he or she becomes uncomfortable with the physical closeness. The child will start backing away from kisses and hugs, feeling uncomfortable about the physical demonstration of affection.

This is a natural process resulting from the bodily changes that take place during puberty. With the production of hormones and the development of the secondary sex characteristics, the adolescent boy or girl begins to experience a surge of sexual desire and drive. The physical closeness of infancy and early childhood becomes threatening; the child begins to feel uncomfortable about being both emotionally and physically close to the parent. The old incest taboo raises its head. This is Mother Nature's way of pushing the child out of the family, as he or she begins to try to find a peer who will ultimately, in some way, duplicate that original nurturing formula that was present in birth. Each adolescent and young adult will hope ultimately to find a person with whom they can be both physically and emotionally close. The drive to experience intimacy in both a physical and an emotional way is a powerful force impelling people toward marriage.

Emotional Maturity

Families either help or hinder young people to grow up and take over their own lives. Some families help people mature, take responsibility, take charge of their own lives. In these families, children have begun leaving their parents in a healthy way in childhood. They are people who, following the completion of high school, go out into the world, live alone for a period of time, and develop their own sense of individuality and individual adequacy. These people thus are ready for the additional intimacy of marriage and are seeking a peer with whom they can become both physically and emotionally close and share the companionship of marriage. Such emotional maturity impels couples toward the intensifying experience of intimacy.

Summary

We have been trying to communicate the idea that marriage is not an accidental and casual event that individuals undergo. Rather, we see marriage as a relationship that has its origin in powerful forces that impel people toward it. Couples look to marriage because they expect some kind of change or growth. The attitude of the couple prior to the wedding is that not of people casually strolling toward an event but rather of couples that are being impelled headlong toward some crucial climax in their relationship. In the vernacular, this is described as being "head over heels in love."

Guldner (1971) has accurately described the powerful way in which people in couples are attracted to each other. He described the premarital state as a state of bliss. That is a way of saying that the attraction that functions in a relationship is indeed intense, powerful, and often all-consuming. When one thinks for a moment about how some marriages can be so intense that they drive people to alcoholism, drug addiction, homicide, or suicide, it should not be surprising that the power that can drive people to extremes in marriage is already functioning prior to the wedding.

All this implies that unless the premarital counselor understands that couples are usually being impelled toward marriage and are in search of healing, he or she will think that couples are casually strolling toward marriage and that a premarital counselor can intervene, change, or stop that movement. We suspect that in most cases, any attempt to do so is unsuccessful, and that the forces are so impelling, so powerful, that the marriage will most often come about one way or another.

3

Psychosocial Dynamics of Marriage: What Is Marriage?

Couples approaching a wedding do so intentionally. The movement toward the wedding for most couples is not a casual meandering that brings them surprisingly and unwittingly to marriage. Rather, as they encounter each other in the relationship, a force builds and moves the couple increasingly toward an interaction that binds them together. By the time the couple reach the wedding, the tapestry of their life is well on its way: patterns are emerging, and the strands have been laced together into a network.

In the previous chapter, we examined some of the forces that bring couples to the wedding. This chapter will focus on the relationship that has developed and examine some of the dimensions of marriage. Earlier we defined the *premarital* state; now we are going to define the *marital* state.

Marriage means many things to many people. It has been defined in thousands of ways. Philosophers have wrestled with its definition; sociologists have struggled to measure it; psychologists have tried to describe it; theologians have attempted to explain its meaning and purpose. Yet no one definition of marriage seems to do it justice. Perhaps that is because no definition by a single discipline encompasses all the dimensions of marriage. This could also be a way of saying that no matter how thoroughly it is described and defined, marriage has a note of mystery about it. It may be the mystery that keeps any definition from being an inclusive and total explanation.

We are not going to attempt in this chapter a comprehensive definition of marriage. Our purpose, rather, is to provide a working definition, a definition of marriage relevant for professionals working with couples in a prewedding counseling context. Our definition will be primarily relationship-oriented.

The Dimensions of Marriage

It seems to us, as practitioners, that marriage can be best defined as multidimensional. In other words, we see marriage as a relationship that functions on many levels. We are not saying that marriage is the only relationship that is multidimensional. There are other relationships that operate on more than one dimension, such as employer-employee, employee-employee, parent-child, and so forth. We are contending, however, that marriage is an intricate tapestry, comprised of many strands and woven and intermingled in a special kind of way (Whitaker and Keith 1977).

We have defined marriage as a multidimensional relationship that functions on many levels. We want to look at some of the dimensions and describe them briefly, so that readers can experience the flavor of the complexity of the marital relationship.

Social dimension. Marriage has a social and companionship dimension. Marriage means a special kind of sharing in social and interpersonal activities, whether they be enjoyed together or separately.

Geographical dimension. Marriage has a geographical dimension. Marriage means an uncommon kind of sharing of space and physical proximity.

Sexual dimension. Marriage has a sexual and/or reproductive dimension. Marriage means a unique kind of sharing of the physical, sensual, reproductive, and sexual aspects of two people.

Emotional dimension. Marriage has a psychological dimension. Marriage means a unique kind of sharing of the emotional and fantasy levels of life.

Intellectual dimension. Marriage has a cognitive and planning dimension. Marriage means a special kind of sharing in thinking about life, making plans, sharing goals, and carving out futures together.

Economic dimension. Marriage has a fiscal and financial nature. Marriage means a particular kind of sharing not only in the accumulation of money, but also in its use and distribution.

Recreational dimension. Marriage has a recreational and pleasure dimension. Marriage means a remarkable kind of sharing in the replenishing and renewal that keep a relationship alive.

Religious dimension. Marriage has an existential and philosophical dimension. Marriage means a specific kind of sharing in regard to the values of life, the sharing of attitudes about living and its meaning.

Legal dimension. Marriage has a legal status in our country. Marriage means a special kind of participation in the incorporation of a relationship in the civil and legal process of society.

Paradoxical dimension. We find couples and their variety of marital relationships fascinating. It intrigues us that there are some couples who, although they have a relationship that is indeed multidimensional, lack a legal dimension. We call them unmarried. There are other couples who, although they possess the legal dimension and are legally married, have been disengaging from or have disconnected the other nine dimensions. Yet we call them married.

It seems to us that our nomenclature, from a psychological perspective, is upside down. Given our definition, the uniqueness of marriage is its multidimensional character. That is a way of saying, then, that it is possible for a couple to be already married, psychologically speaking, before they possess a marriage license. It is also possible for a couple to have a legal marriage but not be or ever have been married psychologically.

The typical definition of marriage is too narrow and simplistic. If marriage is in fact multidimensional, then the tapestry is already being woven during the dating process. The tapestry is already on the loom; the pattern is already emerging. By the time the couple reaches the wedding, the relationship is already operative on all levels, at least in some form, with the exception of the legal dimension. To say that the marriage begins with the wedding is inaccurate. We are suggesting, therefore, that it is more helpful for the premarital counselor to view the marriage as having begun before the wedding. Rather than believing that the wedding begins the marriage, the counselor should understand that the wedding announces what has already taken place on a more private and psychological plane (Broderick 1979; Hoult, Henze, and Hudson 1978).

Bonding

We have been defining marriage as a multidimensional relationship, a relationship that is unique in its operation on many levels. Because we do not think this definition is totally encompassing, we would also like to suggest another definition of marriage that will run parallel to and enrich our definition of marriage as multidimensional.

This way of looking at marriage would be to see it as a relationship that possesses a unique kind of bonding. Perhaps one might think of marriage as a kind of glue. The bonding that takes place between two people in a marriage—the glue that holds together two people, psychologically speaking—can also be described by the word *commitment.*

Our definition of marriage as multidimensional is not mutually exclusive with our definition of marriage as a relationship of bonding or commitment. Obviously, the multileveled connections that exist between a husband and a wife feed into and are a part of bonding. The multifaceted aspect of the connections between a husband and wife is part and parcel not only of what attracts the couples initially, but also of what maintains the relationship on many levels. We are suggesting, however, that other dimensions of the bonding cause the couple not only to weave their lives together, but to find a power in that unique relationship.

Bonding and dependency. One of the dimensions that feeds into the bonding process between a man and a woman as they move through the more serious stages of the dating relationship has to do with dependency needs. The possibilities that the potential mate provides in terms of fulfilling dependency needs is a powerful attracting force that impels people toward a marital relationship. All people, no matter how healthy, have some dependency needs. Although it is true that there tends to be greater "stickiness" to the "glue" when exaggerated dependency needs exist, the counselor needs to understand that dependency needs are a factor in the bonding process for all human beings. It may be true that the glue sets more quickly and tighter when couples have exaggerated dependency needs, but the premarital counselor should not underestimate the degree to which the potential mate represents the possibility of psychological completion. The desire for wholeness—the desire to experience a sense of completion—is a powerful ingredient for bonding or commitment.

Bonding as self-esteem. Another of the ingredients that comprise the dynamic we are calling bonding is self-esteem. All people, regardless of the nature of their self-esteem, see in the marital relationship the possibility of receiving worth and well-being from the other person. As in the case of dependency needs, it is often true that people with low self-esteem look to the marital relationship with the expectation that their mate will in some way make them feel whole, good, attractive, worthy, wanted—in other words, will raise their self-esteem. These expectations, values, and dreams of what the other person can do for the partner in marriage are powerful attracting and maintaining forces in the marital relationship. To be liked, desirable, and wanted is important for all people, regardless of where they are on the continuum between healthy and unhealthy in regard to their own self-esteem. The prospect of raising one's self-esteem because another person likes one is an added ingredient to the glue that establishes and maintains a marital relationship.

The Commitment Process

We have been suggesting that marriage is a unique interpersonal relationship. We have been contending not only that there are strong and particular forces that impel couples toward each other, but that these forces function as a kind of gravitational force in the relationship. We are calling the attracting force and the gravitational force *bonding*. It is important to underscore the concept of bonding, because we contend that it is crucial for the premarital counselor to understand that the marital relationship is rarely a casual relationship. The marital relationship is extremely intense for the majority of couples. The intensity is what we are trying to communicate when we use the words *bonding* and *glue*.

We are also contending that the bonding process is already at work premaritally. It is an integral part of the forces that draw the couple together before marriage. Bonding is the glue that holds the relationship together during the marriage.

We believe that the bonding or commitment process follows a particular progression in most relationships (Bowman and Spanier 1978). In a general way of speaking, we think of the commitment process as beginning privately in each individual in the context of the dating relationship. At some point in time, each person in the relationship says privately and on the inside, "That person is for me." The premarital counselor can usually establish with the help of each individual when that internal event occurred.

The second step in a commitment process is an interactional one. At some point after the first step has been taken, each person begins to indicate, verbally and/or nonverbally, that the other person is being held in special regard. This rarely takes place at one point or event, but is a process. But in some sense and by some point in time, each person has said to the other in some way, "You are for me." By this time, the couple is already deep in the bonding process. The relationship has already connected on many levels. Various aspects of the different dimensions other than the legal dimension are already operative.

As the glue sets more and more firmly, the couple finally make the third step in the commitment process. As a last, public declaration, the couple announce to the world what has already happened to them privately and interactionally on a psychological level. When the couple have the wedding, they are announcing that the bonding or the commitment has already set.

We think it important for the premarital counselor to understand that when the couple come to the wedding, they are psychologically speaking already married.

This brings us to a peculiar dilemma facing the counselor. Although we have suggested that the couple is already married by the time they approach the wedding—that the glue has already set in some sense—the couple does not see it that way on an overt level. Although covertly the couple may sense that they are in some ways especially locked together, on the overt level they still perceive themselves as unmarried. At the same time, society supports the overt view; the couple are not yet married. The premarital counselor is in a dilemma. Psychologically speaking, the couple are already married. On the other hand, the couple do not know that, at least on the overt level. Whereas from the counselor's perspective the task is (in a sense) marital counseling, from the couple's perspective the task is premarital counseling. That is the dilemma.

Conclusion

We have stressed the idea that marriage begins before the wedding. We maintain that the glue that binds a man and a woman together in the unique relationship called marriage begins to thicken and set before the wedding comes along. The acceptance of these ideas will make an important impact on the manner in which the premarital counselor functions.

The premarital counselor operating within a predominantly pathological framework or steeped in traditional therapeutic approaches will experience difficulty in working with premarital couples. Such a counselor may still perceive marriage as beginning with the wedding and will then believe that there is still time to examine the relationship. Although it is true that in some selected instances the couple is still in the process of deciding during premarital counseling, it is rarely true in the majority of cases. With that mind set, both the premarital counselor and the premarital couple will be exasperated with the counseling process, because they will be working in opposite directions.

II
Conjoint Couple Premarital Counseling

4
Structural and Administrative Issues in Premarital Counseling

W ith this chapter, we introduce a new section of the book. Part II will be devoted to developing a model for premarital counseling. The focus of part II will be on the conjoint couple counseling approach and will entail examining structural and administrative issues in premarital counseling. Readers interested in a group premarital counseling approach are referred to part III. Special problems in premarital counseling will be addressed in part IV.

Providers of Premarital Counseling

In our survey of the field, it appears to us that there are three main providers of premarital counseling: the clergy, physicians, and groups sponsored by institutions, churches, or a collection of professionals. Alghough minimal concrete evidence is available in the research about which of these is most active in premarital counseling, we suspect the clergy are the primary providers. As mentioned in chapter 1, Schonick (1975) was able to document in 1972 that 2,745 of 4,000 couples applying for marriage licenses in California received their premarital counseling from the clergy. This datum reflects a 1970 California law requiring premarital counseling for minors under the age of eighteen who apply for a marriage license. Although few other states have such a law, we suspect that the clergy provide more than 50 percent of the counseling for couples planning a wedding.

Without solid evidence, we suspect that counselors in agencies and clinics have been providing premarital counseling in greater numbers during the past ten years (Stahmann and Barclay-Cope 1977). This involvement has usually taken two forms. On the one hand, counselors have been participating in group premarital counseling programs sponsored by groups or institutions in the community. Their role has been primarily that of leader, presenter, or facilitator. On the other hand, couples experiencing more serious conflicts within the premarital relationship, especially in terms of remarriage, have been seeking out counselors for an evaluation of their relationship as part of the process of making their decision to marry.

Although physicians have been involved before the wedding with many couples down through the decades, the work of the physician in prewedding counseling has been rather specific (Spencer, Stahmann, and Hiebert 1977; Trainer 1979). Either the physician has been consulted to provide a premarital physical, or the physician is consulted regarding contraception and family planning (Josimovich 1977). It is true that physicians frequently see individuals before the wedding; however, they usually do not see couples together, nor do they focus on the relationship itself. Thus, although physicians may see a high number of individuals before their marriages, doctors' involvement is of a different nature from that of the other two groups of providers.

Contexts of Premarital Counseling

We believe that the context of premarital counseling is crucial in shaping both the methodology of the counseling and the expectations of the premarital couple. We want to explore a variety of contexts, tracing the impact of each on client expectation and counseling methodology.

Parish Setting

Since a significant percentage of premarital counseling in this country is conducted in the context of the local church in preparation for the wedding, we need to explore this setting in our attempt to trace its impact. With this in mind, we shall explore a variety of expectations.

Denominational Expectations. Because we are a pluralistic nation, we have a large number of religious denominations. Not only do the denominations have different traditions regarding doctrinal issues and religious or liturgical practices; they also have a diversity of traditions regarding the role of the pastor as premarital counselor.

In broad terms, the religious tradition can be divided into large and somewhat distinct categories. On the one hand, there are denominations with a distinctly sacramental orientation. Whether or not these denominations specifically conceive of marriage as a sacrament, the sacramental orientation toward ministry is a distinct kind of responsibility for the clergy. The pastor is responsible for the admission of candidates into all of the sacraments, of which marriage is only one. The sacramental responsibility, then, has within it a kind of guardianship. It is important to understand, however, that this guardianship is not simply implied. Many sacramental denominations are explicit in either their canon law or their constitutional statutes about the nature of marriage and also about the characteristics and nature of the candidates to be admitted to marriage.

On the other hand, in the nonsacramental denominations, there are also denominational expectations. All nonsacramental Christian denominations place an emphasis on marriage, and they explicitly and implicitly have attempted to define not only the nature of marriage in a Christian sense, but also the kind of preparation of and characteristics that need to be present in the couple for the Christian marriage to be consummated. Although the guardianship focus of the nonsacramental denominations is not clear, it is our contention that it is nonetheless active, although subtle and diffused.

In addition to the sacramental and nonsacramental denominational expectations, a third expectation cuts across all denominations. This we call a pastoral counseling expectation. Since the advent of the pastoral counseling movement and the switch in the emphasis of pastoral ministry from the simply and explicitly religious and/or ritualistic, clergy have been expected, particularly through pastoral counseling courses in seminary, to take responsibility for meeting the personal and counseling needs of parishioners. Publishing handbooks on premarital counseling and books and booklets for couples to read in preparation for their marriage are other ways in which denominations encourage the idea that the pastor is to provide premarital counseling. All of these expectations, then, form a composite which suggests that premarital counseling is not only important, but also should be taken seriously.

Although we are dealing with denominational expectations that are part of the context of premarital counseling in the parish setting, it is important to underscore the fact that clergy are not solely agents of their denomination. Each minister is also licensed to perform and thus to ensure the legality of marriages. Ministers therefore carry a dual identity: pastor and civil agent. In spite of the fact that we are a country that has prided itself on the separation of church and state, we specifically give clergy a responsibility to activate the contract and legalize the marriage on behalf of the state.

This dual responsibility causes many ministers to experience a constant state of tension. If the pastor performs a marriage as an agent of the denomination, certain values, expectations, and characteristics will be sought and approved of in the couple coming to be married. If, on the other hand, the pastor performs the wedding in the civil sense, the expectations and characteristics being sought in the couple might be quite different. The tension, then, is enhanced, particularly when couples are primarily interested in having their relationship legalized and are not particularly interested in seeing it either as explicitly Christian in nature or as symbolizing or initiating their participation in active church life.

It would probably be a welcome relief if we could resolve this dilemma for clergy. We strongly believe, however, that there is no resolution to this dilemma as long as clergy have both responsibilities and certifications. Clergy who have difficulty with ambiguity or a need to have their role and path clearly spelled out will no doubt experience tension. They will also seek to resolve that tension and will want to move in one direction or the other. They will either prefer to avoid marriages in which the couple does not meet denominational expectations regarding the Christian nature of their behavior, or they will move in the other direction by giving up any kind of premarital counseling and performing all weddings. We would like to suggest, however, that tension is part of life. To resolve that tension in one direction or another might be easier, but we suspect that such a resolution would make it less challenging, less expanding, and less exciting to be in ministry.

Congregational Expectations. Just as there is a diversity of tradition in denominational expectations, there is also variety among traditions of premarital counseling in local congregations. In some congregations, premarital counseling has been a long-established tradition, begun by earlier pastors. In other congregations, premarital counseling is either brief and superficial or hardly established at all. We suggest that it behooves the pastor to ascertain the local tradition.

If premarital counseling has been established in the congregation, the expectation that the pastor will not only see couples prior to the wedding but also conduct some specialized kind of educational-counseling approach is already entrenched. In congregations in which the premarital counseling expectation is not present, the pastor attempting to introduce such counseling needs to be aware that it will not always be greeted with agreement. Many parishioners, especially in small towns and rural areas where people often already know each other too well and are greatly interested in privacy, shy away from any public exposure. The move toward premarital counseling will often be resisted. Parishioners are likely to respond negatively not only because it is new and different, but also because they might perceive it as meddling. Stuckey and others (1986) found resistance to premarital counseling in a rural sample. The assessment of the congregational expectation is important before any minister attempts to introduce a broad program of premarital counseling. Laying the groundwork is important for a congregation that has not had premarital counseling as part of its expectations of the functions of the pastor. There are some congregations in which premarital counseling might be difficult to establish; conceivably, there are congregations in which premarital counseling should not be attempted.

Couple Expectations. Couples approaching premarital counseling are generally viewing their relationship as positive and are excitedly making plans for their future. This means that they are not approaching counseling with orientation toward problems. They see their relationship not only as something that they want, but also as something that they need. The desire to be together and the intense state of excitement and oneness that they have established has been described by Guldner (1971) as a state of bliss. Although this may not characterize every couple, it certainly characterizes the majority and their expectation of premarital counseling and the premarital counselor.

Summary. The variety of expectations in the parish setting will influence the methodology of the pastoral premarital counselor. If the pastor chooses to follow denominational expectations that prescribe a guardianship aspect to the pastoral function, his or her method of dealing with a premarital couple will have distinct overtones. A pastor influenced by guardianship expectations will likely have a premarital counseling model that could be characterized as investigative and examining. The methodology, then, will be primarily constructed to discern whether the couple meets the institutional expectations. It will essentially place the institution and its desires over the people and their desires. In a similar fashion, the pastor who resolves the dilemma of the civil versus the religious responsibility in the direction of the religious will develop a methodology for premarital counseling that again will primarily attempt to discern whether the candidates meet the institutional expectations and ideals for the marital relationship.

On the other hand, a pastor influenced by the expectations of the pastoral counseling tradition will develop a methodology that is designed to place the people in a more important position than the institution and its ideals or expectations. That methodology will have as its expectation an attempt to meet the people as they are, both in life and in their relationship.

All of this is complicated by the premarital couple's expectations. If it is true, as we believe, that premarital couples are essentially positive in their orientation, then the pastor making use of a screening agent model will find the premarital counseling sessions frequently to be tense and difficult. The pastoral counselor using a developmental model to work with couples premaritally will, we believe, more effectively be able to deal with each couple as they are.

Clinics and Agencies

Social service agencies and counseling clinics are more ambiguous than the clergy about their expectations, which are frequently not spelled out in closely defined terms, as are denominational expectations. Nonetheless, counseling agencies and clinics have subtle and implicit expectations regarding both the role of the counselor and the purpose of their program or therapy.

Theoretical Expectations. The theoretical framework of a counselor will, in fact, influence the premarital counseling methodology. We have already discussed how the individual psychotherapeutic theoretical framework influenced therapists in previous decades. This theoretical framework essentially failed to conceptualize marriage as a bilateral relationship and a focus of therapy. The individual rather than an interactional focus probably had something to do with the fact that psychotherapists in the earlier half of the twentieth century rarely entered the premarital counseling field.

We believe that an interactional and systemic theoretical framework also influences the methodology of a premarital counselor. The systemic framework implies an emphasis on the importance of relationships, motivating the therapist to be interested and willing to work with premarital couples and heightening the reason for involvement. The systemic theoretical model assumes that any change in the behavior and/or attitude of one person automatically changes the relationship. This theoretical framework thus gives reason and motivation to be involved with premarital couples.

The theoretical framework also influences methodology in another way. Because the clinician functioning within an interactional and systemic theoretical framework already values relationships, he or she will be motivated to see the premarital couple together. With a theoretical framework that conceptualizes the relationship as visible only in the presence of both people, the premarital counselor making use of this framework will have his or her methodology influenced by it and will seek to have both parties present for the counseling sessions.

Client Couple Expectations. Couples coming to counseling centers and social service agencies bring with them various expectations about the premarital counseling process. We suspect that premarital couples can be divided into three categories: those with no real conflict or problems, those experiencing difficulty or conflict in the relationship, and those planning to remarry.

Couples who come for premarital counseling for their first marriage and present themselves without premarital conflicts probably have appeared infrequently in the clinic population. Couples preparing for a first marriage, who are generally young in nature and positive in outlook, probably appear more frequently in the premarital counseling population of the clergy. In that sense, perhaps we could say that the couples clergy see are more often "normals." If such a couple come to a clinic because the clinic has stressed its involvement in premarital counseling or provides a group program for premarital counseling, one could anticipate that they will have the same kind of positive outlook that we have already mentioned and that their expectations will be toward not a problem-solving but a skill-enhancement orientation.

Couples who more frequently appear in counseling center populations for premarital counseling are those who are experiencing difficulty in their relationship. In our experience, these couples are different from the couples we outlined in the first category. The presence of conflict and tension means that they are interested in evaluating their relationship and attempting either to get some handle on the nature of the conflict or to make some decision about its continuance. Thus, these couples frequently expect something different from the expectations that characterize the "normals." The expectations of these clients probably more closely approximates the expectations of couples coming for marital therapy. Given these client expectations, we suggest that the premarital therapist should follow a model more influenced by marital therapy, although the model we outline in chapters 5 and 6 would provide a good base for working with the couple experiencing conflict.

The third category of couples who come to a counseling center includes those who are planning remarriage, whether to the same person or to a different person. These couples frequently include people who have had previous marital therapy. Such a couple comes with an expectation that the premarital therapist will provide an evaluation of the relationship, and they are specifically concerned with determining whether patterns that were present in the previous relationship are present in the current one.

Medical Setting

Couples who come to see a physician before marrying also expect certain things about the nature and purpose of the prewedding medical visit and examination. These expectations are often rather specific. The person or couple generally expects two things from the medical consultation, birth control information and sexual information (Josimovich 1977). The premarital individual or couple thus rarely expects the physician to become involved in the psychological dynamics and interactions of the couple, unless there is some conflict regarding either of these areas of focus.

In addition to the particular expectations of patients coming for prewedding consultations, there is a general expectation that is established by both the nature of medicine and medical practice. Obviously, a physician's training about reproductive and sexual functioning and contraception is common knowledge. Patients perceive the physician as knowledgeable about these areas and seek out the physician for a prewedding consultation specifically because of these areas of expertise. In addition, the nature of medical practice, with its characteristic high patient volume, limits the physician's time significantly. With some exceptions (Trainer 1979), physicians simply cannot spend five to ten hours with premarital couples. This is complicated by the fact that physicians, and medicine in general, are still primarily individual oriented and see individuals in prewedding consultations. Few physicians, apparently, have moved toward seeing couples together.

Format for Premarital Counseling

One of the issues that needs to be settled by each premarital counselor is whether the counseling is going to be individual, concurrent, conjoint, or some combination of all three.

Historically speaking, the format of counseling therapy has developed through an evolutionary process. In the beginnings of the psychotherapeutic movement, the format was individual. The one-to-one relationship was sacred. No therapist would have seen the spouse of a patient that was being treated in psychotherapy. The second stage in the evolutionary process was the development of the method of seeing both spouses, but separately. This process, called concurrent psychotherapy, came into prominence as therapists became interested in interactional in addition to intrapsychic aspects. The third stage, the format of seeing the couple together, called conjoint couple counseling, came as therapists became more interested in interactional than in intrapsychic processes or dynamics (Ackerman, Beatman, and Sherman 1961; Glick and Kessler 1974).

Education, like psychotherapy, went through a process of evolution. Although education significantly predates therapy, the process of development was rather similar. In the twelfth through sixteenth centuries in Europe, education was primarily given on a tutorial basis. The relationship of the student to the master was like an apprenticeship. Again, the one-to-one relationship was valued and respected. However, as the demand for education increased, the tutorial process slowly gave way to a class format. Prior to the seventeenth century, the class format was practiced, although all age ranges were present in the class. Today we would refer to that as ungraded education. In the seventeenth century, education moved to a third step, graded education. The process began by separating people into classes by ages (Plumb 1971).

As mentioned earlier, the literature on the development of premarital counseling is lacking. As best as we can determine, prewedding sessions followed the same evolution in terms of format as did education and psychotherapy. In the few references that are available, it appears that premarital counseling was first done on an individual basis, then moved to a concurrent format, then to the use of both a concurrent and a conjoint format, and lastly into an exclusively conjoint format (Stahmann and Barclay-Cope 1977).

Conjoint couple premarital counseling refers to the practice of seeing both the male and the female together, from the very beginning, in the premarital counseling process. The conjoint model uses exclusively the conjoint format.

In our experience, the conjoint couple premarital counseling model is the most productive. We encourage its use for a number of reasons. First, the very use of the conjoint format implicitly suggests to couples that the premarital counselor values not only the individual persons, but the relationship. Second, the use of the conjoint format allows the premarital counselor to have an opportunity to see how the couple interact; it allows the relationship to be seen and observed. Third, by seeing both people together, the premarital counselor heightens the bilateralism of the relationship. Bilateralism means that marriage is a two-way street, a quid pro quo experience. Education that is one-sided, or unilateral, is unproductive and ineffective because marriage is not one-sided. Significant research has shown that relationships achieve the most growth when the effort put into the relationship is two-sided (Watzlawick, Beavin, and Jackson 1967). Fourth, using the conjoint couple format also underscores the idea that the counselor does not want to be the keeper of secrets. Seeing the couple concurrently allows the premarital counselor to be the depository of secrets. We suggest that if a couple are not ready to deal with whatever they need to talk about in the presence of each other, the premarital counselor's private knowledge of some secrets will be of little help in working with the couple (Hiebert and Gillespie 1984).

Goals of Premarital Counseling

The design for the conjoint premarital counseling model sets out to accomplish a number of different goals. Seven specific goals are articulated here.

Clarification of self. The premarital counseling process is a process that involves the establishing of the "I" position of each partner. As the sessions progress, the process is designed to help sketch out each person's thoughts, feelings, beliefs, and fantasies. By the time the sessions have come to a close, the identity of each person as a distinct being will have become clearer.

Clarification of other. As the premarital counseling process helps to clarify who each person is and his or her uniqueness in terms of thoughts, feelings, beliefs and fantasies, the partner gains a clearer picture of who they are in relationship with and to whom they are going to be married. The premarital counseling process helps each person get a clearer picture of the uniqueness of the other's personality.

Binding anxiety. Couples moving toward the wedding are frequently anxious. The anxiety arises from a variety of sources. Couples are anxious that the wedding event should go smoothly and pleasantly. But there is another kind of anxiety, related to the relationship itself. Couples worry about some of its dimensions, whether it will work, whether it will turn out like their parents' marriages. The premarital counseling process, by taking an ordered and methodical look at the relationship, will give the couple a sense of the nature of the relationship and some skills necessary to aid its continuing growth and development. The premarital counseling sessions will also give the couple an opportunity to understand some of the basic mechanics of the wedding and thus relieve that anxiety.

Building adventure. A premarital counseling process, as it seeks to explore not only the nature of a couple's relationship but the kinds of models their parents devised for marriage, will lead a couple into an adventure. If the premarital counselor sets an inquisitive stance and is fascinated with the varieties of marital relationships and their characteristics, he or she can help build within the couple a sense of excitement, adventure, and anticipation of the manner in which their relationship will grow and develop.

Communication. The premarital counseling process has as another of its goals the improvement of communication. This is meant in a twofold way. First, the premarital counseling process itself, being structured, will help each person to become more aware of his or her own thoughts, feelings, and actions. As such, the process will aid the couple to be able to communicate their separate identities more effectively. Second, the premarital counseling process will introduce the couples to a special kind of language; that is, the manner and style of the premarital counselor can introduce couples to the unique language of relationship.

Prediction. Part of the premarital counseling process includes making observations about particular patterns or dynamics in the relationship that in the future may pose areas of conflict. The prediction process is very important for couples. It serves as a warning light, so that if conflict in the predicted area does develop, the couple has a way of interpreting its value and meaning. The prediction also takes the sting of surprise out of the conflict.

Overcoming inhibitions. One of the underlying and perhaps the most important roles of premarital counseling is to help facilitate the couple's talking about specific areas of their relationship that they had not or could not talk about before. The premarital counseling methodology we employ is specifically designed to include areas in their relationship that couples have not previously considered together.

Summary

These goals are important and aid the premarital counselor in applying a facilitative approach to the counseling process. Some premarital counselors will find the presentation of these goals to the couple or group during the first session valuable. The goals can be used as outcome goals in the counseling process. For example, at the beginning of each session, the premarital counselor could review the process as related to the goals from the previous sessions and those of the future sessions. The use of the goals in the counseling session, of course, indicates our bias. It suggests that although the premarital counseling process as we see it is therapeutic, it has education as one of its important ingredients.

Design of Premarital Counseling

We have been hinting at our model of premarital counseling. We now want to outline in brief our design for conjoint couple premarital counseling, exploring five specific areas: time, sessions, contracting, fees, and resources and guides.

Time

In our model, the conjoint couple premarital counseling process contains four basic units: introduction, dynamic relationship history, family-of-origin exploration, and wedding preparation.

The introduction is the time spent at the beginning of the first session to allow the premarital counselor to become acquainted with the couple. The nature of the introduction and some ideas regarding its mechanics will be discussed in chapter 5.

The second part of the premarital counseling process also begins in the first session. The dynamic relationship history (DRH) is a way of looking at the relationship from the time that the couple met to the time that they come to the office for premarital counseling. It is a chronological way of exploring the relationship and its events and patterns. The dynamic relationship history will also be detailed in chapter 5.

The third part of the premarital counseling process consists of an exploration of each person's family of origin. The focus is on each person's parents and their model of marriage. The goal of the family-of-origin sessions has to do with helping the couple understand the kinds of models they have for the construction of their own marriage.

The family-of-origin unit concludes with the optional involvement of the parents in helping to launch the couple's marriage.

The fourth unit is primarily for the clergy, who are involved not only in the premarital counseling process but also in the wedding. This unit consists of the mechanics of the wedding and other theological instructions that the clergy may want to include as part of the process.

Sessions

The premarital counselor needs to make some decisions regarding the structure of the premarital sessions. Two particular decisions need to be made: the length of the individual sessions and the number of sessions.

In regard to the length of the sessions, it appears that premarital counseling is more frequently delivered in two-hour periods than is therapy in general (Stahmann and Barclay-Cope 1977). In this model, we are recommending a two-hour time frame per session.

In regard to the number of sessions, we suggest at least four two-hour sessions for nonclergy. This should be an adequate time for average couples to accomplish in an appropriate fashion the material we are outlining. For clergy, because of the need to include theological and wedding material, we are suggesting five two-hour sessions.

Contracting

As indicated, we suggest a specific number of sessions for premarital counseling, the number to vary depending upon whether the premarital counselor is clergy or nonclergy. At the same time, we are cognizant of the fact that premarital couples have relationships of various lengths and differing histories. The time frame we have outlined is adequate for the couple whose premarital relationship is not more than three years old and whose families of origin are not terribly complex; that is, those that do not include a variety of marriages, many children, or a complexity of events. There are always exceptions, however, and the time frame as outlined will need to be modified to fit those couples. We suggest that in the process of conducting the first part of the first counseling session (the introduction), the premarital counselor should determine the length of the premarital courtship. If the courtship period exceeds three years, the rule of thumb can be altered. We also suggest that in the introduction, the premarital counselor should make a contract with the couples, indicating the number of sessions and the general purpose of each session.

Fees

The setting has something to do with whether or not fees are charged for premarital counseling. Clinicians functioning in counseling settings will no doubt make use of the counseling fee schedule established by the agency in which they are working. The counselor in that setting, then, will need to discuss the fee with the premarital couple as he or she would with any other client.

For clergy, the issue of fees is more complex. Generally speaking, clergy do not charge premarital counseling fees. In some churches, fees for the performance of the wedding are discouraged if one or both of the spouses is a member of that congregation. In other congregations, fees for the performance of the wedding are charged or suggested. Whichever way the clergy member or congregation chooses to deal with fees, the expectation needs to be clarified for the couple. We believe that it would be appropriate for clergy to charge the couple the cost of scoring an assessment instrument such as PREPARE.

Printed Materials

The premarital counseling process is often accompanied by the use of books, pamphlets, and other material. If the premarital counselor, clergy or nonclergy, desires to make use of resources (bibliotherapy) in the counseling process, time and attention should be given to the selection of the material to be used. In addition to making a choice of materials, the premarital counselor needs to determine whether these materials are going to be given by the institution or must be purchased by the couple.

Clergy members are encouraged to develop a brochure or booklet describing the nature of the premarital counseling sessions, the details of the wedding mechanics in the given church, fees, and so forth. This booklet, widely distributed in the congregation, will help set an expectation toward the premarital counseling process and will disseminate the kind of information that is necessary.

5
Dynamic Relationship History

T he premarital couple and premarital counselor approach each premarital counseling session with a myriad of expectations and feelings. Premarital couples are beset with many emotions. There is the bliss, the happiness they have found in each other and the relationship. There is a sense of unreality: Is this really happening to me? In the midst of the joy and the happiness is a strange sense of wondering, How did I get here? With these questions and others, anxious about the wedding and the future of their relationship, the premarital couple approaches the sessions. By the same token, the premarital counselor also has myriad expectations and feelings. As he or she looks at the couple, the premarital counselor wonders, What can I do given their experience of the moment? Where do I begin? What can I do that will be of optimal help at this point in their lives?

In our clinical experience, we have found that both the premarital couple and the premarital counselor are often confused about each other, their expectations, and their goals. They are thrown together at a particular time when neither is quite sure where to go or in what direction to move.

This chapter has a dual purpose: (1) to present a conjoint premarital counseling model which will give the couple an opportunity to look at their relationship, to expand their thinking about their relationship and their lives together, and to begin a process that they hope will be carried on in the future; and (2) to detail for the premarital counselor a methodology that will provide both a sense of direction and an understanding of the appropriate depths of the process.

Design

In the previous chapter we sketched out an overall design for our conjoint couple premarital counseling model. In order to assure that the design is clearly in mind, we briefly review it.

Part 1: Introduction. Part 1 consists of the introductory time spent in becoming acquainted with the couple in the first session. We will characterize part 1 further along in this chapter.

Part 2: Dynamic Relationship History. The second part of our overall design begins in the first session and consists of an evaluation of the couple's relationship. We will outline this procedure further in this chapter.

Part 3: Family-of-Origin Evaluation. The third part of the premarital counseling process is an exploration of the nature and characteristics of the families of origin of the two spouses. This exploration, which is a search for the parental models for marriage, will be described in chapter 6.

Part 3a: Parents (optional). This optional segment is an alternate conclusion to part 3. It consists of inviting the parents of the bride and groom into the session to say good-bye to their children, and allows for the passing on of familial wisdom.

Part 4: Wedding Preparation. This final portion, which consists of an explanation of the mechanics of the wedding and theology, is designed for the clergy.

Part 1: Introduction

The premarital counselor may or may not have any previous knowledge of the couple. In some instances, the premarital counselor may know neither the man nor the woman. In other cases, the premarital counselor may know one better than or exclusively of the other. In still other cases, the premarital counselor may know both parties well.

Although clergy, more frequently than nonclergy, may know one or both parties well, it is nonetheless important for the premarital counselor to spend some time at the beginning of the first premarital counseling session becoming familiar with the couple and establishing a positive relationship with them. In spite of a general knowledge of the couple as individuals, the premarital counselor will rarely have specific knowledge about their relationship.

Getting Acquainted

We believe that the first minutes of the first session should be spent in finding out the basics of the relationship. This is particularly necessary if the premarital counselor does not know one or both of the people to be married.

The introduction should be spent in finding out the basics: names, ages, parents, employment, educational background, overview of the dating relationship in terms of time, the wedding date, and so on. Some premarital counselors find it helpful to use a printed inventory which can provide the basic information about the couple.

Explanation of Process

After the premarital counselor has become acquainted with the couple and has obtained the basic information that provides an overview of the relationship, the premarital counseling process itself can begin to be discussed.

We suggest that the premarital counselor should first introduce part 2, the dynamic relationship history. The counselor can briefly describe the nature of the dynamic relationship history by simply informing the couple that it is a historical view of their relationship, beginning with the time they first met each other and continuing up to the present and on to the wedding.

The couple will probably wonder why the premarital counselor wants to make use of the dynamic relationship history. They may be resistant to or defensive about the process unless an appropriate explanation is made. Thus, we suggest that the premarital counselor should supply the couple with the following rationale. First, the dynamic relationship history provides the premarital counselor with a methodology for becoming acquainted with the couple, for getting to know who they are as individuals. Second, it gives the premarital counselor an opportunity to review with the couple where they have been together and what kinds of experiences and events have influenced their lives. Third, the dynamic relationship history will give the premarital counselor an opportunity to look at the patterns they have established in their relationship. By taking the opportunity to look at these, the couple will gain not only some awareness of their relationship, but also an opportunity to change those things that they feel they want to change for future growth and happiness.

Instrumentation

After the premarital counselor has become acquainted with the couple and has explained the dynamic relationship history, the counselor making use of instrumentation should now introduce the couple to the specific instruments chosen for the sessions. A brief explanation of the instruments should be given and specific instructions as to the taking of the instrument should be imparted.

Some premarital counselors prefer to limit the first session to administrative details, using the first session for the purpose of getting acquainted, explaining the dynamic relationship history, distributing and explaining the inventories, and discussing the contract. If this method is employed, then the dynamic relationship history and the content of the relationship will not begin until the second session. Some adjustment may then need to be made in regard to the total length of the sessions.

Premarital counselors employing instrumentation will need to bear in mind that extra time will be needed between the first sessions in order for the couple to complete the inventories and for the premarital counselor to complete the scoring process. In the case of an instrument such as PREPARE, the premarital counselor needs to allow eight to ten days for the results to be returned. Some instruments, which can be self-scored, can be available sooner, although the counselor needs to allow additional time to score and study the instruments.

Contract

We mentioned earlier that a premarital counseling process can, for most couples, be structured in advance as to the number of sessions. Nonetheless, we think it important for the premarital counselor, after having received the basic information as to the length of the courtship and the amount of time that needs to be covered during the dynamic relationship history, to have the opportunity specifically to contract with the couple regarding the number of sessions it will take to complete the work. If unusual situations are present or emerge in the relationship, the counselor can adjust the number of sessions.

For premarital counselors working outside the parish setting, we are suggesting a basic contract of four two-hour sessions. Since the nonclergy do not need to attend to the material of part 4, they can spend the first session on parts 1 and 2 and devote the next three sessions to part 3—one session on each person's family of origin and one session for the wrap-up. Part 3a, an optional section, includes the parents and would add a fifth two-hour session.

For clergy in parish settings we are suggesting five sessions: one session for parts 1 and 2, three sessions for part 3 (one for each person's family issues and one for wrap-up), and a final session for the mechanics of the wedding, theological issues, and so forth. Part 3a, the optional section including parents, would add more time to the process. Alternatives for the placement of part 3a in the counseling process will be discussed later.

With clergy members who are counseling premarital couples, the central question in the minds of the bride and groom will be, Will this pastor perform the marriage for us? It is our suggestion that premarital counseling will be more effective for the couple if the clergy member agrees to perform the marriage for them, providing they participate in the premarital counseling sessions.

Part 2: Dynamic Relationship History

We are defining the dynamic relationship history (DRH) as a structured way of looking at the history of a relationship from the time the couple first met up to the wedding. It is like a social history, with some significant differences. The DRH is informational in its orientation. The process is that of discovering some of the basic events, dates, dating maneuvers, and conflicts of the premarital process. But the DRH is rhythmic in its conclusions. The purpose is to help the couple become aware of how they behave with each other, how they affect each other, and the patterns they have already established. The DRH is a structured initial interview applied exclusively to the premarital relationship (Hiebert and Gillespie 1984).

Before we move directly into the methodology of the DRH, we want to remind the premarital counselor again of the powerful forces that impel the couple to each other and the marriage, and of the fact that the couple, psychologically speaking, are already married. It is important to accept the relationship of the couple as it is and to go from there. The task of the DRH, thus, is not only to take the couple as they are, but to move from that point to an expansion of their whole understanding of their relationship. The DRH is a way of accomplishing several tasks: helping the couple gain some awareness of the dynamics and patterns of their relationship, giving them some skills and tools for future growth, predicting some sense of the crises or conflicts that might develop, and establishing the possibility of future growth through enrichment and counseling experiences.

Premarital counseling is *not* to be conceived of as a process that can instill in the couple all that they need to prevent any future conflict or divorce. Not only would that be an impossible task, but such an expectation in the mind of the premarital counselor would be debilitating and constricting rather than enhancing and positive.

We like to think of premarital counseling in metaphorical terms, conceiving of the couple's relationship as the coming together of two rivers. The premarital counselor is putting a canoe in the river at some point past the junction. To try to resist a relationship, in view of the force present in the river, means that the premarital counselor would be canoeing upstream. That is a difficult task, at best. We fantasize the premarital counseling process not as an attempt to canoe upriver, but as an attempt to influence the river's course and flow through dredging and the building of wing dams.

Earlier in this chapter, we discussed the rationale for the dynamic relationship history as the premarital counselor explained it to the couple. We are now going to discuss the rationale from the premarital counselor's perspective, providing a more extensive basis for the use of this methodology.

First, the DRH is a way of controlling anxiety. As we indicated earlier, both the couple and the counselor frequently experience anxiety prior to and during the premarital counseling process. Obviously, the anxieties are different. The couple are anxious about the mechanics of the wedding and the future of their relationship. The premarital counselor is anxious about being able to provide the couple with a meaningful experience. We see the DRH as a way of binding anxiety.

The DRH has as one of its results the creation of a sense of direction, orderliness, that something is being accomplished. This sense of purposefulness alleviates anxiety for both couple and counselor.

Second, the DRH is a way of structuring information that is useful to both the couple and the premarital counselor. The use of the DRH will not only help the couple look at what is happening presently in their relationship, but will also aid them in making sense out of earlier happenings. The DRH will provide a methodology that will facilitate the emergence of the patterns and dynamics in the relationship in an orderly and clear manner.

Third, the DRH heightens an awareness of patterns. The process enables the counselor and the couple to become aware of the patterns and to heighten them in such a way that their impact can be more fully recognized and understood.

Fourth, the DRH creates a sense of movement in the lives of the couple. By looking at where they have come from and where they have been, the couple are allowed, in the context of a reflective setting, to get some sense of the transition in their lives from being single to being in relationship.

Fifth, the DRH allows the couple to involve themselves in the process on their own level. People perceive relationships in very concrete terms. The DRH is designed to look at and get at the dynamics of the relationship in the manner in which the couple looks at it. One of the difficulties of other methodologies is that counselors often speak a language that couples do not understand, and the perspective of the therapists or counselors is so different that couples cannot get in touch with the process.

Sixth, the DRH, which involves the use of significant questioning on the part of the premarital counselor, becomes a model for interaction. Because couples have frequently roped off certain areas from discussion, and because questioning is often taken as an attack or criticism, questioning in and of itself is difficult for them. Through the use of questions in the DRH, the premarital counselor models for the couples, helping them to gain some sense of the information and processes for obtaining it that are needed in order to understand another person.

The dating process is, in a certain way, an obscuring process. Couples rope off areas that they do not discuss. Part of this obscuring process is the result of the forces that impel couples toward marriage.

For example, the woman does not ask how much the man really drinks, and he does not ask how frequently she becomes sullen or silent for days on end. In addition, questioning has an underlying risk in intimate relationships: it may open up conflict and negativity, which can dampen the relationship. Thus, in an effort to maintain the peace and to promote the relationship, couples avoid questioning each other so that they do not move into dangerous water.

The DRH has as one of the primary ingredients of its style the art of questioning. The use of many questions is intended specifically to accomplish two tasks with couples. First, active questioning is designed to help expand the awareness of a couple. The questions help a couple to become aware of events or behaviors that they have taken for granted and have developed beneath the level of their awareness. Second, the questioning style of the DRH is designed to expand the thinking process of the couple. The questioning style, therefore, helps the couple to look at events and behaviors differently and to think "unthinkable thoughts" about what is happening in their lives. The primary purpose of the questioning style is to push out the horizons of the couple's thought framework and their awareness of the relationship.

We want to underscore that the goal of the DRH is not to resolve all the problems or conflicts of the couple. The purpose of the DRH is to help the couple to open up. The object is to get them to think and talk about what they have not been able to talk about, *after* they leave the premarital counselor. Although this may seem to be an overstatement, we believe that often what happens to the couple after they leave a session is more important than what happens during the session.

The purpose of the DRH is not to resolve all difficulties for the couple so that they can move into the future without problems, conflict, or fear of divorce. Rather, the DRH is intended to help the couple take responsibility for their lives, for their lives together, and for the joys and problems they create.

In a sense, the value of the DRH is that it serves as a milestone. It is a point at which the adult premarital counselor in a subtle but implicit way helps the couple see that they are no longer children. The couple can no longer blame parents for their lives. They are now moving into a time when they must take responsibility for themselves, if they are going to continue to grow and enjoy the relationship. For the premarital counselor to resolve whatever disagreements may be present between the couple would be to do what their parents did for them when they were children. The task of the premarital counselor is not to be a parent, but to promote the passage from childhood to adulthood, to promote responsibility.

Technique of Dynamic Relationship History

The DRH implies a chronological exploration of the relationship. We have discovered, in our work with premarital couples, that the use of a blackboard or of newsprint is important in the DRH. With a visual time line, the couple can more concretely visualize the movement of their relationship.

A blackboard has the advantage for the counselor of being easily erased, so dates, places, and events can be corrected as the couple move along in their exploration of the relationship. Its disadvantage is that once the material is erased, it is no longer available unless it is placed back on the board. The advantage of newsprint is that the material is available because the counselor can retain the newsprint and time line.

In training people for premarital counseling, we have discovered that there are a number of small issues around the subject matter of technique that can help the counseling process. In the first place, it is important for the counselor, during the DRH, to write down basically what is being said rather than interpretations of it. Second, we suggest that the counselor write the events or happenings on the board or newsprint in simple, short, coded words or short sentences that are large enough to read from a distance.

In terms of style, whenever dates and events are being placed on the time line, it is most efficient for the counselor to stand or move around while writing on the newsprint or blackboard. The counselor's being on his or her feet sets a more informal tone for the sessions, which will aid the couple in feeling more comfortable. At the same time, in a subtle way, the counselor's standing up establishes a definite sense that he or she is directing the session, which is reassuring to the couple.

We suggest that the premarital counselor use a "Y" graph placed on a horizontal dimension for the DRH (figure 5–1). The graph allows for an exploration of the individual lives of the couple before

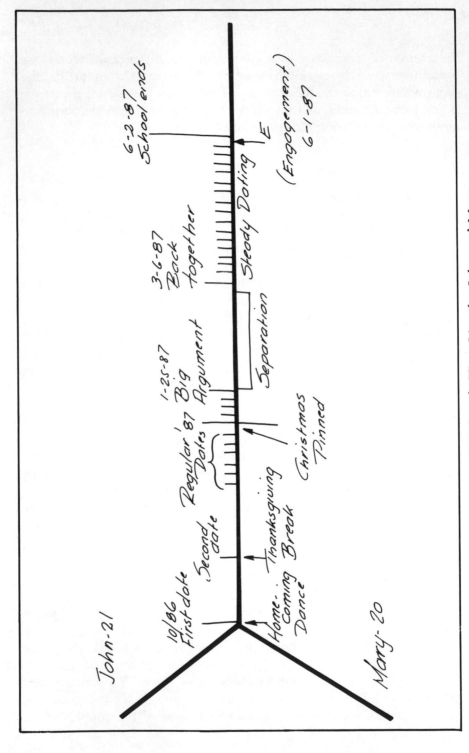

Figure 5–1. DRH Couple Time Line for John and Mary

they came together and began their dating process. The dates and events of the relationship should be plotted clearly and distinctly along the time line as the premarital counselor covers the dating history.

By way of summary, we want to remind the reader that the purpose of the DRH is awareness and expansion. As a result, the focus of the DRH is essentially rhythmic. We are not so much interested in the dates and events as we are in the patterns that are evolving and being established in the process. While we make use of the events and dates to frame the happenings of the relationship, our real interest is an exploration of the manner in which John affects Mary and Mary affects John and how they begin to develop a particular pattern in their relating style.

Because the focus of the DRH is essentially rhythmic, we want to remind the reader of one of the prime goals that we mentioned earlier. We are concerned for the couple to learn to open up areas that they have not explored previously in their communication. Thus, the DRH uses many questions.

Areas of Focus

We are now ready to begin talking about conducting a DRH. We have already indicated the general idea: to explore the relationship from the time the couple first met until the wedding. We now want to outline briefly some of the areas of focus and the kinds of questions we ask, to give the reader some sense of what we do and what we are looking for. We also want to make it clear that the DRH involves moving through the history of the relationship in a month-by-month fashion. Unless the couple has an extensive dating history, there is usually no difficulty in accomplishing this task in the time frame indicated.

If you are making use of an assessment device, such as PREPARE, the instrument(s) should also provide you with supplemental data that may or may not appear while you are conducting the dynamic relationship history. This material, however, can be added and merged with the data presented during the wrap-up.

As you, the premarital counselor, consider the various themes and questions we are now going to outline, recall the premarital factors related to marital quality and stability that were discussed in chapter 1.

The Beginning. At the beginning of the DRH, we are interested in how the couple met. If the couple have a pre-dating relationship going back to grade school, junior high, or high school, then we are interested in their perceptions of each other in those pre-dating years. Did they like each other, were they attracted to each other, did they dislike each other, were they repelled by each other? If they had a pre-dating relationship, how did they make the transition to a dating relationship? How did they move from being classmates or friends to being dating partners? If the couple had little or no previous relationship prior to the first date, how did they meet? Who arranged it, or who initiated it? What did they do on the first date? How did they arrive at the decision to do whatever they did? After their date was over, what were their impressions? What did John think of Mary, and vice versa? What was the attraction that led each other to ask for or to accept the second date? After the first date, what kinds of impressions did each have that caused them to wonder or be surprised or shocked about the other person?

The beginning of the relationship is plotted on the time line at the point at which the sloping lines intersect and become one horizontal line, as illustrated in figure 5–1.

The Second Date. After establishing how the couple first met and dated, move on to the second date. How did the couple get from the first date to the second date? Who initiated the second date? Who accepted the second date? What did they do? How did they arrive at the decisions?

When exploring the second and further dates, the counselor should keep in mind that the issue of what the couple did on the date is a concern not about their activity, but about the decision-making process. Was it a process that both engaged in, arriving at the decision by compromise; did one become the decision maker and the other simply give in or go along with the decision; or did the couple frequently struggle over whose idea they would follow? In other words, we are at the beginning of an exploration of the issue of power in the relationship.

Other Dating Experience. It is our custom when doing the DRH to get the origins of the couple's own dating relationship established before going back to establish previous relationships. Once we get this particular relationship launched, we then go back and take a brief overview of each person's preceding dating experiences.

In pursuing the previous relationships, we explore the beginning of dating in general with each person. We then explore the nature of their dating experiences and relationships prior to meeting their present mate. We are primarily interested in whether the relationships were casual or serious, whether some previous commitment had been made, and, if it had been broken, why?

Our focus on this area is intended to gain some understanding of whether the individuals have had a variety of dating experiences, or whether this is their first and only relationship. It might be suggestive of their level of self-esteem, if we assume that people with better self-esteem do more exploring and find it more comfortable and pleasant. Individuals with low self-esteem or high dependency needs often do little exploring during their early, casual dating period of life, latching on quickly to a dating partner. Some individuals with low self-esteem or high dependency needs show the opposite pattern, staying in an exaggerated casual dating pattern and resisting the development of greater seriousness in previous relationships or in this relationship. In any case, the kind of dating experience prior to this relationship that each person has had should be highlighted by the premarital counselor to give the couple an opportunity to become aware of their history.

The previous dating experiences can be plotted on the two sloping time lines prior to the point at which the time lines intersect, as in figure 5–2.

Dating Pattern. Moving beyond the second and subsequent dates, we begin exploring the regularity of the couple's dating each other. We are interested in how often the couple dates, what they do on the dates, and who makes the decisions.

One of our concerns in this particular part of the DRH is the development of exclusivity in the relationship. When did the couple begin to narrow down their dating? When did they begin to go steady? Did they make the decision verbally and together, or was it made privately and without discussing it openly? We are interested both in when it occurred and in whether there was a mutual discussion process or a nonverbal, covert process.

We are interested in understanding not only the relationship as it

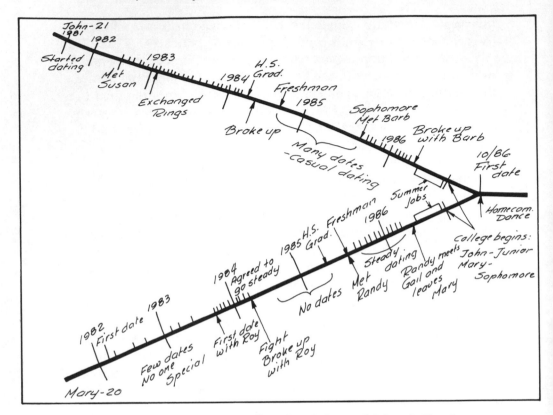

Figure 5–2. DRH Time Line Showing John and Mary's Previous Dating Patterns

narrowed down and became exclusive, but also in what was developing inside each person in regard to private thinking. When did each person begin thinking more seriously about the other? When did each begin to see the other as a candidate for future spouse? In chapter 3, we discussed the process of commitment and bonding and the three stages that process usually goes through. At this point in the relationship history, we are looking for the first stage. As we explore the private thinking, we are interested in what each person thought about the other. What attracted them? What worried them? What did they find unusual or strange about the other? What did they want to change in the other person? How did they plan to bring the change about?

As we continue to document the dating relationship month by

month, we begin to focus on the verbalization process of the couple. When did they begin talking about how they feel about each other? When did their private thought that the other person is indeed a candidate to be their spouse become spoken? Who began verbalizing the thought first? We are looking for stage two in the commitment process.

Events and Conflicts. As we move along the time line, watching the couple's movement from casual to serious dating, we note on the blackboard or newsprint the events or happenings that mark the passage of time for the relationship. We pay particular attention to conflicts and arguments. We ask, What were they about? How did the couple settle conflict? Did someone give in? Did one of them apologize first? How did they make up?

We are interested in the demonstrations of both anger and affection. How does each know when the other is pleased with something the first has said or done? If they do not know, why not? Does each know when the other is angry with something the former has said or done? If not, why not? The inability to risk either giving affection or getting angry may say something about an individual's insecurity (low self-esteem) or need to be taken care of (high dependency needs). Both insecurity and a significant need to be taken care of influence communication patterns, causing people to store up irritations and restrict affection-giving behavior.

We are also concerned about any separations that may have occurred in the dating process. We wonder about the separations. What precipitated the separation? Who initiated it? What contact took place during it? Who initiated getting together? Then, when did they get together? How did it go? Were there any hard feelings? How did they resolve the hard feelings?

We also focus on self-esteem in other ways. What can each do, of which they are as sure as they are of sitting in front of you, that will make the other happy? Or angry? How does each build the other's esteem? If they do not know, why not? These and many more issues are assessed, documented, and wondered about as the relationship is examined month by month.

Engagement. Next we begin to explore the time when the couple moved to the next step in the bonding or commitment process, that of making the nature of the relationship official through an engagement. Did the engagement arise by verbal discussion and mutual agreement, or did one decide that they were ready for engagement and surprise the other with it, either by offering a ring or by asking the question? Did they stumble into it, or walk into it in some fashion?

After the engagement was in some sense official, we begin wondering about impressions again. How did each find the other by this time? What qualities in each person attracted the other and allowed him or her to accept the engagement? What qualities or characteristics in the other caused each to wonder, or worry, or feel negative about the other? As a way of helping the couple to look back to see what has happened in their relationship, we begin to wonder about the changes that have taken place. What has the engagement done for the couple? In what way has it changed the relationship? How is the relationship now different?

Since many couples move to greater physical intimacy either immediately before, during, or after the commitment process, we begin exploring the sexual involvement of the couple. With many, although not all, couples, greater physical intimacy—which may or may not include sexual intercourse—commences around the commitment time. Thus, we are interested in exploring how the physical relationship developed.

If a premarital pregnancy is involved, we are interested in knowing how the decision to have intercourse was reached. We are interested in how it came to be that the couple did not use contraceptives. Did they discuss it? Did one resist? Why did the other accept the lack of contraceptives? We wish to look at the manner in which the couple allowed the pregnancy to take place. Does this say something about the responsibility they exercise in their lives? Or did it have something to do with bringing the couple together? Was it a way to precipitate a marriage? Was it a way of getting out of an unpleasant family of origin? Was it an attempt to soothe loneliness?

Couples can all benefit from some premarital sex education. If the premarital counselor wishes specifically to include a section on sexuality and family planning in the counseling process, he or she will have to allow additional time. We suggest that this material shall be placed at the end of the developmental process, after part 3. This allows for greater comfortableness to be established. A section on sexuality and family planning probably requires a more didactic style of presentation. Placing it at the end of part 3 would thus not change the pace of parts 2 and 3. (See chapter 13.)

Parents. Although couples frequently have involvements with their parents and future parents-in-law prior to their engagement, we generally deal with the parents at one point in the DRH. Thus, at this point we begin to examine the relationship of each person to his or her parents and each person's relationship to the other's parents.

We first begin exploring how each saw his or her parents responding to the dating partner at the beginning of the relationship. How did mother behave? How did father behave? What messages, verbal and nonverbal, did each get about the choice of dating partner? Then, as the couple moved toward greater seriousness, how did each set of parents respond? How did the couple inform the parents of their impending engagement or intention to marry? Was it an announcement of their decision? Or did they ask for permission? Who did the telling? How did each parent respond?

By the time many couples move to the wedding, each person has usually had some experience not only with the other's parents, but with seeing their prospective mate in action with his or her parents. Thus, we begin to ask about the perceptions of each toward the other. How does John see himself getting along with his father? With his mother? How does Mary see John getting along with his father? His mother? And how does Mary see herself getting along with her father and mother? How does John see Mary getting along with her father? Her mother? Then we explore the relationships from the opposite direction. How does John see Mary getting along with his father? His mother? How does Mary see John getting along with her father? Her mother?

Last, we explore the attitude of each set of parents toward the marriage. Is his father supportive? Favorable? How about his mother? Is her mother supportive, favorable? How about her father? If one or both of the parents is negative, why? Are they attempting to intervene in the process? How is the couple coping with that?

Wedding. After this area of focus is examined, the premarital counseling process will be current. At this point, we explore the parents' attitudes and wishes about the wedding. What kind of directives or leadership are Mary's parents attempting to offer? How is she coping with her own desires versus her parents' desires for her wedding? How is John coping with his parents' desires versus his own desires for his wedding? How is each person coping with the other's parents' expectations about the wedding?

There are a number of other issues to which the premarital counselor must attend, issues which do not necessarily occur chronologically but rather have a thematic or topical flavor. These next seven areas can be explored at any one point during the DRH or can be explored at different points along the time line.

Personality issues. We are concerned about how each experiences the other's personality, and whether there are aspects that each tries to change in the other. Is jealousy a problem? Has one or the other experienced the prospective partner as becoming jealous over the other's behavior? What has been done about that? Another area that couples frequently struggle about has to do with anger. How does each see the other's temper? Who becomes the most angry? How does each know when the other is angry? Have they tried to change or alter the manner in which the other expresses anger? Has this succeeded? Another personality dynamic that frequently causes conflict is the issue of moodiness. How does each see the other in regard to moodiness? Does one seem more moody than the other? What brings on the moods? Does one try to help the other's moods? Does it work? Related to the issue of moodiness is the issue of negativity and a sense of being down. We wonder whether one is more negative or down than the other? Who tries to help whom? How do they attempt to counteract the negativity? Does it succeed? Lastly, we wonder about stubbornness or bossy behavior. How does each see the other in regard to stubbornness? Who is the most stubborn? Who can influence whom the most? Who generally wins when push comes to shove? All of these issues have something to do with the couple's relative satisfaction or dissatisfaction with the nature of the prospective mate's personality. All couples will make some attempt to make some changes in the prospective mate. But when a couple has major, ongoing differences that result in repeated conflict and attempts to change the partner, it may be a sign that one has some basic dislike for who the other is.

Communication. Couples have different levels of satisfaction and functionality in regard to communication. Most premarital couples feel that they are communicating well because they are very much involved with each other and very much interested in the other person. Nonetheless, some couples have more difficulty achieving good communication patterns than do others. During the course of the DRH, the premarital counselor needs to assess the functionality of the communication pattern. Thus, we are concerned about whether the couple experiences the communicational pattern as open. Are they able to express their feelings? Are they able to say whatever is on their minds? Or, do they find it difficult to express what they really feel? Does one shut the other off when communication reaches difficult or touchy areas? Some people tend to be much more private and thus inhibited when it comes to disclosing what they really think and feel. It may not be a pattern that is pathological, but rather a pattern prevalent in the family of origin. Nonetheless, differences in regard to openness and closedness can create conflict. Is one more closed than the other? Is one more private and less open? Has this caused conflict? How have they tried to change this quality in the mate? Has it succeeded? Still another aspect of the communicational pattern which we explore is the use of silence. Some families and some people make use of silence, particularly when they are angry, annoyed, or disappointed in the mate's response. In some families, people or spouses may not speak for several days or several weeks. Thus, we are concerned as to whether the couple has experienced silence. Who has become silent? How long did it last? How did they begin speaking again? Was the origin of the silence discovered? How did the recipient of the silent treatment feel? This is an important area because silence can be one of the most vicious forms of anger and can be experienced with a real sense of panic. Lastly, we also like to explore the manner in which the couple handles criticism, either in terms of giving it or receiving it. Do either of them tend to attack the other? If so, who attacks whom? Or, are they mutually attacking?

Conflict resolution. Conflict is part of marital relationships but often premarital couples have limited conflict because of the nature of the premarital dynamics already discussed. In any case, the premarital couple who has some experience in conflict resolution prior to the wedding is more likely to have a satisfactory adjustment to marriage after the wedding because of their ability to experience and practice conflict resolution during the dating process. Thus, we ask about the kinds of conflicts the couple has experienced prior to the wedding. Many couples report few or no conflicts. For those couples who report that the relationship has been all positive with no conflict, we make some observation about the fact that conflict and argument are part of marriage. Two individuals cannot live in a relationship without disagreement and conflict. The issue is not whether the couple experiences conflict, but rather whether they have developed a method to resolve conflicts. For those couples who have experienced conflict, we like to explore the following issues. Can each speak his or her mind to the other? Does one hold back? Why? If each can speak his or her mind, does the other understand? Can they get their point across? And when it comes to resolving differences, how do they go about it? Does each give? Do they take turns giving in? Does one give in more than the other? Sometimes in relationships, one person speaks his or her mind more than the other. When this happens, we are concerned to inquire as to whether one is more concerned to avoid conflict? Does one give in in order to avoid conflict? How did this get started? Does it work for them?

Financial management. As in the area of conflict, some couples report little or no disagreements around issues of financial management. For some couples, this is an area in which they had very similar ideas and similar behaviors. Perhaps they came from similar families of origin. For other couples, conflict over financial management has not arisen because they have not been in the position of needing to make decisions where conflict could arise. Still other couples have had disagreements over financial management. In this area, we are concerned about how the couple has dealt with and reacts to how each spends money. How does each see the other's spending habits? Does one spend too much or too little? How are they similar and how are they different? If they are different, how have they resolved it to date? What plans do they have to resolve the difference in the future? Some couples have been living together prior to the wedding; inquire as to whether they split their expenses or merged their income. If they have merged their income, how did they resolve who did what in regard to financial management? Who banked the money? Who writes the checks? Who has how much spending money? Who has veto power over purchases? Do they like the manner in which they have handled the money? Has it worked out for them? For couples who have split expenses, how do they intend to handle their money after the wedding? If they merge the money, who will write the checks? Who will bank the money? How will they make decisions about purchases? For couples who have been involved in financial decision making of one kind or another during the premarital process, the area of financial management will have greater reality. For couples who are living with parents and not having to confront many decisions in the area of financial management, this particular topic may seem a bit abstract to them.

Leisure activities. Each couple must find some way to deal with their similarities and differences regarding leisure time activities and hobbies. One area of potential conflict has to do with the degree to which the couple needs to be engaged in the same hobbies or activities as opposed to the degree to which the couple needs to engage in separate activities or hobbies. Thus, we explore the degree of similarity or difference between their hobbies and interests. Does one pressure the other to enjoy the other's activities? Do they feel they do too much together? Or, do they feel they do too much separately? Can they find a balance? Have they attempted to do so? Sometimes partners feel that mates are either too busy or too inactive. Has there been struggle in this area? Does one feel the other has too many activities? Does one feel the other has too few activities? Sometimes couples have a different sense of what "having fun" means and thus they disagree over having a good time. Is the couple similar or different in this area? Have they experienced any struggles over the nature of having a good time? And, connected with leisure activities is the area of affection and attentiveness. Some couples have many leisure activities but feel cheated when it comes to enjoying each other. Other couples spend much time with each other but feel they are not active enough in terms of hobbies and activities. In other words, each couple must find some way to balance togetherness and separateness. How has this couple experienced it? Have they had enough time together? Have they felt left out? Have they felt they have had too much time alone? Again, for some premarital couples, this area will be a discussion in the abstract. Because premarital couples usually can't get enough time together, they have not been as concerned about spending time alone. For couples who have lived together prior to the wedding, this area may be discussed with a greater sense of reality because they have had to struggle already with the degree of togetherness as opposed to the degree of separateness. In any case, each marital couple has to decide for themselves how much togetherness they need and when.

Sexual relationship. Each mid-decade the National Center of Health Statistics releases the results of the partial census that is taken in mid-decade. In 1985, the census data indicated that the average marrying age had advanced and that couples were currently marrying, on the average, between the ages of twenty-four and twenty-six. That represented an advance of two years from the 1980 census. If that trend continues, by the year 2000 the average marrying age will probably be around thirty. With couples marrying later, the percentage of couples cohabiting prior to the wedding increases. In addition, the number of couples sexually active prior to the wedding also increases. Currently, premarital counselors can assume that at least eight out of every ten couples are sexually active prior to the wedding. Although prewedding sexual behavior may pose a philosophic problem for clergy, in the premarital counseling context the issue is no longer its appropriateness but rather the functionality of this area of the relationship.

While moving along the time line, we simply ask couples after the dating process has become steady and intense, when they became sexually active. Once we have established the onset of the sexual relationship, then we begin to inquire as to whether the amount of sexual activity was satisfactory? If not, why not? Did the amount of sexual activity change as they moved toward the wedding? As the couple became sexually active, were they comfortable with their sexual activity; was either uncomfortable? Did each know about the other's uncomfortableness? Not only is sexual activity important, but also the degree to which the couple can talk about their sexual relationship. We ask the couple whether they discussed becoming sexually active before the sexual relationship commenced. If so, what did they decide? If they did not talk about it before they first had sex, why? Did they discuss it afterwards? Have they been able to talk about their sexual relationship during their dating? Would they characterize their sexual conversations as open or difficult and tense? Have they been able to share sexual expectations, ideas, behaviors?

Couples who have been sexually active also hopefully will have dealt with the area of birth control. Some couples, however, will not have discussed this area. We think it important to explore the degree of communication in the area of birth control. Has the couple been making use of a birth control method? If so, which one? How did they arrive at that choice? Did they discuss other options? Are they satisfied with the method(s) employed? Would they like to make changes? Have they thought of using a different method at another point in the marriage?

Although we have been specifically discussing the sexual relationship, it is also very necessary to discuss the affectional aspect of the relationship in conjunction with the sexual relationship. Has the couple been satisfied with the amount of affection during the relationship? Has either of them felt unloved? How have they attempted to go about getting more love? Has it worked?

Family and friends. Each couple has to find some way to deal with the separate circle of friends that each partner may have had prior to becoming involved with the other. Some couples find it difficult to merge their friendship circles because one or the other does not like the other's friends. We think it important to check out how the couple handled the merging of their friendship network. We wonder whether each likes the other's friends? Has each felt pressured to like the other's friends? In addition to finding a way of dealing with the other's friendship network, each couple must decide whether there are friends with whom they can socialize individually or whether they must socialize with all friends as a couple. Thus, we wonder whether they have allowed each other to socialize individually with some friends? Must they socialize with all friends as a couple? And, if they can socialize individually with friends, have any friends taken up too much time? Have they fought over whether more time is being spent with friends than with each other?

Each couple must also balance the amount of time spent with families of origin as opposed to time spent with each other. Although this area will be further explored in chapter 6, at this point in the time line we are interested in how they have experienced the involvement with the families of origin. Does each feel the other is too involved with his or her parents? Does each feel the other is too influenced by what his or her parents say? Is each comfortable with his or her in-laws? Have they found a way to resolve the differences?

Comments and Clues about Patterns

We have been outlining some of the areas of focus that the premarital counselor examines as he or she proceeds along the time line, exploring the history of the relationship with the couple. Although we have occasionally made comments as to why we ask the questions we do, we now want to comment generally about what is in the premarital counselor's mind as he or she observes the couple and the relationship unfolding before his or her eyes.

Commitment and Bonding. In chapter 3, we discussed the concept of commitment and bonding. Here, we simply want to call to the reader's attention that while conducting the DRH, we are interested in observing the manner in which the commitment process took place and whether it is following a rather usual or common pattern or has the marks of differentness or difficulty. As we indicated earlier, if the commitment process is following a rather typical development, the three stages of commitment will be evident during the dating history. Difficulties in moving through the three stages can also be easily spotted. Separations may occur when a couple has difficulty in moving from one stage to another. Other relationships may develop and intervene in or prevent the movement to another stage. Difficulties in the commitment process are important to characterize for the couple during the wrap-up.

Dependency. Another of the factors that we bear in mind when watching a couple lay out their relationship has to do with the dependency needs of these two people. How dependent are they? Are they able to articulate their dependency needs? Do they make them clear? Part of the answers to these questions lies in observing the speed of the dating relationship.

Couples who are relatively independent people, who want a relationship but do not need it, follow a more deliberate course as they proceed through the premarital process. Couples with exaggerated dependency needs often take one of two courses. For some, the dependency needs are so strong that they no longer want but need the other person, and rush to stage three in great haste. For others, the dependency needs are so profound that they postpone the commitment process, fearful of being swallowed up in the relationship. They exaggerate the length of the courtship and find ways to postpone commitment, protecting their own esteem.

We have often found it helpful to couples to raise questions about their dependency needs. We often ask them to comment on how they see each other, which seems to be more helpful than asking each to talk about his or her own dependency needs. We sometimes ask John how he sees Mary: How would he rate her on a scale of 1 to 10 in terms of her dependency needs? And the same for Mary: How does she see John? How would she rate him on a scale of 1 to 10?

Self-esteem and Communication. Another factor which we think the premarital counselor should keep in mind is the issue of self-esteem. How each sees the self—whether each sees himself or herself as a person of worth—will have had an influence on the communication process. Couples with good self-esteem can be spotted in the decision-making process. Individuals with good self-esteem speak up; they want decisions about what the couple does and where they go to be made mutually. Individuals with low self-esteem frequently take one of two courses. On the one hand, they are often hesitant to speak up and to give their opinion, because they do not want to be thought stupid or crazy or they do not want to irritate and alienate the prospective mate. Thus, relationships in which one or both partners have low self-esteem are frequently marked by an absence of conflict in the decision-making process, or by a difficulty in making decisions because neither will speak up. On the other hand, some individuals with low self-esteem cover this by being determined to have their own way. They cover their weakness with a kind of dominance. This person can be spotted in a couple in which either one person makes all of the decisions or both people chronically argue about what they are going to do and when. Again, we have often found it helpful to ask each person to comment on how they perceive the other's self-esteem.

Power. Also involved in the exploration of the dating process is the issue of power. The decision-making process, in addition to being affected by each person's self-esteem, is affected by the whole issue of power. During the dating process, couples frequently like to think that neither one is going to have more power than the other, that they are going to have a fifty-fifty relationship. However, whenever two people are intimately involved, the issue of power lies beneath the surface. The question of leadership or control is present anytime two human beings are in a relationship with each other.

Our interest in observing the dating relationship unfold is to get some sense of the nature of power in this relationship. The decision-making process is one area where the issue of power is most clearly visible. As the couple decides how often they will date, where they will go, what they will do, and then, later in the relationship, what they will buy and when they will buy it, their way of making these decisions will reflect issues of power. We find it helpful to raise some questions about that with couples, to wonder about the issue of power, who is in charge of the relationship now, how each of them sees the other in regard to power, and whether they, too, wonder who is in charge.

Intimacy. Another factor which demonstrates itself clearly in a DRH is the dynamic of intimacy. Has the couple been able to establish a closeness, a togetherness, that is healthy? When couples have difficulty with intimacy, it is portrayed in two common ways. Some couples become too close: they absorb each other. These people become obsessed with each other, knowing intuitively each other's thoughts and feelings. To some extent, this is normal for premarital couples. The romantic nature of those who are not yet married or who recently married has been discussed before (Guldner 1971). Nonetheless, some couples clearly are too absorbed in each other. One can predict that at some point in the future, one or both will feel smothered unless they develop more room for individuality in their relationship. Such a couple can benefit from questions designed to raise their awareness about their intense closeness. Can they function when the other is gone for a few days? How much time alone do they each need a day? Can they engage in separate activities and not feel lonely?

On the other hand, some couples have difficulty in becoming close or intimate. These couples set up barriers or distancing behaviors, designed to keep them from becoming too close. Anger, arguments, infrequent contact, separations, and continued dating of others are among the behaviors couples use to keep distant.

We have found it helpful to raise questions about closeness, to wonder how a couple experience their intimacy, to wonder whether they feel smothered or too distant and lonely. Sometimes we have found it helpful to ask each person to rate the level of intimacy at different points in their common history on a scale from 1 to 10.

Religious Practice. In the course of a dating relationship, many issues arise that can produce arguments because of their potential for differences of opinion. Areas such as the handling of money, the use of alcohol and other chemical substances, the disciplining of children, and many others are often battlegrounds for differences of opinion. One such area is the issue of religion and religious practice.

Clerical premarital counselors may want to focus on religion and religious practice at some point during the DRH. It is important, in order to help each person become aware of the other's perspective, to establish a dual focus: religion *and* religious practice. Couples may share similar religious thoughts or a theological framework, but differ widely on practice. On the other hand, couples can share similar religious practices, but differ widely in their philosophical or theological values.

We have found it helpful for couples to explore their religious value systems. Sometimes it is best to have each first speak about what he or she thinks the other believes or values. It will quickly become apparent to the couple how much each knows about the other's thoughts or values. This discussion will naturally flow, then, into a description by each of his or her own religious thoughts and beliefs. Specific questions can be inserted by the clergy member regarding some of the denominational beliefs. If the couple are of the same religious background, the pastor can, by inserting questions, help them to see how each agrees or differs with the religious background. If the couple are from different religious backgrounds, by the use of questions, the clergy member can help them assess their similarities and differences in doctrinal beliefs.

The process of helping the couple to examine their similarities and differences in regard to religion and religious values is a pattern to be followed in the area of religious practice. Again, explore the areas of agreement or disagreement. What was their religious practice or activity in high school? After high school? Were they each a member of a church, synagogue, or religious group? Did they attend? How often—never, once a month, twice a year? What about future plans: Will both attend the same church or religious group? How often?

We suggest that at this point in the DRH, clergy members restrict their work simply to helping the couple explore their similarities and differences in religious values and practices. Specific theological reflection or skill-building should be placed later in the premarital counseling process and will be discussed in chapter 6 as part 4 of the process, the wedding preparation.

The Wrap-up

When we have completed a DRH, we spend some time providing the couple with our observation. The wrap-up is meant to be not judgmental or critical but descriptive. We have found that couples benefit enormously from being able to have the comments of an outsider or third party on their relationship. This kind of information is often helpful for couples, giving them some new sense about themselves and their relationship.

The wrap-up is the time for the counselor to exercise his or her creativity. The more concrete the wrap-up—the more clearly the counselor can illustrate what he or she is describing with the data from the couple's relationship—and the more humor and illustration the counselor can give to the wrap-up, the clearer and more effective it will be for the couple.

As a rule of thumb, we suggest that the premarital counselor mention the kinds of concerns, be they strengths or weaknesses, that he or she sees in the relationship. Each premarital counselor must do the wrap-up in a personal way. The wrap-up must reflect the counselor's sensitivity by including the perceptions that strike him or her most personally.

As noted, it is obvious that we have discussed the areas we are most interested in and the kinds of things we mention to a couple. We are concerned that each couple should have some sense of how we perceive their relationship and the kind of commitment they have. If we see difficulties in the bonding process, we characterize them in a nonjudgmental way. We comment on dependency needs, the manner and nature of the couple's handling of them, the degree to which they have been able to talk about them, the suspicions we have about the problems that the dependency needs might cause. We comment on self-esteem and how we see it either enhancing or detracting from the relationship. We comment on how each person can deal with and begin to work on his or her self-esteem. We talk about power: how we see it operating in the relationship, whether the couple struggle about it, who tends to handle most of it, and so forth.

For premarital counselors making use of instrumentation, especially for those using PREPARE, the data from the instruments can be incorporated in the wrap-up. PREPARE will either substantiate the DRH or provide additional information in regard to seven specific areas of the relationship: personality issues, communication, conflict resolution, financial management, leisure activities, sexual relationship, and family and friends. Not only will PREPARE identify the degree of similarity or differentness on those issues, but it will also point out the areas of strength.

When presenting this information to the couple, the premarital counselor must highlight the strengths of the relationship. Comment on the manner in which they show their affection—by their words, or humor, or teasing—and on their behaviors. Emphasize their caring, their respect for each other's uniqueness, the way they balance each other. By giving them a sense of the way they attend to each other, you can help them attain a sense of the uniqueness of their relationship.

It is important to understand that each premarital counselor probably does the wrap-up differently from every other premarital counselor. We each will be impressed with different factors, different events, different dynamics. The issue is not whether one is right, but whether one gives the couple information that helps them grow while struggling to come to grips with the counselor's impressions. Remember, the issue is to get them talking and to get them to be open to areas that they have not previously been able to identify, look at, discuss. Thus, the emphasis is less on being accurate than it is on being able to raise for the couple's awareness issues that they have not been able to touch.

Conclusion

The dynamic relationship history is, obviously, a dynamic history. It is difficult in written form to give the DRH the kind of life and excitement it can have in reality. It is nonetheless a process that is both easy and fun to use. We feel that as a rule of thumb, if the counselor is enjoying himself or herself, the couple is probably learning from the experience.

By now we have said a number of times that the purpose of premarital counseling is not the resolution of all conflict. Rather, the purpose is to bring issues and patterns to the awareness of the couple, giving them a new way to understand them and some skills to deal with them. We hope that we have underscored the issue of awareness as we have unfolded the DRH. The relationship history keeps moving; it does not get bogged down, but is concerned with raising questions the couple had not raised, with opening up areas the couple had not discussed, with expanding their thinking about the nature of their relationship. If that can be accomplished, the couple will walk into the future with better skills with which to deal with their relationship.

6
On Leaving Home:
Where They Come From

With this chapter we begin part 3 of the premarital counseling process, the family-of-origin exploration (FOE). Before we move directly into the process of the family-of-origin work, we will briefly note the theoretical issues that lie behind the inclusion of this particular aspect. At the end of this chapter, we will explore part 4, the wedding preparation, designed for the clergy.

Separation from Family of Origin

It has been well established in family theory and family therapy theory that the degree of separation a person has from his or her family of origin can be an important indicator of marital success. The degree to which a person is able to move in status from child to adult, to become a peer with his or her parents, has something to do with the ability of that individual to succeed in marriage.

Earlier Cultures

In preindustrial society, the degree of closeness to one's family of origin influenced the success of one's marriage. In such societies, the family existed as an extended unit, with more than one generation in a household. Thus, the family functioned more as a clan. The clan was the depository of knowledge. If a human being was to survive the rigors of life, he or she was dependent on the clan to teach the individual the necessary skills for survival and to provide the appropriate support group for that survival. At best, it was difficult for individuals or a couple to survive outside of a clan. In preindustrial societies, therefore, the individual's connection with and incorporation in the clan were extremely important. In psychological terms, enmeshment in the clan was not only necessary but positive.

Preindustrial societies also did not experience change as it is experienced today. Life was more static; therefore, change came about more slowly. The oldest generations of the family could function as appropriate transmitters of knowledge and skills for survival. The knowledge passed on by the oldest generation might be valid for centuries.

Twentieth Century Cultures

The industrial revolution, which had its beginnings in the eighteenth century, dramatically affected not only society, but family life as well. The advent of the steam engine brought the development of the machine. The machine brought the factory; the factory brought the movement from farm to town. With the nineteenth and twentieth centuries and increasing industrialization, mobility and change became a part of life. The machine brought significant advances in the field of technology. With the advance came change, and with change came the interaction of many other forces.

In preindustrial cultures, the family was relatively immobile. People were born, raised, married, and lived and died in the same home. With the industrial society and the mobility that resulted from it, the clan was disrupted. The kind of mobility that is demanded in twentieth century life means that the enmeshment that was positive in a preindustrial society becomes a liability in an industrial society. Too much enmeshment prevents individuals and couples from appropriate involvement in an industrial society, which demands that people have the ability to move and to change.

It is no longer innovative to talk about the rapid change that is part of our lifestyle. We are familiar with and must continually deal with a rapidly changing world. Our changing world means a change in knowledge. Because of this, parents are no longer the depositors of wisdom that remains fixed and unchanging for centuries. Slowly but surely, experts in a variety of fields have taken the place of the family as the depositors of knowledge. Parents' ways of doing things may no longer be best, or adequate, or right, for children (Lasch 1977).

The industrial revolution and mobility are two factors that have brought about the disappearance of the clan. The clan no longer is necessary for survival. A properly trained individual in an industrial society no longer needs the large support group of the clan either to succeed or to survive in life. In the preindustrial age, the clan was of paramount importance, and individuals were of secondary importance. In an industrial society, the importance of the individual accelerates, as does that of marriage. The clan or extended family unit recedes in importance.

The industrialization of a society, therefore, requires a new kind of maturity on the part of individuals. With the clan no longer around either to support or encourage or to maintain survival, both physical and emotional survival becomes dependent upon the responsibility and the maturity of the individual (Lasch 1977).

Research

Since the early 1950s, significant research has been done in family theory and therapy on the importance of individuals' ability to separate psychologically from their families of origin.

The people who adapt to marital life best in America seem to have two characteristics. First, they are individuals who have been able to leave home, psychologically speaking. By "leaving home" we mean that the individuals no longer ask their parents to take responsibility for their lives. To put it in other terms, the child has become an adult. The person no longer asks his or her parents to mother and father him. Second, people who best adapt to American marital life are also people who have had an opportunity to live alone after they have left home and before they enter marriage. Living alone and being able to survive both emotionally and financially are important in that people must have an opportunity to establish their own psychological identity. These two themes are recounted numerous times in the literature on family theory and therapy (Foley 1974, Barnard and Corrales 1979).

Individuals who have not left home emotionally and psychologically experience greater difficulties in life in a number of ways. First, they keep getting tangled up in family problems. Their own marital relationships are chronically in crisis because of the crises that are going on in the larger family. Struggles between mother and father, between parents and one or more of the children, or between adult children interfere with and cause friction in the marriage.

Second, people who have not left home psychologically tend to look for spouses who will continue the parenting of the biological parents. Because families that hang onto their children prevent their children from growing up psychologically, these individuals look for a spouse not in terms of a peer, a fellow adult with whom they can establish an intimate relationship, but in terms of another person who will take care of them. That kind of relationship, however, is frequently beset with problems, because chances are that the other spouse is looking for the very same kind of partner. Thus, two people who are both looking for a parent depend on each other to be the good, kind, and patient parent who will enable them to be a child forever.

Third, people who have not left home psychologically tend to have more physical and somatic problems than others. The research on psychosomatic illness documents the fact that people who are still emotionally entangled with their families of origin as adults are physically sick more frequently than those who are more independent.

Fourth, people who have not psychologically separated from their parents usually come from homes in which the parents do not want them to do so. They have been encouraged not to grow up, not to take charge of their own lives, to remain children. With this attitude in the family of origin, the young adult will have difficulty functioning as an adult.

Part 3: Family-of-Origin Exploration

The purpose of part 3 of our premarital counseling process, thus, is to take a look at the degree of separation that exists between each of the persons and their family of origin. Part 3 is designed to help the couple assess whether they come from a clan, whether they have an excessive attachment to their parents, and whether they will be able to take responsibility for their own lives, as well as to give them some sense of their need for growth regarding their family of origin.

Parents as Models

There is no doubt that parents are the first human beings that we, as children, come to know. Father is the first male we come to know. Mother is the first female we come to know. Our parents are also the first husband-wife team we come to know. From father, we observe what husbanding is all about. From mother, we observe what wifing is all about.

Marital expectations, marital attitudes, and marital behavior patterns are not born into us. We learn them from parents. Children who have only one parent, or whose parents are absent or deficient in some way, creatively find substitutes or significant others such as grandparents, aunts, uncles, neighbors, and teachers.

The research on family theory and therapy clearly supports the idea that parents are powerful models (Burr et al. 1979). Naturally, some models are better than others. Thus, parents in an indirect fashion either help or hinder couples in establishing and maintaining married life.

Families in which conflict exists in the parental marriage tend to have children who take one of two courses. On the one hand, some of the children will repeat the pattern of the parental marriage. It is almost as if children who see their parents struggling with problems they cannot resolve need to attempt to duplicate those problems and attempt to solve them for themselves and for their parents. Thus it is that many couples will almost identically duplicate the problems or patterns of their parents' marriage. On the other hand, there are some people who try to prevent repeating conflicts of their parents' marriage by behaving in exactly the opposite ways. Sometimes that works, and other times it only creates the opposite problems.

There seems to be a particular kind of pain experienced by people who, as they were growing up, perceived their same-sex parent as losing in the marital relationship. Although marriages are usually well balanced, and husband and wife either both lose or both win, children often do not perceive it that way. If the same-sex parent was perceived as losing, the adult child may be difficult to live with because he or she does not want to duplicate the losing. In like manner, the adult child who saw the same-sex parent winning may seek to dominate or get his or her own way.

In the family-of-origin exploration, our purpose is not only to look at and trace the parental models which a man and woman bring into their relationship, but also to trace how these models influence their own behavior with each other. Again, our purpose has to do with heightening the awareness of the models in the premarital couples.

Format for the Exploration

In our outline of the premarital counseling process, we are placing the family-of-origin exploration after the dynamic relationship history. The reader may be wondering why the family-of-origin work does not come first. We have placed it second because frequently the premarital counselor does not know one or both parties. Placing the dynamic relationship history prior to the family-of-origin exploration allows the premarital counselor a chance to become acquainted with the couple.

We also have found in our own work with premarital couples that people seem to find it easier and to be more motivated to talk about themselves and their dating experience than about their family of origin. Since most couples have experienced their dating relationship as pleasant and are in a state of heightened awareness about their relationship as they move to the wedding, this seems to be an easier starting place for them.

There are some families in which the parental closeness and attachment to the young adult children is so intense that any attempt to discuss the family of origin will be resisted. The young adult often feels that he or she should not be talking about the parents without their explicit approval. He or she may also feel that what happens in the family of origin is no one else's business.

It is important for the premarital counselor to be careful to explain the reasons for the FOE as clearly and as fully as possible. The issue of the impact of parental modeling should be stressed. Some individuals will, upon reflection, see the usefulness of the FOE. Others will remain resistant. If a person or couple is resistant, it is best to respect their feelings. Sometimes focusing on the reason for these feelings will overcome the resistance. The FOE can also be conducted with the willing partner and focus on *both* families. It is important, however, when only one partner is present, for the counselor also to focus on what the reluctant partner's behavior might mean for the future marriage. The use of predictions is useful for the person's reflection on and consideration of the implications of the partner's behavior.

We suggest three sessions as the basic format; one session can be devoted to each family, and a third session can be spent in the wrap-up. We also suggest the addition of one session, to include the parents in a process of saying good-bye, as an optional unit.

The process of looking at each person's family of origin involves an examination of all the interactions and all the levels of functioning in the family. In most premarital counseling cases, this will not be difficult to accomplish, unless the family has many children in it or many marriages, divorces, and other events make the family of origin exceedingly complex to comprehend.

We divide the family-of-origin exploration into eight sections: (1) the siblings as individuals, (2) sibling interactions, (3) parent-child interactions, (4) husband-wife interactions, (5) family interactional style, (6) parental models, (7) wrap-up, and (8) saying good-bye.

Method

As in the dynamic relationship history, we have found that the visual aid is important in effectively dealing with this material. We suggest either a blackboard or newsprint. Since the counselor will want to keep the diagram for future reference, the use of newsprint or a note-pad will save the task of copying the information from the blackboard.

The methodology for the family-of-origin exploration begins with drawing the family as a two-generation genogram. Our basic format is shown in figures 6–1 and 6–2, which illustrate John and Mary's separate families. From figure 6–1, the reader can see that John is 21 years of age and has two older brothers, Joe who is 23, and Mike who is 26 and married to Ellen. He has one younger sister, Susan. John's parents are Henry, 48, and Elsie, 46. Similar information is given for Mary and her family in figure 6–2.

Recently there has been much interest in the use of genograms in marriage and family therapy, with the result that the format has become standardized (McGoldrick and Gerson 1985). As we use the genogram in our premarital family-of-origin exploration, we use both the two-generational figure type diagrams shown in figure 6–1 and 6–2, as well as the standardized format shown in figure 6–3. We have found that the figure-type diagramming can greatly personalize

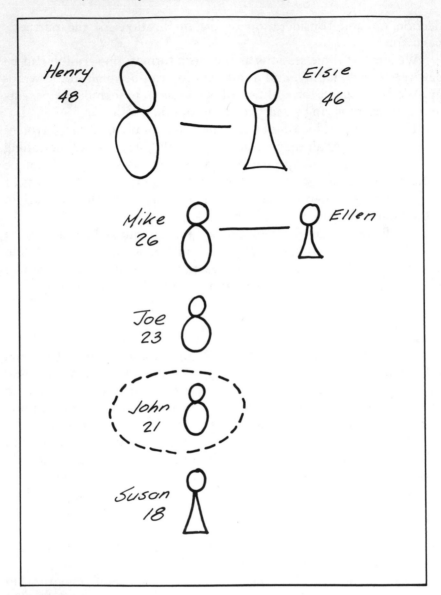

Figure 6–1. John in His Family of Origin

the FOE process by adding faces or similar attributes when discussing and drawing the couple and their families of origin. Thought, creativity, and humor seem to flow from use of the personalized figures

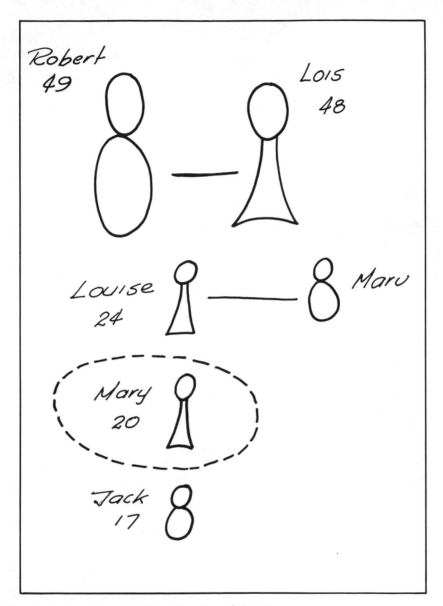

Figure 6–2. Mary in Her Family of Origin

in comparison to the sole use of the square and circle format. We do use the standardized square and circle symbols as we expand the chart to include the details of three or four generations.

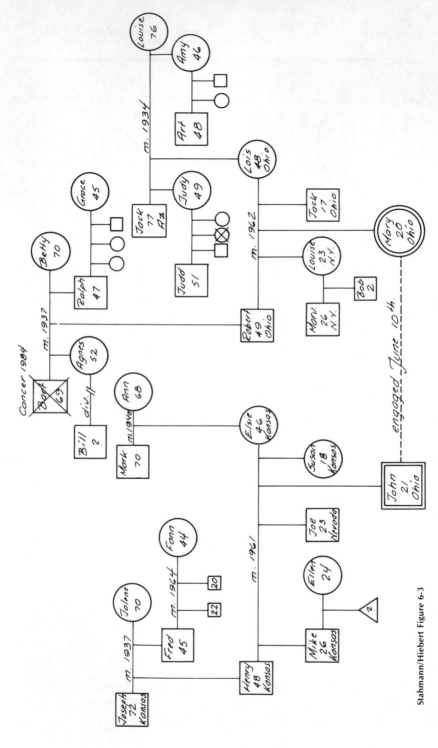

Figure 6–3. Standard Genogram Showing John and Mary and Thier Families of Origin for Three Generations

Stahmann/Hiebert Figure 6-3

Figure 6–3 shows John and Mary in their families of origin using the symbols and notations that have become standardized in genograms (McGoldrick and Gerson 1985). The information shows the engaged couple, John and Mary, and family information back through their grandparents. The reader can easily determine that both John and Mary come from intact families, the only divorce having been Mary's Aunt Agnes. John's family of origin, with four children, is the largest for either family line in the three generations shown. Apparently the families are healthy in that only Mary's Grandpa Bart and one other person are deceased. The genogram shows that Grandpa Bart died of cancer in 1984 at the age of 69. One of Mary's cousins, the middle child of Uncle Judd and Aunt Judy, is dead, but Mary could not recall the reason for the death.

The genogram also shows the birth order position of each family member and the gender of siblings. John is the third child and third son of four children. Mary is the second child and second daughter of three children. What might be the implications for their relationship? Both are middle children, thus have had experience interacting with others. Yet both have same-gender older siblings and an opposite gender younger sib. Perhaps John and Mary will act toward each other somewhat as they did to their younger sibling? We believe that an understanding of family constellation and birth order can be useful to the premarital counselor, not for predictive purposes, but for understanding interpersonal dynamics and behavior. The premarital counselor will benefit from reading further about the use of sibling position in marital relationships (Harper, 1984) and interpreting genograms using family constellation information (McGoldrick and Gerson 1985, Toman 1976).

As we use the genogram, our goal is to obtain both interactional and historical information. Also, demographic information should be obtained and can add to knowledge and insight gained by the couple and counselor. Specifically, such things as age, place of birth, place of current residence, schooling/training completed, and current occupation are basic. In figure 6–3, we see that Mary, her parents, and brother are all living in Ohio. John also lives in Ohio, where he met Mary. Notice that John's family lives in Kansas and Nevada. After marriage will John and Mary live in Ohio near her family? What might be the implications for their marriage if they do live in the same city as her family? What are the implications and expectations regarding John's family living in other geographical areas? Such things are examples of issues that might appropriately be raised by the counselor.

The style of the family-of-origin exploration is similar to that of the DRH. Again, this style makes use of many questions designed to expand the thinking process of the couple. It is important to keep the sessions moving and flowing. Although the premarital counselor needs to take enough time to get the flavor of each of the persons and their interactions with other members of the family, it is necessary not to become bogged down in too much detail and thus not get the family "processed" during the two-hour session. The two-hour time frame should be adequate for most families.

Siblings as Individuals. We begin the family-of-origin work by finding out the names of each of the children in the family, their ages, and where each is living. We are also interested in knowing how each child is faring in terms of his or her success in life. This includes the marital functioning of the siblings if they are married. If any of the siblings have experienced a divorce, we wish to have the person characterize his or her understanding of the reason for and nature of the marital conflict and the subsequent divorce.

We are interested not only in John's characterization of his brothers and sisters by their success in life, but also in the characterization by each of the personality and temperament of his or her brothers and sisters. Are they outgoing or shy, talkative or quiet, easily angered or even-tempered, assertive or passive, opinionated or agreeable?

The issue in this particular segment is the separation of siblings from the family of origin. Generally speaking, the children who are functioning the best in adulthood and are succeeding in marital life are going to be those who have been able to establish some sense of separateness from the family of origin. Sometimes we can pick that up by geography. The children who are within shouting distance of parents or who have gone to the farthest part of the earth are often the children who have had or are having the most difficulty with parents and leaving home. The purpose of this section, then, is to get some idea of the degree to which other members of this family have been able to leave home psychologically.

Sibling Interactions. In this particular segment, we are primarily interested in the manner in which the children in the family got along with each other in their childhood. Our process, for example, is to take the oldest child and look at his or her relationship to the second oldest child, the third oldest child, and so on. Then we take the second oldest child and look at his or her relationship to the oldest child, to the third oldest child, to the fourth oldest child, and on down. We use all the combinations of each child and his or her relationship to every other child until the entire sibling system is explored.

The issue in our study of these dyads has to do with the manner in which these individuals related to each other in the growing up process and whether or not any of the children in the family functioned in a substitute-parent role. It is possible for a person to have been raised in the family in such a way that he or she has developed a close, primary relationship with an older child, which poses as many problems as does leaving the relationship with parents. On the other hand, it is also possible that the child who has functioned as a substitute parent will have difficulty in moving into a relationship in which he or she cannot continue to function in a caretaking role.

We are also concerned about the spacing of the children. If more than five years separate children, it is likely that one or both might have experienced life as an only child does. If there is too much space between children, the possibility of a sense of isolation exists. On the other hand, if children are closely spaced and if there are many of them, the possibility of feelings of inattention exists.

Parent-Child Interaction. The purpose of this section is to examine the nature and the characteristics of the relationship between each parent and each child in the family. What we are interested in is getting some kind of idea of the nature of the interaction between parent and child. How did they get along? How did they express anger toward each other? How did they express affection toward each other? Who won when they fought? How were they similar or dissimilar from each other?

In addition to exploring the kind of interaction each parent had with each child, we are particularly interested in each person's perception of the preference order of parents in dealing with children. In other words, we are interested in knowing from John who he thinks his father liked best and why and who his mother liked best and why.

If the partner has been around the family enough to comment on this issue, we ask for her perception of who the mother in John's family liked best and who the father liked best, and vice versa. It is also valuable to ask about who each parent liked least and why. Again, double-check the perception with the partner's opinion.

The issue in this section is an examination of the role of favorites in the family. People who are the first choice of the parent—the favorites—often have stronger attachments to the parent. Sometimes parents attach their ambitions and dreams to the favorite child and try to live vicariously through him or her. Favorite children may, in fact, find it more difficult to leave home or to have the parent allow them to leave home.

One should not overlook, however, the role of negative attachment. It is also possible that in the dislike or hate for a parent, a child can maintain a negative attachment to the parent, even though positive attachments are denied. The child who feels that he or she is never good enough has a kind of attachment to parents, just as the child who never does wrong does. Again, the issue of attachments has something to do with the psychological freedom of the child in adulthood.

Husband-Wife Interaction. In this section, we are particularly interested in the nature of the parental marital relationship. Our interest in this is very similar to our interest in the relationship of the premarital couple. We wonder about power: who was in charge of the marriage, how did they handle decision making, how was the power balanced? What about anger: how did the child know when mother was angry with father, when father was angry with mother? What happened when they argued: who got hurt, who made up, who initiated peace overtures? Or, if the husband and wife did not argue, how did they demonstrate their disagreement, where did it come out, how far underground was it? How about affection: how did each child know when father was pleased with what mother said and did, when mother was pleased with what father said and did? How comfortable were the parents with affection? Could they both give it and receive it? How about self-esteem: how did each person perceive the level of self-esteem in father, in mother? If low self-esteem was present, how did this affect the relationship? Was each parent oversensitive? Was each vulnerable? How,, then, did they handle their pain?

One of the issues in this section is the nature of the parents' marriage in regard to these dynamics. How parents handled anger, affection, self-esteem, dependency, closeness, and many other issues will have an impact on adult children. Parents will have provided a model; in many and subtle ways, the model will have affected the children.

Another issue in this section has to do with the nature of the parental marriage. If the marital relationship is or was good, if the coalition between mother and father is firm and healthy, the parents will be able to let their children grow up and establish their own lives. If, however, the marital relationship is not good, if it has turned bitter or sour, then one or both parents will frequently attempt to attach themselves to one of the children to make up for what is not happening in the marriage. If there is a psychological split in the parental marital relationship, whether it leads to a divorce or not, the possibility that one or more of the children will be chosen as a surrogate or substitute spouse is high.

Children who are chosen to fill the role of a spouse because of a bad marriage have difficulty in leaving home. Psychologically, the parents in a crippled marriage will attempt to rescue some sense of hopefulness, happiness, and esteem from a child. If a parent has attempted to make a child a substitute mate, that child will have difficulty moving into a marital relationship and maintaining it. It is difficult enough being married to one spouse, let alone two. When a parent chooses a child as a substitute mate, it is a kind of psychological marriage. The child will have difficulty moving to his or her own marriage unless he or she can divorce from the marriage with the parent.

Family Interactional Style. In this particular section, we are interested in two dynamics of the family of origin: family adaptability and family cohesion. See figure 6–4. Premarital counselors interested in a premarital instrument that assesses these two dynamics should consider using PREPARE, which is discussed in chapter 15.

In regard to family adaptability, we focus on two aspects of that dynamic. First, we explore the nature of leadership in the family of origin. Was it easy to identify the leaders in the family? Did the same person or persons exercise leadership roles during the duration of the childraising years? Or, did different individuals at as leaders in that period of the family life cycle? In some families the leadership is am-

Family of Origin
Based on the Circumplex Model

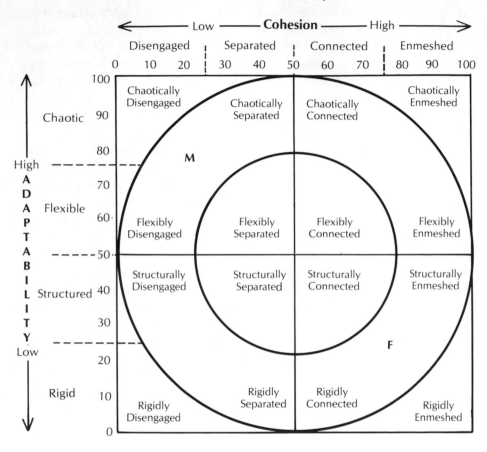

(M) = Male's Family of Origin (F) = Female's Family of Origin

REFER TO THE FAMILY OF ORIGIN HANDOUT FOR HOW TO SHARE THIS INFORMATION WITH A COUPLE

Source: Olson, D.H., Fournier, D.G., and Druckman, J.M. 1986. *PREPARE/ENRICH Counselor's Manual.* Minneapolis, Minn.: Prepare-Enrich, Inc. Reprinted by permission.

Figure 6–4. Circumplex Model or Family Map

biguous. Was it difficult to tell who was in charge of the family? Leadership roles are connected with family rules and how families either maintain their rules rigidly or have no rules at all. Thus, we also explore the nature of the family rules. Were rules constantly changing, or were the rules relatively fixed? Did different people carry out different tasks at different times, or were the same tasks maintained throughout the duration of the growing up years? Was it clear who was to do what when, or were household responsibilities shifted around from person to person? In both of these aspects, family leadership and family rules, we are interested in attempting to assess the nature of the family's adaptability. On one end of the continuum is a leadership style that is very fixed and unchanging, which usually results in rules that are rigidly maintained. At the other end is a leadership style that is constantly changing, which usually results in family rules that are very chaotic and constantly changing. In the middle of this spectrum is a leadership style that has some flexibility in it, with the result being that the family rules also are stable but flexible. Our goal in this section is to assess the family of origin on the adaptability continuum.

In regard to family cohesion, we are also interested in two different aspects. First, we like to explore the degree to which the members of the family of origin were able to cooperate with each other. Could they ask each other for assistance? Did they consult each other in regard to family decisions? In some families there is a great deal of cooperation and in other families people tend to each take care of their own things and manage by themselves. Second, we explore the degree to which the family operated with a high degree of togetherness. Did they spend their free time with each other? Did the family generally do things together? Some families have a great deal of separateness in their activities, spending little free time with each other and generally valuing separateness more than togetherness. Did the family feel close? Did the family feel distant from each other? In regard to both the aspects of requesting assistance and togetherness, we are interested in exploring the continuum of family cohesion. Some families operate with very little cohesion and thus tend to assist each other very little and operate rather independently from each other. The family cohesive style in these families may be described as disengaged. At the other end of the spectrum are families that do almost all things together and assist each other a great deal. These families have a cohesive style that could be described as enmeshed. In the middle of the continuum are families that can operate both with some togetherness and some separateness, thus having a cohesive style that combines both independence and dependence.

Parental Models. At this point in the FOE, the premarital counselor should have a good sense of what kind of modeling the parents provided in psychological and interactional terms. Parents, however, are also models in other ways, showing a variety of styles in handling such things as the demonstration of affection, social life, the use of alcohol and other chemical substances, disciplining children, finances, and religious practices. Counselors who wish to explore the models that parental marriages provide in these and other areas can find further discussion of this theme in chapter 8 and in other literature (Mace 1972, Stahmann and Hiebert 1984).

Clergy may wish at this point in the premarital counseling process to explore the models parents provided in religion and religious practice. Again, the issue is twofold; what values or beliefs did parents directly or indirectly teach, and what were the religious practices of the home? Did both parents attend church? How often? What devotional behavior was part of the family pattern? Did they pray before meals? These and many other questions can be asked to help the couple become more aware of the similarities and differences between the two families of origin and their expectations of each other about religion and religious practice.

The Wrap-up. We have been attempting to outline a process for conducting the FOE. It is an orderly process, but one that is designed to establish how a family works and what makes it tick. We have attempted to provide the reader with some of the kinds of things we look for in our understanding of how families work. Although not all of this information is necessarily meant to be passed along to the couple, it does help explain some of our understandings of family life.

We believe that each premarital counselor would probably see the same family in a somewhat different way. Each must respond to what he or she sees, what impresses him or her, what touches or concerns him or her. A counselor is interested in providing the young person with a new and different way of looking at and understanding his or her family. If one can find a new, different, yet meaningful way for explaining how the family works, one will help the individual and his or her partner to become more aware of what is happening or has happened in the family of origin. This will help both partners to expand their thinking about the nature of human relationships and their own relationship.

We have attempted to provide the premarital counselor with some theoretical background. We want to underscore again that one of the important issues in predicting success in marriage concerns not only the psychological leaving of home, but also the nature of the parental marriage (Barnard and Corrales 1979). When parental marriages do not function well, a psychological split develops between husband and wife. Even if they have not divorced, the presence of the split poses great problems for one or more of the children. When a husband and wife do not get along well and when barriers develop in the relationship and bitterness sets in, the choosing by one or both partners of a child to become a substitute mate means that the child is going to develop a strong attachment to the parent. This may hinder, if not cripple, the child's ability to find a suitable mate and maintain that relationship. The importance of a strong parental alliance or relationship appears again and again in the literature. We wish to underscore for the reader the importance of the parental marriage as a model. The healthy parental marriage and the parental marriage that is psychologically split are both models that have a powerful impact on the premarital couple.

In addition to describing the nature of the parental marriage to the couple, we also discuss the family interactional style in terms of family adaptability and family cohesion. Premarital counselors who make use of the assessment instrument PREPARE can insert the material from the inventory and those two dynamics at this point in time. After discussing the dynamics of adaptability and cohesion with the couple and gaining a sense of where each of the families of origin fell on those two continua, the data on the PREPARE printout will give the premarital counselor a sense of the degree to which the two families of origin are either very similar or very different from each other. As we have said before, the greater the difference the greater the likelihood of conflict. On the other hand, the difference can be seen as enriching and can be used to facilitate the growth of each person to learn something of the other's style.

When presenting the wrap-up on the family of origin to each

person, we suggest that the discussion be addressed to the partner. After one has completed John's family of origin, we suggest, describe it to Mary. If one describes his family of origin to John, he will either defend the material or be preoccupied with relating to the counselor. If one talks to Mary about John's family of origin, John is able to listen and free his mind to absorb what is being said. Similarly, after the counselor has completed Mary's family of origin, he or she should describe it to John. If after the description the child of that family of origin wishes comment on it, the counselor can then answer any questions. The primary focus is reporting the counselor's observations of the family of origin as determined from the information and data generated. Assuming that one is careful and accurate, there should be little rebuttal.

Part 3a: Parents (Optional)

We have added to the FOE an optional session which has to do with bringing both sets of parents into the last session with the premarital couple. If the counseling is being conducted by a nonclergy premarital counselor, this will be the last session. If it is being conducted by a member of the clergy, then the session with the parents can be the last session before part 4 (which deals with the wedding preparation), a part of the session on the wedding preparation, or the session following the one on the wedding preparation.

The premarital counselor does not have a contract to work with the parents on their marriages. He or she can, however, invite the parents to join in the last session. If the counselor wishes to include parents or stepparents in the final stage of the counseling process, we suggest that he or she should inform the couple of this intention at the beginning of the process. Not only is it important for the premarital couples to know, but it is also important for them to be coached by the premarital counselor in how to present the invitation to the parents. They can be instructed to indicate to the parents that marriage is a very special and meaningful event in the lives of people. As young people they are making a step like the one that their parents made many years ago. The counselor's invitation to the parents, then, helps them to connect with and celebrate this event in the lives of their children, which is also a reminder of the similar event that the parents celebrated.

We suggest that when the parents arrive for the session, the counselor begin by explaining why they were asked to come. In this explanation, the premarital counselor can talk about the theory of parental models. The point of this brief introduction is not to underscore any difficulty the children may have with leaving home, but rather to emphasize the concept that parents are indeed important models for children. The counselor explains that the bride and groom have observed sometimes without consciously knowing it their parents' marriages of eighteen, twenty, twenty-four, or however many years, and that these four people, as objects of such observation, have been teaching their young people about marriage and family life.

As part of the explanation to parents, the counselor also can say, in the presence of all six, that he or she has discovered that most parents have had their own struggles with trying to carve out a successful marriage, in their early years especially. He or she can add that each marriage takes adjusting; some marriages take more adjusting than others.

Last, the counselor can indicate that the parents will no longer have the same kind of access to their children after the marriage that they had before. Here one can underscore the sense that marriage is a developmental milestone. Marriage changes the way in which people relate to each other. Not only does it change the way in which a man and woman relate to each other, but it also changes the way in which parents relate to adult children. Marriage is a kind of passage into adulthood, a milestone in the maturing process of human beings. While children are single, parents frequently feel they can offer the children plentiful advice. Once a child makes the move to marriage, that child is in effect saying to parents, "I am becoming an adult; I am going to do the very same things you do." Although not all people experience marriage as the passage to adulthood, it is still valuable in helping the generations to separate for the premarital counselor to stress the importance of marriage as a developmental milestone.

All of this is a way of saying that with the marriage of their children, parents are experiencing a kind of loss. Children are also experiencing a kind of loss. Marriage marks a passage of time. The focus of the session with the parents, then, is an attempt to wrap up two basic elements: the changing nature of the parent-adult child relationship and the passing on of family wisdom (last advice).

We think it well for the premarital counselor to structure the session rather than turn it over to the family. Indicate to the parents that in this setting, they are being asked to give a last piece of wisdom to their children. Each will have his or her time to talk. This is their opportunity to say good-bye. The premarital counselor can aid the parents by asking or helping them to discuss two areas. First, what one piece of advice would they give their child about how to succeed in marriage—advice they learned in their own marriage? Second, how are they going to continue their own marriage now that the child is moving on? How will their relationship now be different?

It is helpful for the premarital counselor to structure the rest of the session as well. Indicate which parents should go first; if one needs more time to think, pass on to the other. The premarital counselor has the responsibility of keeping the session moving, but the parents have the responsibility of doing the talking.

When the parents have finished with what they have to say, the premarital counselor can summarize what the parents said as a way of recapping and heightening both the happiness and the poignancy of this session.

The session with the parents will probably be experienced as somewhat strange and tense but rewarding by the premarital counselor who has not had the opportunity to experience this process before. The more of these sessions that the premarital counselor conducts, the more efficient and successful they will be. It is important, however, to underscore our idea that if the premarital counselor is enjoying the task and having fun, the couple and the parents will too—and they will benefit from the process.

Part 4: Wedding Preparation

The purpose of part 4 in our premarital counseling process is to focus on the special role and task of the clergy in the wedding itself. This segment is designed to assist the clergy member in thinking about the wedding preparation section of the premarital counseling process and in deciding on the nature of this unit.

We assume that the clergy will routinely discuss with the couple the mechanics of the wedding and the reception, the meaning of the various parts of the wedding service, and any other liturgical considerations. Some clergy members will involve the couple in writing a portion or all of the service. Others will prefer to follow established liturgies. In either case, couples are likely to appreciate the service more if they understand it fully.

Every clergy member confronts the issues of whether or not to include religious or theological issues in the premarital counseling process and if so, what kind. Two approaches to the inclusion of specifically religious or theological issues will be explored.

Method 1

One method of approaching such issues is to integrate them into the premarital counseling process. This method does not use a specific, formal discussion or lecture on the theology of marriage, or on the nature and meaning of marriage within the perspective of faith. The focus of method 1 is not on the presentation of an established theological perspective, whether of the denomination or of the pastor. Rather, the focus is on the couple and helping them to become aware of (1) each person's previous religious belief system, (2) their similarities and differences in their religious value systems, (3) each person's practice of their faith, (4) their similarities and differences in their religious practices, and (5) their future plans regarding their religious practices.

The goals of method 1 are to heighten the couple's awareness of the uniqueness of each, to enhance their enjoyment of the values and practices they share in common, and to increase their respect for each other's beliefs as they plan to encompass their desires in their future.

The approach of method 1 has already been integrated into the outlined counseling process. For our purpose here, we want to highlight this approach. In part 2, when describing the DRH, we suggested an exploration of the area of religion and religious practice. As described in chapter 5, the clergy member has an excellent opportunity to focus on both religious values and religious practice at this point in the process. If that suggestion is followed as outlined, the result should be a clarification of who these two people are in regard to their religious orientation and practice. In part 3, when describing the FOE, we suggested an exploration of the religious orientation and practices of the parents and the kinds of models they provided in this area. If the FOE in this area is followed as outlined earlier in this chapter, the couple should develop a heightened awareness of both their differences and their similarities.

When a couple have pronounced differences, the use of the prescribed sections of the DRH and FOE should help them appreciate their differences. However, when the differences seem pronounced, the clergy member can enhance in the couple both the development of respect for the differences and the beginning of negotiation of a resolution to the conflict.

Implicit in method 1 are several concepts. First, the focus is on the couple—not the institution—and where they are coming from and going toward, religiously speaking. Second, the purpose of premarital counseling is to explore and enhance the new relaionship, and counseling is concentrated at one time. Concern for the spiritual dimension of the individuals and the relationship is an ongoing pastoral theme and covers the entire lifespan of the individuals and the couple. The relationship, then, takes primary focus, whereas spiritual growth becomes more important in postmarital groups, retreats, enrichment programs, and other religious education experiences. Third, the DRH and FOE have implicit within them a deeply theological task. The writer of Genesis 2 spoke of the nature of the man-woman relationship: "It is not good that man should be alone; I will make him a helper fit for him." Although many have incorrectly interpreted the word *helper* to mean *helpmate,* it would be better translated "another human being like or corresponding to him." The original Hebrew says "another person (woman) to live *alongside* him." This passage thus suggests that a man shall leave his parents and take a wife. That is, they shall live alongside each other. They shall have a bond between them greater than the bond that each has with his or her parents. When the Genesis account says that a man and a woman become one flesh, it means that a husband and wife create a new home, separate from their parents and from which their children will leave. The man and woman are to marry each other, not their parents or their children. The DRH and FOE are designed to deal with the important process of life's pilgrimage, in a familial and psychological sense, but also in a deeply theological one.

Method 2

The other method of approaching religious or theological issues involves the addition of a separate unit to the premarital counseling process. This method makes use of specific exercises and/or formal discussion and presentation of the theology of marriage and the nature and meaning of marriage within a perspective of faith.

Method 2 has two focuses: helping the couple to explore and expand the spiritual dimension of their relationship; and formally discussing or presenting the meaning of marriage from a perspective of faith. Ministers may choose one or both of these.

Clergy who wish to present a formal discussion or lecture on the theology of marriage will need to decide whether they will present their own theological or scriptural understanding or their denomination's interpretation. We are not going to develop a theology of marriage here. There are too many differing theological and denominational perspectives to encompass. Ministers should, however, have little difficulty in finding ample material in their libraries or from denominational resources.

Ministers who wish to focus on helping couples to explore their spiritual dimension may use a new body of literature that is developing in this area. Those interested in pursuing the use of a specific methodology for building the spiritual dimension should explore Clinebell's "intentional marriage method" (1975). The intentional marriage method uses a four-step formula for teaching couples a process for spiritual growth. Other methodologies are also available for use both in conjoint premarital counseling and in group premarital counseling (Allen 1973; Clinebell 1972, 1973–1974, 1977; James 1973; Morrison and Price 1974; Simon 1972; Stewart 1970).

The separation of part 4 into two methods is not meant to imply that clergy cannot borrow from both methods. Methods 1 and 2 can be put together. The issue will be one of choice of emphasis and time.

Postwedding Session

Although we have not previously mentioned the idea of a postwedding session, we have found that a session with the couple six months following the wedding has been a very helpful and valuable interview. By that time the couple has been cohabiting long enough that they have had an opportunity to confront the differences that appear as a result of the day-to-day living process. Many of the issues that previously during the prewedding sessions seemed more abstract are often now more real and vivid. It is our suggestion, if the reader wishes to experiment with the postwedding session, that the appointment be set up at the time of the last prewedding session and then a reminder be sent to the couple just prior to the session. Our experience indicates that a high number of the couples not only keep the appointment but find the sessions most profitable.

III
Group Premarital Counseling

7
Design and Structural Considerations in Group Premarital Counseling

U nfortunately, there has not been very much written on the delivery or evaluation of group premarital counseling. This may seem surprising to the casual observer for it appears, from a clinical point of view, that many of the premarital counseling programs offered on a regular basis take a group form. Nonetheless, in our review of the literature, we found relatively few reports of group premarital counseling. Those programs that were reported often would not provide enough detail for evaluation or enough information for duplication of the programs being described (Gleason and Prescott 1977, Glendening and Wilson 1972, Horejsi 1974, Olsen 1975, Rolfe 1977a,b, Ross 1977).

Defining Group Premarital Counseling

In this chapter, group premarital counseling is, by our definition, more a counseling process than a teaching process. In a counseling process, the couples involved have the opportunity to work in a small group setting and focus on various significant aspects of their personalities and their relationships. In other words, the primary distinguishing factor between a counseling process and an educational process, for our purpose here, is the setting: a small group for counseling and a large group for education.

Format is another distinguishing characteristic. In a counseling process, couples in a small group setting have the opportunity for both structure and individual and couple exploration of issues that are significant for them at an appropriate psychological and/or emotional level. In the educational approach, with a larger group of persons, the structure hinders individual exploration or deviation from the prearranged format.

Kilgo (1975) concisely summarized the differences among group guidance, group counseling, and group therapy. He indicated that *group guidance* is basically an educational approach, with the main focus upon the acquisition of information and skills of learning by the participants. In group guidance, the role of the group leader is primarily that of an instructor or teacher. In *group counseling,* the focus is on small group interaction which is designed to facilitate self-understanding, increase the participants' awareness of self and others, and improve interpersonal relationship skills. In group counseling, the primary role of the leader is that of a counselor. In *group therapy,* the purpose is similar to that of counseling, but a greater concern is given to unconscious motivations, emotional problems, and the goal of personality reorganization. In group therapy, the role of the leader is that of a psychotherapist.

In our consideration of group premarital counseling, we most closely follow the aspects of group counseling as described by Kilgo. The focus of our approach is upon the facilitation of self-understanding and relationship understanding of the participants in the context of a small group of several couples. The role of the leader is that of a counselor and facilitator who guides the couples in their exploration and awareness process.

Advantages and Disadvantages of Group Premarital Counseling

In evaluating the advantages and disadvantages of using the group format in premarital counseling, we want to keep in mind our overall goal of premarital counseling as discussed in chapter 1: to enhance the premarital relationship so that it might develop into a satisfactory and stable marital relationship. Keeping this definition in mind, we have found the considerations offered by Kilgo (1975) a useful guide in deciding whether or not to use a group approach. We have separated Kilgo's eight considerations into two categories, advantages and disadvantages. We also have reranked and elaborated on his short descriptions of the eight considerations. For the premarital counselor making a decision between conjoint couple premarital counseling and group premarital counseling, we suggest placing the considerations in two columns and tallying them.

Advantages

More Economical Use of Counselor Time and Client Money. If the same outcome can be achieved in a small group process as in a conjoint couple process, obviously it is more economical to use the group format. It is often the case however, that the premarital couple pays a minimal fee or no fee at all, which makes this a less important consideration. In addition, the group process counselor often uses more questionnaires or assessment devices than does the individual premarital counselor. The time required for the counselor to work with these various assessment devices may be such that in the overall picture, the time-saving per client served may not be significantly greater in the group process than in the individual couple process.

Influence of Peers. In group counseling, the influence of peers is generally a helpful factor in the process. Our experience in group premarital counseling, however, is that while a couple are interested in and influenced by their peers, their highly emotional involvement with each other is such that the influence of peers is significantly less than it would be in other forms of group counseling or at other points in the persons' lives.

Reality Reflections. Kilgo referred to this as the "many mirrors" aspect of the group. Reality reflection is the phenomenon of persons' pointing out something to a group member and keeping the member focused upon it, even though he or she is attempting to avoid looking at or dealing with it. We really consider this to be a weak advantage in premarital counseling groups. The focus in such groups is usually less intensely upon the individual group members and more intensely on the couples or the relationships. The reality reflection does operate, however, on a broad level when the couples are concentrating on issues as couples and when the larger group is concentrating upon specific aspects of the group process (the need for affection, role as wife or husband, and so forth).

The "Not Alone" Feeling. It is a common and positive experience of couples in a group premarital counseling program to realize that the questions and adjustments which they may be experiencing are shared by other couples. David and Vera Mace have identified this as the intermarital taboo. Couples in marriage enrichment groups often find that other couples are experiencing or have experienced the same kinds of problems and questions (Mace and Mace 1977).

Direct Education. It is helpful for couples to see how others have worked out similar problems or are presently working them out. It is also easier for a person or couple to see others' problems than it may be to see their own. We like to think of group premarital counseling as a consciousness-raising experience for the participants, who learn from other couples in the group context.

Satisfaction of Helping Others. In a group process, all members are in some ways counselors as well as participants and thereby help one another. Kilgo pointed out that this particularly increases the self-esteem of all group members. We agree with him and would add that the helpfulness of the group can serve as a very important model for continued growth throughout the marital relationship. We suspect that couples who have satisfactorily completed a group premarital counseling experience will be likely to participate in marriage enrichment experiences later in life, with the goal of continuing to help themselves, their relationship, and others.

Disadvantages

Spouse Inhibition. The possibility exists that either or both of the premarital partners might feel less free to talk in a group because of the presence of other group members. This has implications for the screening of group members, which is discussed later in the chapter.

Problems That Are Too Intimate. Some couples might be reluctant to discuss certain problems because they might feel they are too intimate to be exposed to the entire group. In addition, in group premarital counseling, where some of the relationships may be relatively new and somewhat insecure, the individuals may have rather strong inhibitions about discussing some topics or concerns in front of their prospective spouse, not knowing how he or she may react or respond.

Premarital counselors need to consider all of these factors in deciding whether or not the group process is appropriate for them and their particular clients. We suggest that in making your decision, you create a tally list as described and consider the eight factors. Perhaps this will also enable you to generate additional considerations of your own.

Design Issues and Group Premarital Counseling

There are a number of design or structural issues that must be addressed as the counselor considers the use of the group counseling format. We have found several factors that are of most relevance to the premarital counseling situation.

Pregroup Screening Interview

We believe that it is essential for the counselor to have an interview with each couple prior to the onset of the group process. The primary goal of this interview is to ascertain whether or not the couple is appropriate for and will benefit from group counseling. We have found that the majority of couples seeking premarital counseling are appropriate for the group process; however, there are some who are not. Those who should routinely be screened out are couples who have a primary relationship dysfunction, couples who are for some reason opposed to the group context, and couples who are not voluntarily committed to the counseling process itself. The reader will see that the underlying concern here is to keep out those couples who are atypical and who would be disruptive to the other couples in the group.

We recommend that the screening interview should be conjoint, like the group counseling sessions themselves. Occasionally, because of a specific need that arises with a couple or an individual, we arrange for individual or conjoint sessions outside of the group once the process has begun. However, these are arranged on an ad hoc basis and are not a routine part of the group process.

The screening interview needs to be more than an explanation of what the group counseling process is all about. The counselor needs to ascertain whether the couple will be appropriate for the process. In the majority of our cases, our clinical impression, along with the client's self-perception of participation, has been adequate. We do not, therefore, routinely employ a psychological test or screening device as part of the screening interview.

Co-counselor

In establishing a premarital counseling group, the counselor must consider whether or not to use a co-counselor. We believe that a co-counselor is desirable, particularly if the counselors are of opposite sexes. The reasons for our preference for this model may be obvious. We can not overemphasize the importance and impact of male-female modeling, particularly in the discussions, which are a significant aspect of the counseling process. In the group context, where there will be four to six heterosexual couples, we believe that it is desirable to have a man and a woman as co-counselors.

The co-counselors do not need to be (and usually are not) married to each other. They do, however, need to be well acquainted and to have a positive relationship. As one can imagine, the various content and value considerations in premarital counseling are a significant part of the process. It is important, therefore, for the co-counselors to have resolved any major differences or questions between themselves on such topics.

Group Size

Although the size of the group can vary, it appears that groups of four to six couples provide the most exciting and productive experiences. Groups that contain fewer than four couples, we find, tend to exhibit less vitality. The smallness of the group tends to eliminate discussion, because the variety of backgrounds necessary to stimulate group discussion is not present. In groups with more than six couples, we find that it is difficult to have enough time to interact with and attend to all the persons involved. We have also found that with more than fourteen people in a group process, patterns can develop regarding involvement and withdrawal from the group that are difficult to change. Discussion and interaction by all participants are important aspects of the group process, and these can be eased by the recommended group size. In addition, we have also found that if couples are selected in the pregroup screening who have committed themselves to the process, all six couples (and never fewer than five couples) will complete the counseling process as outlined.

Frequency and Length of Sessions

We recommend that each group session should last two and a half hours. Articles dealing with group premarital counseling, have noted that session length varied greatly. The range is from two hours to six hours, with some programs including marathon sessions of eight or more hours. Our goal here is to attempt to structure a meaningful time block that will be repeated weekly for a number of consecutive weeks. We have found that two and a half hours is long enough to accomplish significant amounts of work, yet not so long that it becomes tiring. This consideration is particularly important because counselors frequently will need to conduct the sessions in the evening, after a full day's activity in other pursuits.

We believe that the goals of premarital counseling can be accomplished in five consecutive sessions of two and a half hours each. We recommend that the sessions be held on a weekly basis. Such a procedure communicates to the participants the time span during which the experience will take place and suggests to them the involvement that will be necessary in order for them to accomplish as much as possible within the relatively short period of time.

Group Composition, Setting, and Environment

One issue that needs to be considered in any group counseling program is whether or not the group is to be open or closed. The open group allows for the addition of couples as the group is in process. Because of the structured format and the time-limited nature of the premarital counseling process, we require the group to be closed.

Once the process has begun, other couples are not permitted to join the group.

Little needs to be said regarding the group setting other than that the room should be adequate in size and that it should be comfortably furnished, lighted, and heated. These are administrative assumptions which must be taken care of by the counselors prior to the group sessions. Another environmental consideration which should be discussed with the participants during the pregroup screening interview is appropriate dress and attire. The goal here is to have the participants wear comfortable and nonrestrictive clothing that allows them to move without inhibition yet is modest and inoffensive to other group members. We would concur with the suggestion of Barnard and Corrales (1979) that women and men wear slacks and other nonrestrictive clothing.

Homework and Assessment Devices

As will be explained further in the discussion of the premarital counseling process, we believe that an important aspect of that process is participants' completion of various types of homework assignments between the group sessions. Our group process requires the participants to complete questionnaires and assessment devices. The homework assignments are vital in translating into reality the experiences that have been generated or discussed in the group setting. We believe that effective exploration and change requires application and work, and that is the goal of the homework assignments. Although a number of specific homework assignments will be discussed, counselors must be ready and able to generate specific assignments to assist in the counseling process. Counselors will also need to follow up on the homework assignments routinely at the beginning of the next session in order to tie together in a coherent fashion the counseling process and events that are transpiring in the lives of the participants.

Confidentiality

Confidentiality is crucial in all counseling, including group counseling. Confidentiality needs to be explained in the precounseling screening interview and reinforced throughout the counseling process. Counselors will need to define and implement their own methods of insuring confidentiality. For example, whenever assessment devices or questionnaires are used, counselors must ask themselves (and explain to the participants) whether or not the results of the questionnaire or the device are to be shared with the entire group, or between the counselors and individual couple, or between the counselors and the individual participants. The guidelines are to keep confidentiality in focus and clearly understood. We know of no instances where confidentiality has been violated to the detriment of the group or its participants once the issue has been dealt with and is an ongoing part of the group process. In fact, the issue itself becomes an important aspect of bonding and group cohesiveness.

Approaches to Group Premarital Counseling

As indicated previously, there are few detailed discussions of specific programs for group premarital counseling in the literature. Our purpose in this section of the chapter is to present a number of significant concepts and techniques useful in the group premarital counseling process. We have selected three programs which appear to us to be the most valuable, most fairly researched, and most clinically documented. Interestingly, all three of the programs have been developed for use in marital counseling. Two have been specifically extended into the area of group premarital counseling.

Conjugal Relationship Enhancement Program

The conjugational relationship enhancement program is basically an educational model, designed as a group program that focuses upon the improvement of dyadic communication. The model emphasizes Rogerian client-centered therapeutic principles and has been applied to a variety of dyadic relationships such as husband-wife, parent-child, parent-teenager, and premarital dating partners. The rationale for the program is that of a communication model and appears to be valid and well documented (Rappaport 1976). The model has been specifically tested with premarital dating couples and found to be very effective in improving communication and the general quality of the relationship between the premarital partners (Avery et al. 1980, D'Angelli et al. 1974).

Typically, three or four couples are present in a group with two counselors. The sessions are held weekly for an hour and a half to two hours, in a series of eight to ten sessions. The primary content of the program consists of a supervised practice involving interpersonal skills, particularly emphatic understanding, acceptance of others' feelings, and openness and honesty about one's personal feelings. Role-playing by the counselors serves as the core in teaching the interpersonal skills to the clients. Two primary roles are taught: a warm, emphatic, and accepting listener, and an open and honest speaker.

The hypothesis underlying the program is that if a premarital couple can be trained to utilize the communication skills of listening and speaking appropriately, their marital relationship will be enhanced. Although this hypothesis is certainly still open to additional testing, it is one that is shared by the majority of marital counselors, who agree that effective communication is at the heart of stable and satisfying marital relationships (Barnard and Corrales 1979, Gurney 1977).

Rappaport (1976) provides a look at the procedures and process that comprise the conjugal relationship program. We have modified the program slightly for use with premarital couples.

Session 1: Learning the Speaker and Listener Roles. This session, as Rappaport discusses it, is an eight-hour marathon that introduces the participants to the rationale and philosophy of the program. Lectures and role-playing techniques are used by the coleaders to teach the techniques. After the leaders have explained the process and modeled it for the participants, each premarital couple performs the speaker and listener roles, while other group members and the leaders serve as coaches and facilitators. Apparently, in some of the groups, the members also played the listener and speaker roles with group members other than their fiancés in an effort to build cohesion in the group. At the close of the session, time is spent in discussing and processing the experiences of the group. Homework is assigned, including reading a manual, role-playing outside the counseling session on nonthreatening topics for a half-hour every other day, and making a tape recording of one of the half-hour homework sessions and bringing it to the next group meeting.

Session 2: Practicing the Roles. This was initially designed as a four-hour session. The focus and emphasis is upon the previously learned roles of speaker and listener, using them in topic areas that are more threatening for the couples. Some of the homework tapes which have been brought to the sessions by couples are reviewed by the entire group at the beginning of the session. At the conclusion, the same homework as in the previous sessions is assigned: four sessions in the workbook, role-playing, and taping one of the half-hour role-playing sessions and bringing to the next session. Additionally, each partner is to prepare independently a list of the two most serious problems or areas of potential conflict in the premarital relationship and to bring it to the next counseling session. Couples are instructed not to share the list with one another; however, they are expected to share the list with their partner, and likely with other group members, at the next session.

Session 3: Communication of Specific Conflict Areas. The third session is an eight-hour marathon devoted primarily to communication on specific areas of conflict for each of the premarital dyads. During the first three hours, each couple discusses the second problem on their list, in front of the entire group and using the previously learned listener and speaker roles. After a break, each couple independently spends approximately an hour communicating about the primary problems on their lists. During this time, the co-counselors circulate among the dyads, helping and consulting with them as appropriate. The remainder of the day is spent with the couples coming back together and meeting as a group to focus on and communicate about the positive areas of their relationships. During the last half-hour or so, the group also focuses on and discusses the day's process and homework assignments for the final session. Homework consists of the three steps that have been used previously: role-playing on positive or negative areas in the relationship for at least a half-hour every other day, tape-recording at least one of the sessions and bringing it to the next group session, and independently preparing a list of possible solutions for two of the problems that were presented at the last group session. Suggestions regarding changes or modifications in behavior are to be specific and to focus upon the process by which they might be achieved in the relationship.

Session 4: Communication in Problem-Solving. The fourth and last group session is a four-hour session focusing on conflict resolution within the premarital relationship. The primary technique is to have each person demonstrate certain behaviors, such as compromise and bargaining, in front of the entire group. Group members other than the fiance serve as the facilitators for the couple as they deal with problem-solving skills and methods.

Premarital Program for Marital Enrichment

The reader is probably familiar with the terms *marital enrichment* and *marriage encounter* and may have participated in one of these programs. The acknowledged leaders of the marital enrichment emphasis in this country, David and Vera Mace, have suggested that marital enrichment can begin in the initial stages of marriage. In fact, one of David Mace's recent books, *Getting Ready for Marriage* (1985), very closely follows the Maces' recent work on marriage enrichment, *We Can Have Better Marriages If We Really Want Them* (1974), *Marriage Enrichment in the Church* (1976), and *How To Have a Happy Marriage* (1984). Because marriage enrichment is so directly applicable to the premarital relationship and because it is designed primarily as a conjoint couple group process, we will briefly review it here.

The approach of David and Vera Mace is refreshing and realistic and points out the fallacy of the idea that a couple gets married and lives "happily ever after." The idea, they say, is a myth because it indicates that marriages are stable, static, and stagnant. Yet in subtle ways, people apparently still believe the myth. For a relationship to be enriched, it must be growing. For a marriage to be growing, three vital components are necessary: commitment, communication, and conflict.

A premarital counseling program can be designed to deal adequately with each of the three broad areas as well as specific offshoots of them. Our discussion here will focus upon the three areas, purposefully omitting the more detailed structure and formation and leaving those to the creativity of the leaders or counselors.

Commitment Is Crucial. Commitment in the premarital and marital relationship is of obvious importance. However, commitment is a complex issue involving several questions: Commitment to what? How much commitment? In the group premarital counseling process, exercises should be structured to guide and enable the couples to look at their degree of commitment to the forthcoming marital relationship, to their future spouse, and to themselves as individuals. Two things are important here: first, assessing the degree of commitment of the partners to the present, premarital relationship; second, assessing the commitment of the partners to a continually growing and developing marital relationship.

Techniques for assessing commitment and commitment potential in a relationship vary according to the counselors' styles and desires to structure and use written or verbal aides in the counseling process. Adapting from the work of the Maces, we have found that the following simple checklist can be useful in assisting a couple to look at their commitment to the present, premarital relationship. Instruct the couple to list independently, on a sheet of paper, the following areas of a marital relationship:

 1. Common goals and values
 2. Commitment to growth
 3. Communications skills
 4. Creative use of conflict
 5. Appreciation and affection
 6. Agreement on gender roles
 7. Cooperation and teamwork
 8. Sexual fulfillment
 9. Money management
10. Childrearing expectations
11. Decision making

Then, instruct the couple to put a plus sign following each of the eleven items which they believe is currently an active part of their relationship. Second, instruct them to put a plus in a second column by those items which they believe will be a part of their relationship three months after they have been married. By using techniques such as this, the counselor can assess with the couples in the group their degree of commitment and the conformance of commitment both premaritally and postmaritally.

Creative Use of Conflict. The second primary area identified by the Maces in the healthy marital relationship is the appropriate use of conflict. The Maces have called marital conflict the phantom in disguise. They are realistic in pointing out that conflict does and will exist in all interpersonal relationships. The best thing for a couple to do is to learn to use it wisely and deal with it appropriately. We believe that this is certainly true for premarital relationships as well as marital relationships.

In discussing conflict in marriage, the Maces have identified three patterns which we believe are of importance in premarital relationships:

1. *Conflict exclusion.* The conflict-excluding premarital relationship is one in which one partner dominates and thereby excludes conflict in the relationship. When one partner is such a dominant force or person, there is no room for conflict, just as there is no room for discussion of alternatives. Because one person is dominant and the other is submissive and obedient, communication is one-way. One partner tells the other partner what will be done. Differences and disagreements are excluded through the simple yet powerful process of repression.

2. *Conflict avoidance.* The second pattern is conflict-avoiding. In this pattern, the couple is on a par as far as dominance and power are concerned. However, the partners avoid conflict by not bringing up conflicting matters or problems. This system often manifests itself in very passive people by the failure to make decisions and minimal progress in the relationship or their individual lives.

It is also possible for two powerful people to be involved in a conflict-avoiding relationship. Here the pattern is that of two headstrong individuals who do their own thing and avoid one another. Either the powerful or the submissive conflict-avoiding pattern for a premarital couple is obviously destructive to the potential growth of the marriage.

3. *Conflict resolution.* The third pattern identified by the Maces is that of conflict-resolving. In this pattern, the couple stands side by side, joined in physical and emotional contact with one another. When it surfaces in such a relationship, conflict will almost always be resolved through the process of negotiation and compromise. This is a healthy mode of conflict resolution for two healthy persons. Both give up a bit of themselves in order to have a positive interpersonal rela-

tionship. Seen in this light, compromise, which is necessary for conflict-resolving, is appropriate.

The Maces have identified a process for conflict resolution: identifying a difference which may lead to a disagreement, but which then can be followed by a healthy form of conflict and result in an appropriate resolution for the couple.

Communication. As a third vital ingredient, communication is the master key for an effective premarital and future marital relationship. Within their program, the Maces do not go into great detail regarding communication programs or models. Rather, they endorse a number of models, including the Minnesota Couple's Communication Program (MCCP), which will be discussed in this chapter.

It is important to note in considering communication that although the focus is upon verbal communication, nonverbal and body languages are also extremely important and should be included in any training program in couple communication.

Minnesota Couple's Communication Program (MCCP)

The Minnesota Couple's Communication Program (MCCP), also known as the Interpersonal Communication Program (ICP), is a significant program that is receiving wide attention and acclaim in marital, premarital, and marriage preparation courses. The MCCP is a small group dyadic program in which couples participate for three-hour sessions, usually in a series of four meetings. The dimensions underlining the MCCP, as identified by Miller, Nunnally, and Wackman 1975, include the following:

1. *An educational-developmental orientation.* This dimension focuses upon the goals of the MCCP as preventive and designed to equip participants for real situations, rather than as remedial or designed to repair dysfunctional relationships. The idea is to take people who have satisfactory communication skills and to enhance and increase those skills.

2. *A focus on the system.* The MCCP focuses upon the dyad or couple versus the individual or a group of individuals. This is in specific harmony with the goals of premarital counseling as stated previously. Although the focus is upon the couple or dyad, it does not

exclude the individual or group. The secondary focus on the system relates to communication of messages. The focus is on *how* messages are sent, along with *why* they are sent. Because understanding and correctly interpreting messages is a goal of effective communication, the *how* is equally important as the *why*. The MCCP also teaches four specific styles of communication in an attempt to increase the flexibility and adaptability in verbal communication of the participants.

3. *The MCCP is skill-oriented.* As Miller and his associates state, "Our research indicates that the ingredients of effective communication can be discovered, taught, and used by couples to improve their ability to communicate directly, congruently, and supportively together" (Miller, Nunnally, and Wackman 1975, p. 26). Their assumption is that because the couple have joined together in the training program, the transfer and lasting effects of the skills learned in the MCCP will be reinforced and carried into their everyday life.

4. *The presentation of conceptual frameworks.* Four conceptual frameworks are presented: the awareness wheel; shared meaning process; communication spouse; and I count/I count you. These frameworks are taught to the couples in order to assist them in understanding predictable priorities and properties of relationships. They also provide a common basis for communication. Once couples are aware of such communication patterns and styles, they presumably find it easier to modify or change them.

5. *Volunteerism and participant choice.* The MCCP is a refreshing approach to participation. It assumes that individuals and couples are attending the program through their own free will and choice. Couples choosing to join the program can benefit from it if both partners want (1) to identify communication skills that they wish to improve; (2) to practice these skills during group sessions; (3) to transfer and experiment with these skills outside the group sessions and report back to the group on their experiences; and (4) to attend all four group sessions together.

6. *A Group context as the learning environment.* This last dimension is rather self-explanatory, but indicates that the group context is of crucial importance to the conduct and effectiveness of the MCCP. "The function of the group is to create a self-learning environment where couples can discover that exploring and experimenting with their own patterns of relationship can be interesting and rewarding" (Miller, Nunnally, and Wackman 1975, p. 28). The authors go on to

discuss the particularly positive aspects of the group context for the premarital couple. Premarital couples are frequently in an isolated environment for receiving information from people regarding themselves and their relationship. Significant friends or family members often choose to leave a premarital couple alone for fear of interrupting or meddling in a process. The couple themselves are often too blinded or infatuated to see reality or to have healthy perceptions about themselves and their relationship. Thus, a structured, safe environment such as the MCCP can offer premarital couples an opportunity for learning in a constructive context.

Summary

In this chapter, we have looked at a number of the serious aspects which need to be considered in the structured organization of a group premarital counseling program. In addition, we have attempted to highlight the primary components of three successful premarital counseling programs. In the next chapter, we will specifically outline a program that we have synthesized from literature about and the practice of group premarital counseling.

8
Content and Methods in Group Premarital Counseling

Most of the points outlined and discussed in the previous chapter are basic to the specific program for group premarital counseling that is presented here. It is assumed that the structural and administrative issues will have been raised and resolved prior to the first meeting of the group. In this chapter, we will describe a process that begins with the first group meeting and carries through to the conclusion of the group.

What is proposed in this chapter is really only one of many variations on satisfactory content and methods in group premarital counseling. It has been our experience and the experience of most others who conduct counseling groups that each group will vary to some extent because of the particular participants in the group and the particular issues that are of importance to them. We are providing a basic model, knowing in advance that this model may need to be modified to fit the needs of each premarital counseling group.

We find that there is an appropriate overlap and redundancy between the processes used in group premarital counseling and in conjoint couple premarital counseling. Certain aspects of the group approach, therefore, will be familiar from earlier chapters. Similarly, some ideas that are presented in this chapter would work very well in a session in which a counselor is seeing an individual couple.

A Group Premarital Counseling Procedure

There are a number of decisions that the counselors will make regarding the structure and format for the premarital counseling sessions. These have been discussed in detail in the previous chapter. We assume that these decisions have been made: (1) the leaders for the counseling group will be a man and woman functioning as co-counselors; (2) a screening interview will have been held by the counselors with each of the couples; (3) five couples will have been selected for the group; (4) the group will meet for two-and-a-half-hour sessions during five consecutive weeks; (5) the couples in the group will represent an age range of the late teens to the late twenties; (6) all couples will have been in their present relationship for at least three months; (7) all couples will have sought counseling voluntarily, to strengthen their current and future relationship.

The following general outline was developed to serve as an overall guide to co-counselor planning for the five sessions.

Session 1. In the first session, the initial focus is upon the process of getting acquainted. The authors believe that it is extremely important for the twelve persons (two counselors plus five couples) to establish trust and rapport at the outset. The primary way for group members to get acquainted is for each of the group members, beginning with the co-counselors, to introduce himself or herself briefly to the rest of the group. After the introductions of individuals are made, the counselors introduce themselves as a counseling team to the group and discuss their professional relationship. The counselors then ask each of the couples together to introduce their relationship or their plans for the marriage to the group, specifically explaining briefly where they met, interesting and relevant facts related to their courtship to date, and, if applicable, what wedding plans or goals they have set for themselves. The counselors then discuss in capsule form an overview of the proposed five-session group counseling format.

The next task for the group is to identify the specific goals that each couple wish to achieve from the premarital counseling process. A procedure for the goal-articulating process is demonstrated by the counselors. Speaker and listener role-playing, from the Conjugal Relationship Enhancement Program which was discussed in the previous chapter, is used in articulating the goals (Rappaport 1976). During the remainder of the session, each couple have the opportunity to practice the speaker and listener roles, focusing on the content of specific goals or outcomes that they hope to accomplish in the premarital counseling process. The homework assignment is to continue to use the speaker and listener role exercise with nonthreatening topics; for thirty minutes daily on five of the upcoming seven days.

Session 2. Session two begins with a review of the speaker and listener role exercise and looks for any problems that have been encountered, reinforcing the success which the couples have had with it. The aim in this session is to explore with the couples their personal life histories and the model for marriage that their parents or home environment provided for them. The homework assignment generated from this session consists of several requirements: the couple are to continue to discuss and develop their personal histories; they are to discuss their parental model; the couple is to use the speaker-listener exercise for a period of thirty minutes on four occasions during the coming week; and they are to complete the FIRO-B, an assessment instrument discussed in chapter 15 and bring it with them to the next session.

Session 3. The third session begins with a review of the homework assignment, collection of the FIRO-B, and discussion of couples' continued exploration of their personal and parental modeling histories. Specifically, responses are solicited regarding the FIRO-B and any problems or comments that arose with that particular instrument. The primary content of this session is a focus upon the interpersonal dimensions generated by the FIRO-B instrument. The homework assignment is for each of the couples to discuss the ten interpersonal areas discussed later in this chapter, that were introduced in this session, at the rate of two areas per day, and to bring to the next session any problems and specific strengths that they identify in each of the ten areas.

Session 4. The fourth session begins with a follow-up on the homework assignment on the ten interpersonal dimensions. Particular attention is paid to any strengths that the couple have noted. The counselors should be listening for and pointing out areas of conflict or potential problems that the couples identify. The main focus of this session is to teach a system for the appropriate handling of conflict (Bach and Wyden 1969, Mace and Mace 1974, Scoresby 1977). The homework assignment is for the couples to practice the conflict negotiation skills that have been demonstrated for a period of thirty minutes on each of five days. Although the counselor might ask the couple to review the listening and speaking skills discussed and practiced during earlier group sessions, these skills are such an integral part of the conflict negotiation process that to separate them at this time is unnecessary.

Session 5. The fifth and final session consists of summarizing and reviewing the process and content of the previous sessions and looking at the present status of the group in relation to the goals that were discussed during the first and second sessions.

Session 6 (optional). The clergy, who may be providing premarital counseling as preparation for the wedding which they will conduct, will likely include a group session dealing with wedding preparation. Even if the counselor is not the person who will perform the wedding, dealing with wedding preparation and expectations in a sixth group session can be of value if the couples are of the same religious denomination. This session should be designed in a format similar to the one discussed in chapter 6.

As previously stated, this is the basic model for a group premarital counseling program. The remainder of the chapter will detail many aspects of this outline.

Goal-Setting in Premarital Group Counseling

In chapter 4, the various goals that direct the premarital counseling process were discussed. Goals for group premarital counseling do not differ greatly; however, we wish to articulate the following goals related to the outcome of group premarital counseling.

1. *Discovering and clarifying the basic identity of each partner.* In relation to this goal, the group premarital counseling process aims to develop the sense of identity and establish the "I" of each person. Helping each person to a heightened awareness of his or her thoughts, feelings, and fantasies establishes a clearer sense of who he or she is.

2. *Discovering and articulating the other's identity.* Another goal is to fill in the partner's "I" position. By sketching out and attending to the other's thoughts, feelings, and fantasies, the partner will develop a sense of who the other person is.

3. *Making sense of and understanding behavior.* During the premarital counseling group process, many opportunities arise, spontaneously or not, for the counselor to assist partners in understanding each other's behavior. Group premarital counseling can enhance the understanding of behavior and the meaning behind it, as well as aid the creation of new behavior by the individuals and couples.

4. *Developing communication skills.* The premarital counseling process is structured so that each person becomes more aware of his or her thoughts, feelings, and actions and interpersonal skills in communicating about them. Checking out the meaning of messages is a crucial part in the communication process. Another aspect of the group process is the building of communication skills.

5. *Opening up significant areas for communication.* Another goal is to help couples to talk about topics and areas that they could not or had not previously talked about. Content such as that described earlier—empirically documented premarital variables (Lewis and Spanier 1979) and areas from the Premarital Counseling Inventory (Stuart and Stuart 1975)—is consciously and systematically included in the group process to open up areas of communication.

6. *Teaching of conflict-resolution skills.* Just as communication skill building is important to the premarital counseling process, so is developing and enhancing conflict-resolution skills. Thus, as a part of the group process, at least one session is spent on the teaching and practicing of conflict resolution. It is interesting to note that the premarital counseling content, like life itself, is not free of conflict, as the various aspects of the relationship are looked at and examined. It is not only appropriate, therefore, but often necessary for the focus of a segment of the group process to relate to conflict negotiation and resolution.

These six general goals will assist counselors working in a group context to articulate participant outcomes. The characteristics of congruency and flexibility are extremely important and need to be present in the counselors. We suggest that the goals be presented to the couples during the first group session as ultimate or outcome goals of the counseling process. We also recommend that at the beginning of each counseling session, the counselors review the process and goals from the previous session and summarize the particular goals of the current session. That is, we suggest that counselors should present an overview of the goals, relating both to the entire process and also to specific goals for each session.

Our assumption regarding group premarital counseling is that it is a combination of an educational and a therapeutic process. Thus, a contract regarding the total number of sessions can be agreed upon at the beginning of the process. Specific components, such as communication skill building and conflict negotiation, can be taught as part of the process. Although structure and goal direction are part of our group premarital counseling process, modification can be made for particular couples as appropriate. For example, it is possible that in some instances, some couples or an entire group may need virtually no training in communication skill building. In that case, time can be spent on other matters important to the group.

The Role of the Counselor

The counselor's role in group premarital counseling can most appropriately be described as that of a guiding facilitator. Because the process is structured, the element of guidance exists. But because the goal of the premarital counseling is also to aid individual and relationship development, the element of counseling also exists.

As the reader may have surmised from the outline of the group process, we recommend for the counselor to be quite active in the sessions. This activity consists primarily of the introduction of topics and concepts that relate to the specific goals of the session. The focus should be on the couple, and therefore the talk and interaction should be primarily between them and not between them and the counselors or other group members. Although the main focus is on the premarital couple and their relationship, however, significant relationships can also exist between the couple and the counselors and among other couples or individuals in the group. Counselors who are aware of this can use the relationships in assisting couples to develop and grow. Counselors need to be sensitive to client expectations regarding this role and to be aware of the nature of their influence with the couples. We think that it is important to understand that counselors serve as models and create safe and trusting environments in which the couples can understand each other and grow together. All of this is a way of saying that counselors are models of communication, teaching skills in communication and conflict negotiation.

As the final group session approaches, it is important for counselors to remember that above all, they are persons involved in significant relationships with premarital couples. "While the couple will perceive the counselor in a variety of ways, he/she will facilitate the couples' growth when he/she is perceived as person who clarifies, understands, and enables couples to change in positive ways. Thus, the counselor sets the tone in premarital/prewedding counseling for future help in marital crises" (Stahmann and Hiebert 1977b, p. 314).

Instruction about the Group Process Model

Throughout the group premarital counseling process, the various sessions focus upon the premarital relationship as well as introduce specific areas of content. Generally, the counselors will have established broad goals for each session in order to guide its particular focus. Our outline earlier in the chapter of the goals for each of the five sessions is an example of this pregroup planning. Our experience suggests that premarital couples desire and expect some formal structure and guidance as to the content of the premarital counseling process. We believe that this is particularly true in group procedures involving a number of couples.

Session 1

The purpose of the first session is to establish rapport and build a warm, empathic, and trusting relationship between the couples and the counselors. This is not difficult to accomplish. However, there may be a tendency on the part of the counselors to rush through the initial interview, rather than to proceed in a relaxed yet systematic manner. We suggest that counselors need to keep in mind that each of the partners in each relationship, and each of the couples present, has unique and important contributions to make in the process of getting to know one another.

A getting acquainted procedure involving all of the persons in the group is essential as a part of the first session. Some counselors prefer to use name tags to assist couples in identifying other persons by name. Other counselors use a verbal procedure, asking each individual in the group to introduce himself or herself and tell of some significant event or fact which would help the group remember and know the person. We have found this to be useful. In addition, we have found that after names have been given, it is useful for the couples to introduce themselves as a couple, stating something of significance about their relationship, past history, or future plans. The goal is not to gain a great deal of information about the individuals and couples, but to give them a chance to talk and become somewhat involved in identifying themselves, their partners, and other group participants.

After the initial introductions and getting acquainted, the group will undoubtedly be somewhat relaxed. The counselors can then provide additional structure by a brief presentation of administrative or procedural issues such as length of meeting time, scheduling of breaks, review of expectations about confidentiality, and related matters. The remainder of the first session will be used to present and practice the speaker and listener roles from the Conjugal Relationship Enhancement Program. At the end of the session, the counselors present the homework assignments. In this case, the requirement is for couples to practice the communication exercise five times during the next week, for a period of thirty minutes daily. At the conclusion of this session, counselors who wish to offer to consult with individual couples can make their availability known.

Session 2

In the second group session, the homework assignment follow-up is the first procedure. Any problems that have been found with the process are discussed and corrected. Discussion of and information about the process are solicited from all group participants. Particular successes with the speaking and listening roles are also discussed. If it is appropriate, a couple may be asked to role-play or recall one of their homework interactions that was particularly stimulating or problematic.

The primary goal of the second session is to explore the personal history and parental modeling of each of the individuals. In order to assist our work with this process, we use the procedure we discussed in chapter 4 of drawing two time lines in the shape of a "Y" on newsprint. We have found it useful to obtain a large piece of newsprint and marking pencils for each couple, leaving tape around the room so that couples can go to the wall and write on the newsprint as they discuss their time line. The counselors begin by drawing a "Y" and explaining that one fork of the "Y" indicates John and the other fork of the "Y" indicates Mary. The intersection of the forks of the "Y," resulting in a single line, is the point at which their relationship began. The counselor then begins by asking Mary (or John) to discuss the significant aspects in her childhood that helped her to evolve to the person that she was when she met John. The events are placed on their separate time lines.

It is assumed that John and Mary volunteered from the couples in the group to help the counselors demonstrate this particular aspect of the group process. The counselors may have already obtained some demographic and background information on the couple through a questionnaire or inventory such as the Premarital Counseling Inventory that was completed by the couple when they applied for group counseling. Throughout the individual life history process, the counselors listen for various influences that parents, schools, jobs, and other dating relationships have had upon the individuals.

As discussed in detail in chapter 6, parents are models for husband-wife interactions. One goal of the premarital counseling process is to assist the couple in identifying the impact that parental modeling has had upon them and at the same time in growing and progressing beyond the model that the parents provided. Growth beyond the parental models is frequently necessary and appropriate. Although the model the parents devised may have worked well for them, it is unlikely that it will work well for the adult child, who will be joining another person with another history of parental modeling to form a new marital relationship. The counselors, then, serve as guiding facilitators, assisting the couple in identifying the path and moving beyond it.

In assisting the couple to examine the effects of parental modeling, the counselors need to explore five areas (Stahmann and Hiebert 1977b). These areas are provided as suggestions and are not all-inclusive. Counselors are encouraged to expand or modify these areas as they deem appropriate. We suggest that counselors present and discuss as many areas of parental modeling as there are couples in the group. The procedure, then, is to have each couple discuss one of the areas of parental modeling with the counselors. With five couples, we would explore with each couple one of the following areas.

1. *Demonstrating affection.* The first area deals with the demonstration of affection as modeled by the parents. It is important to explore when, where, and how affection was demonstrated by the couples' parents. Was affection openly displayed, or were there very few displays of affection? Was touching a natural and frequent occurrence, or was it taboo? Misunderstandings and problems can arise

in premarital and marital relationships if the partners have different expectations and interpretations regarding affectional practices. For example, if Larry is undemonstrative and does not put his arm around Susan, Susan may feel unloved; or Larry may feel rejected if every time he attempts to hold Susan's hand in public, she feels uncomfortable and rejects the hand-holding, an affectionate move by Larry. As differences in parental modeling and home experiences are discussed and discovered, a notation is made on the time line for the couple to discuss this area further. It is important for couples to resolve their different expectations for their relationship. (The counselor will note here that topics such as affection will be excellent content for the later focus on conflict negotiation and resolution.)

2. *Companionship and shared activities.* The counselors move on and focus on a different couple. The second area of exploration for the individuals relates to companionship and shared activities. Did the parents socialize as a couple, or primarily as individuals? In some families, the husband's primary form of companionship is with other men, in such activities as fishing, hunting, and so on. How about parent-child companionship? Did the parents tend to socialize with the children, or did they socialize without them.? Were there sex-linked pairings, such as Dad doing things with the boys (his son or other men) and the mother doing things with the girls (daughters or other women)? What social modeling did the individuals observe in other adult couples? What individual expectations does each have regarding social activities that include or exclude the future mate?

3. *Money and finances.* Moving on to a different couple, the counselors explore a third area of parental modeling, money and finances. Here we explore not only the standards of living of each parental family, but also the spending habits and methods of handling money of the parents. What value was placed upon money and material things by parents? How was money handled by them? Who paid the bills? Who managed the money? Was some of the responsibility shared? How were the decisions about spending the money made?

4. *Religion.* The counselors next focus on another couple and move into the area of religion. Religion or values is another area in which parents will have influenced a child. By religion, we do not mean simply the avowed denominational affiliation of the parents, but, more important, their religious activity and involvement. Was religious activity practiced by both parents in the family? Was it ab-

sent? Or a part of only one parent's life? Based upon the parents' influences, what expectations and practices relating to religious habits and customs does the young person currently have and expect in the marital relationship (Clinebell 1977)?

5. *Discipline and children.* Moving on to the last couple (assuming a five-couple group), we consider the modeling of the parental home regarding children and discipline. At some point, the parents began a family. How did the parents handle the children? What did each learn about being a parent from a child in his or her home? Young couples frequently have many ideas about raising children based upon their own experience of being a child and being raised according to certain guidelines and assumptions (Satir 1972). Each person's understanding of the meaning of being a child has much to do with the particular parental home in which he or she was raised (Allred 1976).

These areas, then, should be explored individually by each of the persons in each of the couples in the group. As was mentioned previously, the counselors should not be limited to a consideration of the topics that have been suggested. By listening carefully, counselors can discover other topics to pursue. For example, it is not uncommon for topics such as parental use of alcohol and other chemicals or drugs or handling of physical illness to be explored in the same manner as the five suggested areas.

The homework assignment for this second session is for the couples to continue to discuss all of the areas. If five couples and five areas were discussed in the group session, each couple would have discussed only one of the topics. At home during the coming week, the couples can focus on the other four areas. A very short review of the speaker and listener roles can again be offered, with the admonition that as couples talk together about the content areas, they should attempt to increase their communicative effectiveness. In addition, the FIRO-B, a brief paper-and-pencil instrument, is handed out for the couples to complete in the few minutes after the session has concluded.

Session 3

The counselors begin the third session by asking the couples for their reactions to the FIRO-B. Any problems with or concerns about the instrument which are expressed are appropriately discussed with the group. Similarly, reactions regarding the homework assignment of continued dialogue on the various content areas is solicited.

After these items have been adequately dealt with, the counselors shift the focus from the past history of the individuals to the present premarital relationship. They start by again constructing the time line, beginning at the point at which the couple first met or first noticed one another and continuing up to the present time, the base of the "Y." The counselors demonstrate the process by asking one of the couples to serve as a model. The counselors ask, When did you first meet? How did you first meet? What year was this, and what were you doing? What are your recollections of your first meeting? Who initiated dates or continued the relationship? When did you each individually become more interested in the other? What attracted you to the other person? As you got to know the other person, what did you like and dislike about him or her? How were the two of you different from each other? How were you similar to each other? How did your level of commitment change over time? What first entered your mind when you thought you might marry this person? When did the two of you initially discuss marriage? When did you tell someone else about your intent to marry? Who did you tell? What were the reactions of others who matter to you to your relationship with this person? These questions and many others are asked. As this process unfolds, the counselors can make brief notations on the time line indicating important dates and events.

The focus here is upon helping the couple further to discover and uncover what it is about the relationship that attracted them and has led them to this point. The counselors need to keep in mind that at this time, most of the couples will, in fact, be psychologically married, as was discussed in previous chapters. Each partner has already committed himself or herself to the other person and has no intent of changing or altering that commitment. Sometimes, however, one person in a premarital relationship may not have made a commitment. Occasionally, neither person has really done so. The exploration—discovering the nature of the commitment—is therefore crucial.

At this point in the session, the counselors will introduce and discuss the concepts of the FIRO-B, which has been taken by all of the group participants. The specific model for using information derived from the FIRO-B, is discussed in detail in chapter 15, "Instrumentation in Premarital Counseling." Suffice it to say here that the presentation of the FIRO-B concepts and specific scores obtained by each couple is intended to provide the couples with a meaningful framework in which to explore interpersonal relationships in terms of affection, control, and inclusion. The FIRO-B also helps them examine their needs to express and to receive these dimensions from other persons, particularly their future mates.

Based upon the framework of the FIRO-B, the later part of this session shifts to those areas that are identified as interpersonal dimensions in marital relationships. By now, each couple should know something about their individual developmental histories, have reviewed the salient dimensions of their own relationship and courtship history to the present time, and have developed improved communication skills. The goal of providing these interpersonal relationship dimensions is to assist the couple in exploring these areas and to discover how they might deal with each other and the suggested content or topics. Thus, the counselors are concerned with the *what* or *content* focus and also with the *how* or *interactional* process.

The areas are quite similar to those discussed earlier in this book. We present them here for your continued consideration in the group context.

1. *Friends and socialization.* Exploration here focuses on the extent to which friends are primarily his, her, or mutual friends. Do the couple see themselves as continuing to make new friends as the relationship develops, or are they likely to carry over old friends from the days prior to their relationship?

2. *Activities.* What kinds of recreational and nonvocational activities does each of the persons enjoy alone? Together? What are their individual vocational or professional plans and goals? How does their future mate fit into these plans? How do they feel about each partner's vocational plans and goals?

3. *Religion or values.* This area focuses on the meaning of marriage to each partner and explores the psychological, emotional, and legal dimensions of the marital relationship. What is going to be the religious practice that the couple wish to maintain in their life? What will be the nature of the religious activity that each desires to pursue in marriage? What about the spouse? How are the partners similar and different in this area?

4. *Geography.* In this area, counselors ask each participant, What was your geographical environment as you grew up with your family

of origin? Did the geographical experiences which you had coincide or conflict with those of your future spouse? What are your geographical preferences after marriage?

5. *Affection and sex.* Assuming that there has been an affectional component in the relationship to this point, counselors ask whether it has been what each expects and desires. They ask each partner, How might your upbringing and previous experience influence your demonstration of affection in this relationship? Do you have adequate sex information? Have you and your future mate discussed male and female physiology and contraception? What do you believe are your expectations about giving and receiving affection in your relationship now? After marriage?

6. *Budget and finances.* Ask such questions as, Have you discussed your financial situation? Are the two of you comfortable with it? After marriage, who will handle the money that you have? As you begin the marital relationship, who will earn the money? What are your short-term and long-term goals and plans regarding financing and budgeting?

7. *In-laws and parents.* Questions in this area include, Was your premarital relationship with this person supported and encouraged by your parents? What expectations do parents have for you individually? As a couple? What has been your reaction to your future in-laws during your premarital relationship? How might this affect your marriage? What are your particular ideas and expectations regarding your future mate's interaction with your parents?

8. *Roles.* Counselors ask what roles each person expects to fulfill as a husband or wife in the marital relationship, what it means for each to be his or her partner's wife or husband, and how various roles in the relationship will be negotiated and changed.

9. *Physical health.* Questions in this area might be, Have there been any major illnesses in your personal medical history that might have an impact on your marriage? What is likely to be your reaction and how might you cope with illness in your spouse? Do you have specific activities or plans which you will implement to maintain your physical health? Do these include your spouse?

10. *Children.* Counselors should ask each person, What are your individual goals regarding the number and spacing of children? Have you discussed family planning and contraception? If you do have

children, what will be your goals as parents? What specific goals will you have for your children?

At the end of this counseling session, the couples are instructed to discuss two of the ten areas per day and to mention at the next session those areas that were a problem to them as well as those that were relatively easy to discuss. It might be useful for the premarital counselors to prepare a page summarizing the ten areas and listing sample questions which the couples can use in their dialogue during the week.

Session 4

At this point in our group process, we are at the beginning of the fourth counseling session. It should be apparent from the material presented so far that there will undoubtedly be variations in the tempo and fullness with which various groups and counselors will deal with the material. Thus, it may be that this point represents the beginning of the fourth, fifth, or even sixth counseling session. For consistency, we will assume that we are beginning the fourth.

This section begins with a follow-up on the homework assignment in which couples discussed the ten interpersonal dimensions presented the week before. Particular attention is given to each of the couples as they identify briefly those areas that were easy for them to discuss as well as those that were difficult to discuss or around which some conflict appeared. The counselors then instruct each couple to identify one of the areas that contained some conflict for them as they discussed it. This area then will be the content upon which the skill building of conflict negotiation will be based. A volunteer couple is solicited and the counselors coach them and teach a conflict-resolution and negotiation approach.

At least three different couples should have the opportunity to practice the conflict-resolution model during the group session. This allows them to experience the process firsthand and also allows each couple to observe at least two other couples using the skills that they have themselves learned. It is ideal to structure the time and experience so that each of the couples has an opportunity to participate in the learning process. This is a primary reason for keeping the groups relatively small. Each couple will have an opportunity to participate actively in the learning process when no more than five couples are involved.

At the conclusion of this session, the homework assignment is given: Each couple is to practice the conflict-negotiation skills that have been introduced. They are also asked to review their previously learned skills in communication, those of speaking and listening effectively. As the couples do this, it will be apparent to them that the communication and conflict-resolution skills go hand in hand. It is difficult to negotiate and resolve conflicts without effective communication.

Session 5

In the fifth and final session of the group premarital process, the primary goal is to summarize and synthesize the learning and experimental components of the previous four sessions. The previous sessions have been involved in skill building in communication and conflict negotiation, as well as introducing specific areas of content and focus for the couples. The counselors assist the couples in reviewing the material they have covered together.

Counselors should be aware of a number of possible alternatives that may be appropriate at termination. First, it is assumed that most couples will have progressed well and will continue their plans for the upcoming wedding and marriage. It is important at this point, we believe, for the counselors to discuss with the couples the possibility that they should come back for a few sessions of postmarital counseling after they have been married for a period of six months to a year.

The focus of this postmarital counseling is to assess the current status of their relationship and strengthen it even further (Guldner 1971, Bader et al. 1980).

The second alternative involves further premarital counseling. This would be the case if particular difficulties have arisen (Peck and Swarts 1975). On the other hand, it is possible that through the premarital counseling process, the couple has determined that their commitment to marriage as previously planned has changed and that they wish to continue the counseling process to explore the nature of this change. We recommend that if continued counseling is appropriate, it is most effectively done on an individual conjoint couple basis rather than in a continuation of a group setting.

A third alternative is to move from a dynamic premarital counseling format into a format that includes other family members (Rolfe 1976, 1977 a,b). This approach has been discussed in detail in chapter 5. It should be noted that this alternative—having each couple meet with the counselors and the couple's parents—is being adopted as a routine procedure in some settings. Because of the large size of the group if each of the five couples were to bring their two sets of parents (a total of thirty persons plus the counselors), we recommend that a session for each couple and their parents be conducted separately from the group process.

There may be other alternatives and other types of conclusions which could cap the group premarital counseling sessions. Again, the counselors need to be sensitive, conscientious, and creative in developing specific approaches to closure that will have meaning for and impact on the particular couples that are in the group. The termination should be planned by the counselors with the help of the couples.

IV
Marrying Again

9
Remarriage Counseling

It has been estimated that in approximately fourteen million marriages in the United States, at least one of the spouses has been married previously (Knox 1979). Divorce is the most common way for ending marriage, with the current divorce rate at about 50 percent. Approximately 1,180,000 divorces occurred in the United States in 1986 (National Center for Health Statistics 1987). In spite of the relatively high rate, 75 to 80 percent of divorced people remarry (Carter 1986). The rate of divorce in remarried families is projected to reach 60 percent in 1987 (Carter 1986). It is clear that large numbers of persons who voluntarily or involuntarily terminate marital relationships enter into new marriages. Thus, the phenomenon of remarriage is prevalent in American society.

The premarital counselor will likely be confronted with couples in which at least one partner has been previously married. In recent years, there has been a tremendous increase in professional and lay publications that focus upon the problems of remarriage, particularly those involving the adjustments of a divorced person and children to a remarriage. The competent premarital counselor needs to be sensitive to the potential problems confronting those who wish to remarry. This chapter will examine the process of premarital counseling for the remarriage of a childless couple. In chapter 10, we will explore remarriage premarital counseling for reconstituted families, that is couples who will have a child or children present from a preceding relationship or relationships.

Theoretical Issues in Remarriage

It has been well established in family theory and family therapy theory that the degree of separation a person has from his or her previous marital relationship can be an important indicator of marital success in remarriage. Before we move directly into the process of premarital work with remarriage couples, we will briefly note the theoretical issues that lie behind work with these particular couples.

Leaving the Previous Marriage

If a person has been married and that marriage has been terminated by death, divorce, annulment, separation, or desertion, the experience of that marital relationship will have a lasting impact upon the person. We would agree with and expand upon the point made by Whitaker and Keith (1977) that a person cannot really be psychologically divorced. We believe that regardless of the cause of the termination of a marriage, the partners can rarely completely get over or ignore the impact of that previous marital relationship. People are unable to dismiss significant intimate relationships from their life. Although it is possible to remove oneself physically from a relationship, it is rarely possible to remove every trace of that relationship so that a person is as he or she was prior to the time it began.

Decourting

Therapists speak of the decourting process, a divorce counseling process in which the goals are to help the partners get back as much of their original emotional and personal investment as possible and to clarify the practical factors in the new relationship, such as childrearing (Whitaker and Keith 1977).

The task of the premarital counselor in working with a remarriage couple is similarly to assist the persons in adequately resolving and dealing with their previous marital relationship. Previous relationships have a significant impact upon persons, and that impact may be positive or negative. Even though the previous marriage may have been forgotten for the present time, or may perhaps have been satisfactorily discussed and resolved by the couple, a part of the counseling process for remarriage should include a discussion of the experience of each person in his or her previous marriage.

Continuation of Previous Dysfunction

It might generally be expected that because a high percentage of persons who have terminated their marriage tend to remarry, marriage is viewed as a satisfying and valuable lifestyle. Often people voluntarily terminate marriages because of discomfort and dysfunction in their particular relationship. One would expect, therefore, that people would carefully select a second marital relationship and prepare for it well so that the previous dysfunction might not be repeated. However, there is evidence that this is not the case; many persons enter into a second marriage carrying with them the dysfunction and hurt that they experienced in the first marriage (DeBurger 1977).

In dealing with a remarriage, the premarital counseler needs to be particularly alert to the probable dysfunction in or cause of the termination of the previous marriage and to assist the couple in assessing the extent to which previous dysfunctions have or have not been resolved. When such problems are found, the counselor must responsibly assist the individuals in resolving them. Such a counseling process often takes longer than the five- or six-session premarital counseling process discussed in the earlier parts of this book. The sessions may go on for several months, and may continue after the wedding. In contrast to premarital counseling involving first marriages, a satisfactory outcome may be for the couple to decide not to enter into the remarriage at the particular time as originally planned. The counseling process for the remarriage couple without children is similar to the process described in chapter 5, uses the DRH to focus on the dynamic of any dysfunction in the previous marriage, and will be described in greater detail later in this chapter.

Blaming Previous Relationships

It is not uncommon for persons who have been divorced to focus a great deal of blame on the previous marital relationship or previous spouse. Often this is seen as healthy by the couple, and can have the effect of seeming to strengthen the current relationship by downplaying the previous relationship. However, in the long run, such blaming is frequently dysfunctional. The task of the remarriage counselor, therefore, is to assist the couple in adequately differentiating the present marital relationship from the previous marital history, so that the couple can deal with the current relationship without needing to downplay the previous one.

DeBurger (1977) pointed out that the converse can be true of the blaming often found in remarriages. He pointed out that discomfort in the remarriage may result in one partner blaming the other for the loss of the previous marriage which, as time passes, may look as if it were not so bad after all. There may also be resentment because the second marriage is not as satisfying or fulfilling as the first marriage, which was voluntarily terminated.

Contexts of Remarriage Counseling

We believe that the context of marriage counseling shapes, to some degree, both the expectations of the remarriage couple and the methodology of the remarriage counseling.

Parish Setting

Although more first marriages take place in local church settings than do remarriages, still a significant number of remarriages take place in the context of the local congregation. Although there have been no studies comparing and contrasting the difference between couples who go to pastors for remarriage counseling and couples who seek remarriage counseling from social service agencies, it is our suspicion that couples who seek remarriage premarital counseling from their pastor perceive the forthcoming remarriage in generally positive terms and have a minimum amount of concern regarding the success of the remarriage. This means that they are not approaching the remarriage counseling with an orientation toward problems. Thus, the expectational level is somewhat similar, but not totally so, to the couple approaching the first marriage.

Another factor affecting remarriage counseling in parish settings is that several denominations require remarriage premarital counseling before giving permission for a church wedding. Couples approaching remarriage premarital counseling in this context expect the parish pastor to not only explore the current remarriage relationship with an eye toward functionality, but also expect the pastor to pay attention to the dysfunction in the previous relationship and the possibility of its continuation in this current relationship. Thus, these couples expect scrutinization of the current and previous relationships. Many couples are cooperative and believe that the process is aimed toward helping them improve their relationship. But, some couples are irritated and annoyed by the process and see it more as an obstacle than as an attempt to help improve their relationship.

Agency Setting

It is our experience that there are two types of remarriage couples who seek out remarriage counseling from social service agencies and clinics: the previous client and the conflicted couple.

Some couples seeking premarriage counseling in agency and clinic settings are couples in which one or both partners have had previous marital therapy. Sometimes the former clients return to the previous marital therapist, expecting the therapist to examine the current relationship to detect any signs of continuing dysfunction. Although the couple expectation in this situation is appropriate, many counselors functioning with a family therapy orientation would choose to refer this couple so that a new therapist can begin working with the couple with no previous alliance or relationship with the former client. In addition, it should be noted that many marital therapists working with a divorcing couple caution them about forthcoming relationships and suggest remarriage counseling as a check on the possibility of perpetuating the dysfunction of the earlier marriage.

There are other couples, who may or may not be former clients, who are currently experiencing significant conflict in the prospective premarital relationship and are wondering whether they should terminate the relationship or go forward to the wedding. This couple expects the remarriage counselor to help them explore the relationship, identify the cause(s) of the dysfunction, and move toward some resolution. On occasion, counseling seriously conflicted premarital couples may seem more like marital therapy than premarital counseling. We will explore more fully working with seriously conflicted couples in chapter 12.

Design of Remarriage Counseling

We have been hinting at our model of remarriage counseling. We now want to briefly outline the design of remarriage counseling and explore a number of administrative issues.

Administrative Issues

Although there are a number of administrative issues regarding remarriage counseling that are similar to administrative issues regarding premarital counseling with couples preparing for the first marriage, there are several specific issues which we need to consider in the case of remarriage counseling.

Framework. In our remarriage counseling model, the conjoint couple counseling process contains five basic units: introduction, dynamic relationship history, exploration of previous marriages, family-of-origin exploration, and wedding preparation. These basic units will be discussed in greater detail later in this chapter.

Sessions. The remarriage counselor needs to make some decisions regarding the structure of the premarital sessions, particularly in regard to the length of each session and the number of sessions.

In regard to the length of the sessions, the two-hour framework, as is typically employed in counseling couples preparing for their first marriage, seems to be an appropriate model for remarriage counseling as well.

In regard to the number of sessions, we suggest at least five two-hour sessions for nonclergy. This should be an adequate time for remarriage couples to accomplish the remarriage counseling. Clergy, who need to include theological and wedding material, would need to add another session.

The discussion regarding contracting, fees, and printed material in chapter 4 related to premarital counseling of first marriages would apply to the remarriage couple.

Instrumentation. In remarriage counseling, we have found the use of assessment devices very valuable. Both PREPARE and the Taylor-Johnson Temperament Analysis are excellent resources in exploring the current relationship. If the remarriage counselor makes use of assessment devices, these then need to be administered in the first session. Any fees applying to the instrument need also to be discussed at the onset of the remarriage counseling.

Part 1: The Introduction

The introduction is the time set at the beginning of the first session to allow the remarriage counselor to become acquainted with the couple. Part 1 of remarriage counseling is identical to part 1 of premarital counseling. All of the aspects discussed in part 1 of chapter 5 apply to the remarriage counseling context, including the issues of getting acquainted, explanation of the process, instrumentation, and contract.

Part 2: Dynamic Relationship History

We believe that the second part of the remarriage counseling process should consist of an exploration of the history of the current relationship from the time the couple first met up to the proposed wedding through the use of the dynamic relationship history (DRH). In this sense, part 2 of remarriage counseling is similar and identical to part 2 of premarital counseling with couples preparing for the first marriage. Thus, the rationale for the DRH and the techniques for the DRH, as discussed in part 2 of chapter 5, apply in remarriage counseling.

Areas of Focus. In conducting the DRH for remarriage couples, the remarriage counselor can follow the process as previously presented, exploring the relationship from the time the couple first met until they present themselves for counseling. Through use of the DRH, the remarriage counselor can move through the history of the current relationship in a month by month fashion.

All of the various themes and questions enumerated in conducting the DRH in chapter 5 apply when conducting the DRH with remarriage couples.

Prewedding Pattern. In working with remarriage couples, the remarriage counselor is seeking clues about the nature of the current relationship, attempting to determine the kinds of patterns that are unfolding in the relationship. Thus, all of the themes mentioned in chapter 5 in "Comments and Clues about Patterns" will apply in working with the remarriage couple. Thus, the remarriage counselor should be observant about the following themes and/or patterns: commitment and bonding, dependency, self-esteem, communication patterns, power, intimacy, and religious practice.

The Wrap-up. When the remarriage counselor has completed the DRH, it is important that the counselor spend time providing the couple with his or her observations about the relationship. The wrap-up is neither meant to be judgmental nor critical but descriptive. Remarriage couples benefit enormously from being able to have the comments of an outsider or third party on their relationship. Thus, the remarriage counselor can fashion the wrap-up in the same manner as a counselor would in working with a couple preparing for the first marriage. Thus, the themes and items mentioned in chapter 5 in "The Wrap-up" would apply to the remarriage counseling process at this point.

Part 3: Previous Marriages

In our model of remarriage counseling, we have placed the examination of the previous marriages following the completion of the current relationship. This placement is designed to reduce the resistance of the remarriage couple. If the remarriage counselor begins by exploring the previous relationships, it generally irritates the remarriage couple. They are coming to the counselor because of the current relationship, are usually excited and happy about the relationship, and are in some sense coming to celebrate it. Thus, by attending to the current relationship first and focusing on it as the primary relationship, it is easier then to move backwards and explore the previous marriages. We suggest it is met with less resistance by the couple and also it is more productive at this stage of the remarriage counseling process.

The purpose of part 3 is to explore the previous marriages in order to determine both the degree of resolution of the previous relationships and whether any dysfunctional patterns are going forward into the current relationship.

In many ways, part 3 is similar to a DRH, although it is shorter and more intense and offers a more specific focus on seeking to determine the nature of the dysfunction(s) that brought about this marital breakdown.

Methodology. In conducting the exploration of the previous marriage, we ask the couple to choose which partner wants to go first. After the couple has chosen who will initiate the examination (provided both have been married previously), we then focus primarily on the individual chosen and his or her previous marital relationship. While conducting the exploration, we not only ask the individual to describe the previous marriage, but also ask the individual what the ex-partner would say to the questions as we go along the time line. In addition, if the prospective mate has some knowledge of the previous marriage because of friendship with one or both of the previous partners, we invite the prospective partner to add his or her observations to the nature of the previous marriage. As in conducting the DRH, we make use of the time line and proceed in a forward fashion, although not so much month by month but rather in larger time frame units.

Areas of Focus. Although any of the areas of focus that were used with the DRH can be used in regard to previous marriages, we attempt to condense the previous marriage exploration by focusing on larger time frames. These will be evident in the areas of focus that follow.

> *Dating relationship.* As in the DRH of the current relationship, we explore the dating relationship in the previous marriage, looking at it as an entire unit. We are interested in how the person perceived the dating relationship, what indications now, in looking back on it, are there regarding the problems that occurred in the marriage. We ask about any peculiarities in the dating process, any items that now appear to be strange even though they were not perceived so at the time.

> *Beginning of conflict.* Rather than moving through the time line month by month, we begin the marital portion by exploring the onset of conflict. We are interested in when the conflict began and

how it manifested itself. In addition, we are interested in early attempts of the couple to either manage the conflict or resolve it.

Attempts to change. As we move along the time line, we inquire about attempts to change the previous relationship, whether these were through professional counseling or through the use of ideas generated by the couple.

Nature of breakdown. We inquire as to the nature of the conflict, its ongoing manifestation, and the shape of the struggle as it began to occur in the relationship.

Decisions to separate/divorce. As couples move towards increasing marital conflict, it is not uncommon that they separate, come back together, separate, and ultimately divorce. We are interested in what precipitated separation or the divorce action, how the decision-making process evolved, and the actions of both of the previous mates in dealing with the decisions.

Process of parting. We are interested in how each of the former partners dealt with the pain of the separation and dissolving of the marital relationship. We are particularly interested in how each mate handled the pain of the divorcing process, whether any professional help was sought at the time. In some remarriage situations, the current relationship began as one or the other attempted to help the partner through the pain of a divorce. Thus, a current relationship may have evolved as a way of dealing with a previous marriage. If that is the case, we believe it is important to look at that therapeutic process and what it means for the current relationship both now and in the future.

Similarities. After we have moved through the previous marriage, we are interested in spending time with the couple looking at the similarities between this current relationship and the previous marital relationship. We are interested in seeking patterns that are similar to those in the previous dissolved relationship.

Differences. In addition to the similarities, we are also interested in the differences between the current relationship and the previous dissolved marriage. In other words, in what ways is the couple trying to shape this relationship that are different from the previous dissolved marriage?

The Wrap-up. Like the wrap-up following the DRH, the wrap-up of the exploration of the previous marriage(s) is designed to indicate to the couple what the counselor perceives in the previous dissolved marriage. This wrap-up, like the wrap-up following the DRH, is not meant to be judgmental but descriptive. The idea is to help the couple focus on what is new and different in this relationship and what is similar and holds the prospect of causing conflict in the new marriage. Thus, in style and shape, this wrap-up is no different than the items discussed in "The Wrap-up" in chapter 5.

Part 4: Family-of-Origin Exploration

The purpose of part 4 of the remarriage counseling process is to explore the separation that exists between each of the persons and their family of origin. As in the case of working with a couple preparing for their first marriage, part 4 is designed to help the couple assess the nature of the parental marriages, whether they have an excessive attachment to their parents, and whether they will be able to take responsibility for their own lives. The issues discussed in chapter 6 regarding parents as models, the format for exploration, the method, the wrap-up, and saying good-bye all apply in the remarriage counseling process.

Part 5: Wedding Preparation

This final portion consists of an exploration of the mechanics of the wedding and theology, and is designed especially for clergy. This portion of remarriage counseling is identical to part 4 discussed in chapter 6.

10
Counseling the Blended or Stepfamily

I t is widely acknowledged that the great majority of those who divorce will remarry. The previous chapter outlined a process for premarital counseling for couples who have been previously married. The purpose of this chapter is to expand on that discussion and to focus specifically on remarriage where one or both of the partners have children.

The *blended family* or *stepfamily* "is a family where one parent is a stepparent and the children may live full time in the family or visit frequently or infrequently (Martin and Martin 1985, p. 1)." The term *reconstituted family* has also been used to describe remarriage where one or both of the partners bring children into the remarital relationship (Landau, Egan, and Rhode 1978). Current data indicate that some fifteen million children and twenty-five million adults live in stepfamilies in the United States. Furthermore, each year, approximately one million children and 500,000 adults become members of stepfamilies (Martin and Martin 1985).

Issues Facing Stepfamilies

Clinicians will generally agree with the observation of researchers who were studying divorce and remarriage and concluded that "despite the growing interest in remarriages, there is much that we do not know about them (Albrecht, Bahr, and Goodman 1983, p. 143)." Their data support earlier findings that remarriages are slightly more likely to end in divorce than first marriages. As we pointed out in chapter 9, one major cause for the failure of remarriages is due to unresolved issues from the previous marriage(s). Other factors also can contribute to the failure or success of remarriages, particularly stepfamilies. The counselor must be aware of these factors and needs to assist the couple in identifying and working through them.

1. *Inadequate role models.* It is likely that persons entering the stepfamily situation have not been there before. The influence of family of origin and the modeling of significant persons in one's life is well established. Generally, the previous history of the premarital couple and their children does not include direct experience in the stepfamily life. Although family roles and functions in the stepfamily will be similar to those in the previous family, there will also be new and different roles and expectations. The counselor will need to work with the couple to identify and confront them.

2. *Losses.* As Martin and Martin (1985) point out, the stepfamily members have suffered the loss of an intimate and significant relationship. This is particularly true in the case of death of a spouse/parent, yet is also true in the case of divorce. In the case of divorce, the recognition and dealing with the loss of the previous relationship may be confused by the behavior of the former spouse, who may encourage a continuation of the relationship in a manner not comfortable to the partner entering into the new marriage. Feelings of confusion, guilt, anger, and anxiety are some of the feelings that the partner(s) will have to deal with as they exit the previous marriage and enter into the stepfamily marriage.

3. *Old traditions.* Memories and behaviors from the previous marriage will likely be very much alive as the stepfamily begins. The counselor needs to assist the couple and children in drawing from the past so that some continuity and stability are maintained (Martin and Martin 1985). Yet, the emphasis and focus needs to be on the current stepfamily situation in an attempt to create bonding and the feeling of psychological belonging and commitment to the new marriage and family.

Parental Problems

The problems facing a stepfamily involve the roles of both the adults and the children, and we have found it useful to separate them into these two categories. Ransom, Schlesinger, and Derdeyn (1979) have identified three developmental phases through which the reconstituted family typically passes. In the remarital counseling process, the counselor can appropriately assist the couple with each of these growth phases.

1. *Recovery and entrance.* The first developmental phase which the reconstituted family passes through is recovery from the previous marital relationship and entrance into the new marital relationship. Here the appropriate focus in counseling is to assist the individuals in resolving as much as possible their feelings of loss of the earlier marital and family relationship. Similarly, positive anticipation and expectations regarding entering into the new marital relationship are of great importance and must be worked through prior to the entrance into the remarriage.

2. *Understanding and planning.* A second developmental phase which the family passes through and works with is the understanding and planning of the new marital relationship. This can be processed by using the dynamic relationship history with a specific focus upon children, finances, and role expectations.

3. *Reconstitution of the family.* Although the first two developmental phases might primarily involve the couple in conjoint counseling, in this third phase, the children should be added to the process. The aim at this point in the counseling is to deal specifically with the expectations and functions of a newly constituted family. We suggest that the counseling take place over a long term, beginning before the marriage and continuing after it as the family experiences their actual reconstituted nature and adjusts to the process of such living.

In addition to the developmental phases which the couple and family typically follow, Landau, Egan, and Rhode (1978) have identified several problems facing the adults in the reconstituted family. The first problem is relationships with the ex-spouse. The second area relates to problems facing the new couple in the reconstituted family situation. Both of these have been discussed in previous sections of the chapter.

A third problem facing the adults in a reconstituted family relates to grandparents and other significant adults in the lives of the children. What will be the nature of such intergenerational relationships? Counselors have often found it useful to invite the grandparents of the reconstituted family to the counseling process. In such cases, the counseling room will contain at least three generations (parents, children, and grandparents), and, depending upon the numbers involved, the group may be a rather complex network. Even though this may seem to be an overwhelming number to cope with in a counseling situation, we have found the event to be very useful and significant in the counseling process and the lives of the clients.

The issue of maintaining a relationship with children who are living in the custody of the other parent rather than in the parental home on a regular basis is a difficult one. As we pointed out previously, this can cause problems of jealousy, commitment to the new spouse, and financial resources.

The final adult problem discussed by Landau, Egan, and Rhode is that of building new relationships as a stepparent to children who are not biologically related. The problem of the new stepparent arises (Landau, Egan, and Rhode 1978; Messinger 1976; Ransom, Schlesinger, and Derdeyn 1979; Visher and Visher 1978). There are many problems associated with a person's joining a family in the role of a stepparent. A primary problem is one in which the stepparent does not meet the expectations of the spouse in the role of being a parent to the spouse's biological children. From the children's perspective, there are also problems associated with the assumption by the new spouse of the role of a parent in the home.

In counseling situations in which children are involved, either in the custody of the new partner or in the custody of a previous mate, issues related to handling of the children must be dealt with prior to the marriage. Expectations of both partners must be thoroughly considered, along with potential problems based upon the partners' or counselor's previous experience with such situations. The primary vehicle for dealing with this subject matter is an expanded section of the dynamic relationship history on children and the style of parenting in previous marriages.

It is often useful to devote some counseling sessions to a clarification and discussion of expectations and agreements. The children and former spouse should be present in these sessions, along with the remarrying couple. While it may be difficult to involve the former spouse in the counseling sessions, it is usually fairly easy to arrange to have the children involved.

Increased Financial Burden

Another significant problem area reported by divorced and remarried persons is finances (Messinger 1976). In cases involving divorce in which one of the spouses is paying either alimony or child support, severe financial strains may devolve upon the person and his or her remarital relationship. Alimony and child support can be a significant part of a moderate-income earner's disposable money. If this is the case, the financial expectations and obligations of the couple may be difficult or impossible to meet. In order to assist with the financial burden, the spouse is frequently forced to work outside the home. A careful financial analysis must be part of the remarital counseling process so that the couple completely understand the financial resources and strains which will be a part of their relationship.

The person who receives alimony or child support may often initially be thought of as bringing a financial asset to the remarital relationship. However, this is not always the case. Frequently, the remarrying couple finds that the alimony which they had counted on has been discontinued or reduced because of the remarriage, or the child support payments do not adequately cover the anticipated expenses of the spouse and children in the reconstituted family. This may be particularly true in the case where a person with children marries a person who has not been a parent or has not lived in a marital situation in which there are children. Again, the indication for remarital counseling is that careful and significant discussion should revolve around anticipated financial resources and expenditures so that the couple can accurately and openly assess their financial resources and goals.

Issues Related to Children

In a great majority of instances, the children will provide a permanent link between the spouses of the terminated marriage, a link that must constantly be dealt with. Messinger (1976) studied seventy couples who had been divorced and remarried and found that children were the biggest source of difficulty in the second marriage. One of the primary reasons for this difficulty was that the spouse's children often are regarded as competition for the new spouse. There may be feelings of jealousy when the spouse directly feels that the partner's children are of greater significance to him or her than the current marital relationship is. There may be feelings of resentment when the children from the previous marriage spend time with the remarried couple.

A problem that often occurs relates primarily to the man who marries a woman with children from a previous marriage. Here the man is entering into the family relationship as an outsider, and he often will have difficulty in becoming a member of the family. Although this is particularly true because of the typically closer bonding between mothers and children than between fathers and children, the same problem can occur in a situation in which a woman marries a man with children in the home.

There appear to be three primary problem areas that are unique to children in a reconstituted family (Landau, Egan, and Rhode 1978). Of course, the adult problems include the children, and there are undoubtedly many more than three problem areas which affect children.

A first problem facing children in a reconstituted family has to do with their continuance and maintainance of relationships with the biological parent with whom they are not living. It is likely that the child will spend some time with this parent; however, because he or she may not be in the legal custody of the parent, the nature of the relationship is different from what it has been or is with the other parent. Children are frequently more sensitive to this issue than are the parents. They are frequently put in the position of a go-between or scapegoat for the parents. In counseling for remarriage, therefore, counselors should include sessions involving both of the children's biological parents, the new spouse, and the children.

A second problem area confronting children is the building of a relationship with the new stepparent, who is not biologically related. In many ways this is the flip side of the problem that the stepparent has in attempting to build a relationship with children who are not biologically related. This particular problem is most adequately dealt with in the counseling process after the wedding has taken place and the family is formally reconstituted.

A third problem area for children relates to the relationships that are maintained in the family network of the biological parents and the stepparent. What will be the nature of the relationship and contact between the child and grandparents, aunts, uncles, and cousins of their divorced father or mother? Similarly, what will be the relationship and interaction between the child and the greater family of the stepparent? The resolution of the relationships in the greater family networks requires years of interaction. The reconstituted family's expectations are initially processed in counseling, but several years later, they may wish to make appointments to deal with issues that are unresolved.

Continued Counseling for Stepfamilies

As we have demonstrated, additional concerns, beyond those encountered by couples entering first marriages, confront stepfamily couples. Although the specific nature of these problems will vary with the history and family composition of the persons involved, a common element is that of children. We also emphasize that it is not all problems with stepfamilies. There are many strengths which these couples have which should be built upon in the counseling process. Specifically, such things as greater maturity and high motivation to achieve success as a marriage partner and stepparent should be identified and focused upon as the counseling proceeds.

In this regard, we have found the inventory PREPARE-MC (Marriage with Children) to be very useful for working with stepfamily couples. PREPARE-MC contains the same eleven categories as does PREPARE, which is discussed in chapter 9. However, the PREPARE-MC includes specific items related to stepchildren and parenting in the marriage. Thus, this form of the inventory can be used by the counselor to help identify strengths and weaknesses in the premarital relationship which then become part of the counseling process.

If there are children in the stepfamily that are age thirteen or older, the premarital counselor could consider using the T-JTA (Taylor-Johnson Temperament Analysis, discussed in chapter 9). The T-JTA, when used with the criss-cross of family members describing each other, or some combination of family members describing other family members, can provide very useful information to the counselor and family.

Counseling the stepfamily usually involves a longer process than the four to six sessions suggested for first marriages. This is true whether the process is conjoint for the individual couple and family or whether the context is that of a group (Stroup et al. 1984).

Experience indicates that the couple facing a stepfamily relationship will frequently want to become involved in counseling prior to the wedding and to continue the counseling after the wedding as the new marriage and family experience begins. The counselor needs to be aware of this expectation and should, we believe, routinely plan to work with the couple or family for the first several months of the new marital experience. The counseling format prior to the wedding should follow and expand on the dynamic relationship history, focusing upon such areas as finances, children, and other specifics that may be of relevance to the particular couple or family. After the wedding has occurred and as the new family life is experienced, counseling will aim to increase positive growth by assisting the persons appropriately to identify and deal with problems and challenges that are stressful to them.

V
Special Topics in Premarital Counseling

11
The Very Young, the Late Marrying, and Forced Premarital Situations

T he intent of this chapter is to discuss the dynamics and process information which is available regarding the very young premarital couple, the late marrying couple, and the couple that are forced to marry. There is, of course, a severe limitation upon a discussion of topics of this nature in that statements and conclusions are generalizations based upon large samples of persons. The premarital counselors must be cognizant of the fact that the individuals or couples in a counseling situation may or may not be similar to the larger group upon which generalizations have been based. Thus, it is the responsibility of the counselor to apply the information contained in this chapter carefully to each premarital couple.

There is a fairly large body of literature, generated primarily from marital and family sociology, that points to a number of trends and generalized conclusions with which the competent premarital counselor should be familiar (Knox 1979). The reader will recall our contention earlier in the book that once a couple has committed themselves or decided to marry, it is very unusual for them to change that commitment. In the California study of couples seeking premarital counseling cited earlier (Schonick 1975), the data showed that of 1,300 couples who had applied for marriage licenses and were involved in premarital counseling, only thirteen, or one percent, decided not to marry! As premarital counselors, we must raise the question of the role of the counselors of these 1,300 couples. We are not suggesting that counselors should accept any overt responsibility for telling a couple not to marry. There were factors, among these couples, however—such as the fact that half of the women were pregnant at the time of counseling—that would indicate that the prognosis for satisfactory and stable marriages was questionable.

In many instances, the premarital counselor may want to share some of the information regarding the prognosis of marital satisfaction and stability with the couple as a part of the premarital counseling process. In other instances, when specific factors pointing to an unsatisfactory or unstable marriage are covered as a part of the routine premarital counseling, the premarital counselor may appropriately refer the couple to another counselor who has more specific training for the kind of therapeutic, long-term counseling that may be indicated.

The Younger and Older Premarital Couple

There appears to be great consensus among family sociologists that one of the most reliable predictors of marital stability and success is the age of the partners at the time of marriage. Generally speaking, the younger the couples are at marriage, the more likely they are to divorce. The divorce rate is highest among those who marry before their late teens or early twenties. Data have shown that for men who marry under age twenty, the expected divorce rate is two to three times higher than for those who marry at age twenty-one and above (Cannon 1978; Knox 1979; Albrecht, Bahr, and Goodman 1983). For females, the data show that women marrying under age seventeen have a divorce rate two to three times that of women marrying after age eighteen.

Recently information has become available that indicates that the couple, particularly women, entering a first marriage after the age of thirty tend to have less stable marriages than those who marry in their twenties (Glick 1986). "Older brides apparently are more independent and more willing to terminate a bad marriage than is true of those who marry in their twenties (Albrecht, Bahr, and Goodman 1983, p. 77)."

Although this generalization, based on large national samples, is true for *groups,* the premarital counselor must be aware that group averages may not apply for the specific couple in counseling. There are also differences in groups and group characteristics that should emphasize the need for the counselor to know well the sample that is being served. For example, Albrecht, Bahr, and Goodman (1983) found that for a sample of older marrying couples from western states, educational level seemed to counteract marital instability. They found that college graduate couples, who were likely to delay marriage until a later age, had the most stable marriages in their sample.

A logical question is, Why is the age at marriage such a determining factor in marital happiness and stability? The answer is not clear. It appears that the older a person is at the age of marriage, the greater the likelihood that he or she will be emotionally and psychologically mature. Such a person is more likely to have completed schooling and to be in a stable financial situation. Also, those who are older will more probably have prepared for marriage by clarifying their values and life goals and working out good relationships with parents and future in-laws (Knox 1979). Yet, with the older person, it is possible that style of living as a single person, as well as personal habits and preferences, can contribute to difficulty in marital adjustment.

The premarital counselor may be interested in attempting to determine what age is "old enough" to marry. Fortunately or unfortunately, depending upon one's point of view, there is no specific answer to such a question. The data indicate that men below twenty years of age and women below eighteen years of age who marry would be in a "high-risk" category for divorce. Research reported by Knox (1979) indicated that women who married at the age of twenty-five and men who married at the age of twenty-eight reported greater marital satisfaction and showed greater marital stability (lower divorce rates) than those who married earlier. It is unlikely, however, that the majority of couples seeking marriage or premarriage counseling will be in the twenty-five to twenty-eight year old age category.

A second major factor which Knox discusses as significantly related to marital happiness and stability is the amount of education each partner has and whether or not that partner's mate has more education. Studies indicate that those men who complete college have lower divorce rates than those who complete only high school or who leave college without graduating. The trend is for college-educated women to be more satisfied with their marriages than non-college-educated women. Also, it appears that more highly educated women are more satisfied with affection in their marriages and tend to be more sexually responsive to their spouses. An apparent caution, however, emerges in relation to education: when a wife has achieved a higher level of education than her husband, there is a greater risk of divorce than if the husband has obtained more education than the wife.

The primary reason for the positive correlation between higher education, particularly for men, and marital satisfaction and stability appears to be that the higher level of education is associated with a higher income level and economic potential. It is likely, therefore, that income level is a significant variable in marital stability and happiness. This is demonstrated by the finding that well-educated men with low incomes are more likely to divorce than men with a lower level of education and higher income. A rule of thumb, then, is that the higher the educational level the higher the income potential, but this is not always the case since the income generalization also holds.

David Knox, himself a marriage counselor, has appropriately summarized four crucial points that, if present in a premarital relationship, may well warrant a counselor's suggesting the extension of the courtship or engagement period (1979). In fact, Knox suggests that when the factors are present in any combination or process, the couple should be encouraged to extend the courtship.

Indication number one is a short courtship. A one-year courtship seems to be ideal as the minimum before marriage. The longer the couple have been involved before marriage, the better will be their opportunity to get to know and observe each other in a wide variety of settings. Thus, a longer courtship offers less possibility of premarital deception and greater possibility of a true knowledge and understanding of the other person.

The second indication is a lack of money or a poor financial condition at the time of marriage. As we indicated previously, there is a significant positive correlation between the husband's income level and the chance that a couple will stay married. This is not to say that a couple cannot live on a shoestring for awhile. However, a poor financial condition apparently must be temporary for a couple to achieve satisfaction and stability in marriage.

The third factor identified by Knox is that of parental disapproval. If parents disapprove of or have reservations about a potential mate, the most appropriate action is for the adult child to attempt to evaluate the parental objections objectively. Often parental concerns and predictions of marital failure are based upon their own experience as adult observers of marriages and upon what might be termed an intimate knowledge of their offspring. A direct implication is the idea that the premarital counselor should meet with the parents and the couple in an attempt to assist in discussing openly and accurately parental concerns and the couple's resistance to these. This can be done in the FOE, as discussed in chapter 6.

The fourth reason for prolonging an engagement or courtship is often viewed as a reason to speed up the process and get married immediately: the condition of premarital pregnancy. However, it is documented by statisticians and clinicians that if the woman is pregnant, that factor alone greatly increases the likelihood of marital unhappiness and divorce.

The Forced Marriage

As we have noted, it is difficult to establish exactly what age is "too young" in regard to marriage. Similarly, it is difficult to establish exactly when a forced marriage or forced premarital situation is occurring. For example, until recent times it was widely accepted that marriage was the answer to a premarital pregnancy, and the result was a forced or hurried marriage. Similarly, a person living in our society is often expected to be married by a certain age. When reaching the age when they "should" be married, some people may enter into less than ideal marriages. In considering the issue of forced marriage, therefore, we will regard any marriage as forced when either or both of the partners have the feeling or impression of being coerced into that particular marital relationship.

Earlier chapters in this book, which focused on the various factors relating to the premarital period and the technique of the dynamic relationship history, discussed in detail the personal and interpersonal dynamics of the courtship period. As a way of addressing the topic of the forced marriage and in an attempt to refrain from repeating some of the earlier discussions, we will briefly discuss four positive ways in which the courtship and/or engagement period can be used by a couple.

The dynamic relationship history, discussed in chapter 5, is an important and effective way to assist the couple in examining their relationship. An important part of the DRH is the discussion between counseling sessions, in which the couple continue to examine and explore their premarital relationship on specific topics and interpersonal areas. If during the DRH the counselor finds that the couple are very deficient and do not know one another well, then a direct implication is to expand counseling or the engagement period by continuing their examination of their relationship, focusing on getting to know each other.

A second appropriate use of the engagement or courtship period and the DRH in counseling is for couples to recognize danger signals that may assist in predicting marital problems. Knox identifies two danger signals, the on-and-off engagement and frequent and intense arguments (Knox 1979). An on-and-off engagement is predictive of a marital relationship with a similar pattern. The same is true of arguments. In a premarital relationship, an argument is a quarrel and often does not last long or become permanent. When a couple is married, an argument becomes a fight; it often builds up until frustration, dissatisfaction, or lack of the ability to cope with or change the situation leads to divorce. In this book, we have taken the position that conflict is unavoidable in premarital and marital relationships. A significant proportion of the premarital counseling process therefore focuses upon anger and disagreements in order to develop skills in dealing with conflict and conflict resolution.

Similarly, we suggest that the engagement or courtship period and the FOE in counseling can be used to increase interaction with future in-laws and each partner's parents. Significant interaction with parents would include visits to allow the potential spouse to observe firsthand the interpersonal relationships in the family, as well as other factors such as life style and living habits of the family. Of course, it is possible for a person to change and to be quite different from his or her parents. However, the likelihood is that there are many similarities between the prospective spouse and his or her parents. A very appropriate capstone to the premarital counseling process is to include the parents in a final counseling session, as was discussed in chapter 6.

Research has indicated that it is useful for premarital couples to assess the relationship comfort level, which is an indication of how each partner feels in relation to the other person. In looking at the combined results of several studies, Knox reported six variables as indications of relationship comfort level (Knox 1979):

1. Empathy, or the ability to put oneself in the emotional place of the other and to see things freely from the other person's point of view;
2. Spontaneity, or the open and unguarded expression of feelings;
3. Trust, the ability and willingness to trust the other person and to be honest and unafraid in the dyadic relationship;
4. "Interest-care," or the ability to have a genuine interest in and concern for the other person;
5. Respect, or the ability to have a regard for the uniqueness and individuality of the other person; and
6. "Criticalness-hostility," or the tendency to criticize and express hostility toward the other person when the other person takes different actions.

The goal of the counselor in assisting a premarital couple to examine their relationship is to have them resolve the many complex issues in a manner most appropriate to their relationship. In data cited earlier, it appeared that it would be unusual for a couple who has reached the engagement stage of a premarital relationship to change their minds and cancel the forthcoming marriage. The great majority of relationships are ended by the initiative of one person.

It appears that perhaps more women than men end premarital relationships. Knox indicated that a possible explanation for this is that women may be more sensitive than men to the signs of continued or serious trouble in the relationship.

12
The Seriously Conflicted Premarital Couple

A s pointed out previously in this book, the typical couple who seeks premarital counseling does so with the idea that the premarital counseling process will encourage the upcoming marriage. However, there are couples who show up in the counseling office to seek counseling because of a serious conflict or dysfunction in the premarital relationship. Often such a couple has been referred to the counselor by a friend, pastor, or physician who may have discovered the conflict or dysfunction during contact with the couple. However, we are also finding that an increasing number of couples seek premarital counseling on their own when a dysfunction is present. Perhaps this reflects the decrease in the stigma attached to counseling and therapy, or perhaps it reflects a greater concern for having the approaching marriage be a successful and satisfactory experience. Whatever the reason, the premarital counselor wil need to be alert to the seriously conflicted or dysfunctional couple.

Treatment Options

The identification and dynamics of the seriously conflicted premarital couple will be discussed later in the chapter. However, if the counselor has identified a couple as seriously conflicted or dysfunctional, he or she has at least three options. Of course, these options vary in specific instances depending upon the background, clinical experience, and qualifications of the premarital counselor.

The first option is for the couple to complete the premarital counseling process as described in chapters 5 and 6 of this book. Here the couple is treated as if they are not seriously conflicted or dysfunctional, and the counseling process in most ways ignores or overlooks their dysfunction. We do not believe that this is an appropriate treatment for premarital dysfunction. However, in instances in which the couple is not aware of the dysfunction or conflict or the counselor is not alert to the signs of conflict and dysfunction, such blind counseling likely occurs.

A second option open to the premarital counselor who is confronted with a dysfunctional couple is to refer that couple to another counselor. A referral can be made whenever the premarital counselor does not have the time or training to treat the dysfunctional couple appropriately. A referral to a professional who is better trained in dealing with interpersonal conflict and dysfunction is desirable. Even though the premarital counselor may have the training, experience, and skills to treat the dysfunctional couple, since such couples represent a minority of the premarital counseling population, the counselor may well choose to refer them because of a lack of time or interest in working with them.

The conscientious premarital counselor will establish a working relationship with professionals who can serve as referral sources. Although the referral sources will vary among specific localities depending upon available resources, professionals who are competent in working with conflicted and dysfunctional premarital couples are often clinical members of the American Association for Marriage and Family Therapy (AAMFT), which has members throughout the United States. The national office for the association provides a referral list of clinical members for specific geographic regions, which can be obtained from AAMFT, 1717 K Street NW, Suite 407, Washington, D.C. 20006, telephone (202) 429-1825.

A third option available to the premarital counselor confronted with a dysfunctional premarital couple is to treat the couple in counseling or therapy according to their specific dynamics. The dysfunction is identified in the counseling processes of the DRH and FOE (see chapters 5 and 6). In such cases, the counseling is extended and follows the therapeutic techniques used with marital conflict and dysfunction (Beavers 1985, Framo 1982, Gurman 1985, Humphrey 1983, Jacobson and Gurman 1986, L'Abate and McHenry 1983, Stahmann and Hiebert 1984). It is beyond the scope of this book to detail specifically the treatment of the dysfunctional or seriously conflicted premarital couple. The reader is referred to resources such as the six books cited for specific treatment procedures.

The remainder of this chapter will focus upon the dynamics and factors that can assist the premarital counselor in appropriately identifying the problematic premarital relationship.

Identification of the Seriously Conflicted Couple

In discussing the conflicted premarital couple, we must keep in mind that we mean the *seriously* conflicted or dysfunctional relationship. Every experienced counselor realizes that conflict is a part of the dynamics of any relationship. One of the tasks of premarital counseling is to help a couple to identify and deal constructively with conflict in their relationship. Here, however, we are discussing couples whose conflict is severe and, in the judgment of the counselor and/or the couple, a primary problem atypical of problems manifested in other couples.

It is possible that the dysfunction will be identified by the couple. It is also likely that the dysfunction will be identified as part of the routine premarital counseling process. The conflict may also be uncovered or discovered by the counselor or couple through some of the questionnaires or instruments used in counseling. Therefore, the counselor needs to be alert and sensitive to the identification of potential dysfunctional dynamics in the premarital couple.

When there is an indication of dysfunction in the relationship, the counselor needs to assess the extent of that dysfunction. This is accomplished by focusing upon the area of concern in a conjoint counseling session. If the couple is involved in a group counseling process, the counselor would probably be wise to schedule a conjoint counseling session with the couple outside of the group. As the counselor attempts to assess the nature and extent of the conflict or dysfunction, he or she should gather whatever additional data will aid in accurately understanding the dynamics of the interaction or problems. Therefore, an assessment instrument often can yield useful information on the personality of the individuals and the nature of the premarital relationship. The Taylor-Johnson Temperament Analysis (T-JTA) is particularly appropriate for this purpose, and will serve as the reference for our discussion of dysfunctional relationships.

The manual for the T-JTA (Taylor and Morrison 1984) and related publications identify and discuss the number of personality trait or temperament patterns that appear to occur as problematic or dysfunctional in premarital relationships. These patterns are discussed in some detail here; however, the reader is referred to the T-JTA manual for a more detailed discussion of them and of appropriate use of the instrument.

Figure 12–1 shows the profile for the T-JTA. The reader is referred to this figure for assistance in understanding more thoroughly the traits discussed here. The reader will also note that the profile identifies a pattern of traits in one person rather than in both persons. The discussion implies interactional dynamics for the relationship, but begins with an understanding of the dynamics of each person and therefore focuses upon these dynamics. Since the trait patterns of the five types that are presented can occur in virtually any combination, it is beyond the scope of this book to present a detailed discussion of all possible interactional patterns.

The Uncommitted Partner

The uncommitted partner in a premarital relationship is the person who, for one reason or another, is not able to make a firm commitment to the relationship at this time. Uncommitted patterns may be present in one or both of the persons in the premarital relationship. Even though the premarital counselor may have a tendency to assume that a person knows consciously whether or not he or she is committed to a relationship, this is not always the case. Therefore, these patterns can occur in a premarital counseling situation even when the partners believe or behave overtly as if they are committed to the relationship.

Refer to figure 12–1. In looking at the specific scales of the T-JTA, we would identify the uncommitted partner as someone who scores in the areas implying unhealthy behavior and the urgent need for improvement on three or four of the following six scales: relatively high, above the seventy-fifth percentile, on nervous, depressive, and/

TAYLOR-JOHNSON TEMPERAMENT ANALYSIS PROFILE
Profile Revision of 1967

Name _____ Age _____ Sex _____ Date _____

School _____ Grade ____ Degree _____ Major _____ Occupation _____ Counselor _____

Single _____ Years Married _____ Years Divorced _____ Years Widowed _____ Children: M ____ Ages ____ F ____ Ages ____

Answers made by: SELF and/or husband, wife, father, mother, son, daughter, brother, sister, or _____ of the person described

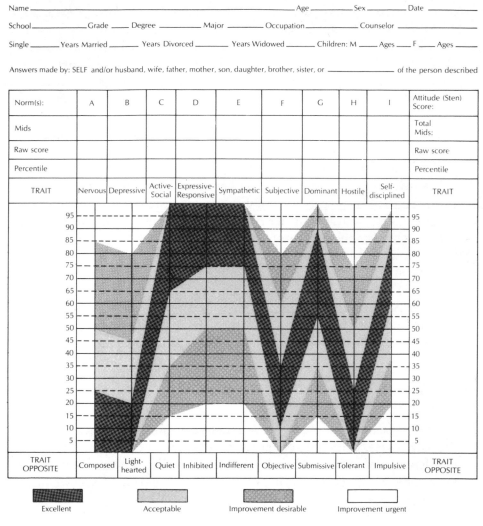

Norm(s):	A	B	C	D	E	F	G	H	I	Attitude (Sten) Score:
Mids										Total Mids:
Raw score										Raw score
Percentile										Percentile
TRAIT	Nervous	Depressive	Active-Social	Expressive-Responsive	Sympathetic	Subjective	Dominant	Hostile	Self-disciplined	TRAIT
TRAIT OPPOSITE	Composed	Light-hearted	Quiet	Inhibited	Indifferent	Objective	Submissive	Tolerant	Impulsive	TRAIT OPPOSITE

Excellent Acceptable Improvement desirable Improvement urgent

Definitions

TRAITS

Nervous—Tense, high-strung, apprehensive.
Depressive—Pessimistic, discouraged, dejected.
Active-Social—Energetic, enthusiastic, socially involved.
Expressive-Responsive—Spontaneous, affectionate, demonstrative.
Sympathetic—Kind, understanding, compassionate.
Subjective—Emotional, illogical, self-absorbed.
Dominant—Confident, assertive, competitive.
Hostile—Cricital, argumentative, punitive.
Self-disciplined—Controlled, methodical, persevering.

OPPOSITES

Composed—Calm, relaxed, tranquil.
Light-hearted—Happy, cheerful, optimistic.
Quiet—Socially inactive, lethargic, withdrawn.
Inhibited—Restrained, unresponsive, repressed.
Indifferent—Unsympathetic, insensitive, unfeeling.
Objective—Fair-minded, reasonable, logical.
Submissive—Passive, compliant, dependent.
Tolerant—Accepting, patient, humane.
Impulsive—Uncontrolled, disorganized, changeable.

Source: Taylor, R.M., and Morrison, L.P. 1966–1977. *Taylor-Johnson Temperament Analysis* (T-JTA). Los Angeles, Calif.: Psychological Publications, Inc. Reprinted by permission.

Figure 12–1. Profile for the T-JTA

or hostile; relatively low, below the twentieth percentile, on quiet, inhibited, and/or impulsive.

The following brief description of the uncommitted partner is based upon the T-JTA. This partner, whether male or female, is probably tense and apprehensive, pessimistic, and easily discouraged in most situations at the present time. There is likely a sense of argumentativeness, hostility, or inappropriate criticalness in relation to much interaction. He or she may also manifest impulsiveness or apparent disorganization and flightiness. Depending upon the extent of hostility and impulsiveness, the person may or may not appear to be unresponsive or restrained in his or her behavior and interactions. In sum, the pattern reveals a person who is unable to commit much to what is going on in his or her life. It may be that the person believes that a commitment can be or has been made to the marital propositions; however, because of the pervasiveness of the pattern in other aspects of his or her life, the possibility of lack of commitment or change in commitment should be thoroughly explored.

It may be that some of the identified traits, such as depression and anxiety, are temporary and transient, related to specific occurrences in the life of the person. Nonetheless, these need to be brought to the awareness of the couple and appropriately resolved.

The Passive-Inactive Partner

On the T-JTA profile, the passive-inactive person will typically attain the low scores, below the twentieth percentile, on the quiet, inhibited, indifferent, and submissive scales. He or she will score relatively highly (above the eightieth percentile) on the subjective scale. Thus, we have a description of a person who tends to be socially inactive, unresponsive or repressed, insensitive, and passive or dependent in interpersonal relationships. The high subjective score indicates that the person has a corresponding tendency to be illogical or perhaps self-absorbed or self-centered. The T-JTA manual points out that this person may be regarded as having an introverted personality, a pattern which has wide identification and acknowledgement in psychological nomenclature and description.

We frequently find that this passive-inactive person may be seeking the premarital and marital relationship as an attempt to gain personal strength and support. This is often true of the dependent person who is fulfilling dependency needs as he or she looks toward the marital relationship. The dynamics of the passive-inactive person can become severe as a marital relationship progresses.

The Unresponsive and Insensitive Partner

In this pattern, we find the person usually scoring below the twentieth percentile on the inhibited and indifferent scales. He or she often scores, in addition, relatively highly, above the seventy-fifth percentile, on the hostile scale. The description of the unresponsive-insensitive person, therefore, is of someone who is overly restrained, repressed, and insensitive or unfeeling in interpersonal relationships. When the T-JTA indicates that hostility is present in the person, the additional dynamic of argumentativeness or criticalness is present in his or her interpersonal interactions.

It appears that of the patterns that are identified as indicators of potential problems or serious conflict in premarital couples, this may be among the most easily changed. This pattern is often based upon the early learning and experience of the person and can be modified with appropriate new learning. This pattern may emerge as the counselor is conducting the DRH in the early conjoint interview.

The Apprehensive and Pessimistic Partner

As might be expected from an examination of the T-JTA profile, this pattern is indicated by relatively high scores above the eightieth percentile, on the nervous and depressive scales. This pattern is supported by a score of the same magnitude on the subjective scale and usually by a score of somewhat lesser magnitude, above the seventieth percentile, on the hostile scale. Thus, we have a person who is tense, apprehensive, pessimistic, and discouraged, as well as emotional and perhaps illogical. The relatively high hostile score indicates that the apprehension and pessimism of this person is likely to be acted out in argumentative and critical ways. Our clinical experience indicates that it is the anger and hostility that are identified as the primary problem or dysfunction in the relationship. Once those dynamics have been identified, the underlining apprehension or pessimism emerges.

This pattern will perhaps be discovered during the DRH, particularly in the exploration of the courtship experience of the couple.

The primary concern for the counselor is whether the pattern is long standing and related to the life-style of the person, or whether it is situational and perhaps somewhat typical of persons as they approach marriage. Even though marriage is ordinarily a time of joy and excitement, moments and experiences of anxiety accompany it. Thus, the apprehension and pessimism may be temporary and transitory, in which case the treatment would be rather clear-cut and the relationship would not be identified as dysfunctional. However, if the dynamics are such that the causes appear to be long standing and related to earlier emotional experiences or learning, appropriate treatment must be rendered before the partner can function in a healthy manner in the marital relationship.

The Angry and Aggressive Partner

In this pattern, the partner will score relatively highly on the dominant and hostile scales of the T-JTA. Frequently, although not always, there will be a similar score on the subjective scale and a relatively low score, below the twentieth percentile, on the indifferent scale. Our description of this person is of one who is aggressive and argumentative, as well as frequently verbally or physically punitive in interpersonal relationships. The subjective scale adds a degree of emotionality and illogical manner to the pattern, and the indifferent dimension adds unfeeling and insensitive responses.

As the reader might surmise, this is probably the most readily identifiable of the dysfunctional patterns in premarital couples. Frequently, when one of the partners is of the angry and aggressive type, the other partner will request premarital counseling in an attempt to reconcile differences prior to the marriage. Often, too, friends or family members will identify this pattern as problematic for the forthcoming marriage and refer the couple to premarital counseling. On the other hand, we are all aware of instances in which, although the pattern was identified premaritally, the couple went ahead with the marriage because of the inappropriate belief that the pattern would change after marriage without intervention.

This pattern is difficult to treat. It appears that conjoint couple therapy is most appropriate for assisting the person in modifying this behavior pattern. Modification of the abrasive interpersonal style can best be accomplished in the interpersonal context. The potential spouse appears to be the most significant person for involvement in the modification and therapy. Although this is a difficult pattern to change, the treatment process itself can serve as a significant bonding process, which might lead to an even more significant marital relationship than many couples who function well might experience.

13
Sexuality and Premarital Counseling

I n parts II and III of this book, we outlined the process and content of conjoint couple premarital counseling and group premarital counseling without specifically mentioning the place of sex education in the prewedding counseling process. This chapter will specifically discuss sexual education as an optional unit for inclusion in the premarital counseling process.

Changing Trends

We believe that the changing trends in sexual behavior and in sexual education runs parallel to and are exemplified by our own writing in the field of premarital counseling. Ten years ago, in our first published material on premarital counseling, we advocated the inclusion of a specific unit on sexual education (Stahmann and Hiebert 1977a). In the early to mid-seventies, the number of couples who were still virgins at the onset of the marriage was substantial. Couples marrying then were on the average younger compared to the current average marriage age of twenty-three to twenty-five. In addition, the practice of cohabitation prior to the wedding has increased dramatically, increasing some 400 percent in the last five years. Thus, when we wrote our first material on premarital counseling, we were speaking to professionals who were working with couples who were not typically sexually active to the extent that they appear to be now.

In 1980, when we published the first edition of this book, we decided to omit a unit on sexuality and focus primarily on the emotional and relational aspects of the couple. Couples presenting themselves for a wedding now, in contrast to couples in the early 1970s, are considerably older on the average, may have been sexually active (perhaps as many as eight out of ten couples), have experienced more sex education in the public and parochial schools, and frequently have cohabited prior to the wedding. In this sense, the couples marrying in the mid- to late 1980s are more sexually sophisticated and experienced than couples marrying fifteen years ago. Not only, thus, has the sexual climate changed, but also the trends mentioned in the previous paragraph will probably continue, with Americans gradually pushing the average marrying age toward thirty and with cohabitation occurring on a common basis between the engagement and the wedding. Whether the premarital counselor agrees with these happenings or not is really immaterial; these are the trends.

In this edition, we have chosen to return to our earlier custom and include a unit on sexual education in premarital counseling. The reasons are twofold. In spite of the average marrying age moving towards thirty, there are still numerous couples who marry at earlier ages and who are not sexually active or educated. Second, regardless of the marrying age and regardless of the amount of sexual activity, some couples are ignorant of sexual information and practices. For these individuals, sexual education at the onset of the marriage is invaluable.

Premarital Counseling Context

The issue of whether, when, and what sexual information to include in the premarital counseling process depends greatly on the nature of the premarital counseling setting. Parish ministers face different issues than do counselors in clinics and agency settings.

Parish Setting

As mentioned previously, a significant proportion of first marriages are performed in the context of the local church. With this in mind, we shall explore a variety of expectations related to sexual education in premarital counseling.

Denominational Expectations. Because we are a pluralistic nation, we have a large number of religious denominations. In addition, within each denomination, there are a variety of opinions and attitudes towards appropriate sexual behavior and explicit sex education. Denominations also have a diversity of opinions and traditions regarding the role of the pastor as a sexual educator.

In a general sense, the major denominations, and especially the Protestant denominations, have officially spoken to the issue of the importance of sexual expression in marriage, perceive sexuality as a gift of God, and encourage positive and wholesome attitudes towards appropriate sexual expression and behavior. In addition, most of the major Protestant denominations have developed curricula for the teaching of sex education to grade school and high school students, and adults. Thus, on an official and national level, the major denominations are supportive of sex education, especially in the context of prewedding counseling. In fact, most of the official handbooks for preparation for marriage, published by the denominations, include material on sexuality and direct the pastor to discuss this with couples.

In broad terms, then, it can be said that the national church bodies encourage and support sexual education, particularly in the context of pastoral care in regard to prewedding counseling. Nonetheless, there are always specific congregations within the context of a major denomination that may be reluctant or negative towards the inclusion of sexual material in a premarital counseling setting. Pastors of some of the more conservative and evangelical denominations, however, may find explicit support of sex education lacking in their denominational statements and social creeds.

Congregational Expectations. Just as there is a diversity of tradition in denominational expectations in regard to sexual education, there are also a variety of traditions in regard to the comfortableness with sexual education in local congregations. In some local churches, sexual education as part of premarital counseling has a long-established tradition, begun by earlier pastors. In other local churches, prewedding counseling is either brief and superficial, or hardly established at all. In these congregations, the attempt to introduce sexual education in the context of premarital counseling might be met with great resistance, to say the least. We suggest that it behooves the pastor to know the local attitude in regard to sexual education. In congregations where parishioners do not perceive the pastor as either being knowledgeable or the appropriate one for sexual education, the pastor might consider making use of a nonclergy professional for the sexual education portion. A nurse, physician, or psychological counselor could appropriately provide the sex education material for premarital couples.

Couple Expectations. Couples approaching the premarital session do so with a variety of expectations in regard to sexual content in the course of the counseling. Couples who have been active in their growing up years in their own denomination and congregation, and who come from denominations and congregations that are encouraging of sexual education, will probably expect the pastor to address sexual issues in the context of premarital counseling. Couples from denominational and congregational experiences that were more negative regarding sexuality may not expect the pastor to deal with sexual education and may be angered if such content is introduced. To some extent, therefore, it means that each couple must be evaluated by the pastor before pursuing sexual education with the couple.

Clinics and Agencies

Social service agencies and counseling clinics are more ambiguous regarding their expectations about the role of sexual education in premarital counseling. Nonetheless, counseling agencies and clinics have implicit expectations regarding the role of the counselor and the program in helping couples obtain an adequate sexual adjustment.

For physicians in medical clinics conducting prewedding medical examinations, the theoretical expectations are rather specific. The physician's responsibility is to provide both sexual information and birth control information.

Couple Expectations. Couples coming to counseling centers and social service agencies bring with them expectations about the premarital counseling process. We suspect, however, that couples coming for prewedding counseling come with the expectation that the counselor will, in some way, discuss their sexual relationship. This attitude is supported by the fact that today so much is being written and said in the popular literature and in the news media about the importance of a good sexual relationship in maintaining a satisfying marriage. Since millions of Americans are exposed via the popular literature and media regarding the importance of the sexual relationship, we believe most couples would anticipate the premarital counselor's inclusion of sexual material.

Design

For premarital counselors who wish to include a unit on sexual education, we have identified a number of topical areas that we believe are important for the counselor to include in order to provide relatively complete sexual information. In addition to providing a discussion of the three topical areas for inclusion, we will also provide several primary sources in each of the topical areas for the purposes of both expanding the counselor's knowledge and providing direct resources to the couple.

Biology and Anatomy

First, topics related to anatomy and the biological functioning of the human sexual system must be included in a sexual unit. This portion of the material should include such areas as sexual anatomy and physiology of the male and female, including anatomical structure and function.

Books are available that can enrich the knowledge of counselors who wish to either refresh or expand their sexual information. Excellent books for the counselor would include Kolodny, Masters and Johnson's *Textbook of Sexual Medicine* (1979) and James Leslie McCary's *Human Sexuality* (1978). Two older but classic books containing much professional information are Frederick Cohn's *Understanding Human Sexuality* (1974) and Frank Netter's *Illustrated Atlas of Human Reproductive Systems* (1974), as well as other books.

Two excellent resources are available for use with clients. An excellent audiovisual on the sexual anatomy of the male and female is available from Multi-Focus, Inc. (333 West 52nd Street, New York, New York 10019). This audiovisual is available in a filmstrip format or slide format with a lecture cassette tape accompanying either format. The audiovisual combines a comprehensive factual review with insights for care and treatment. This audiovisual was specifically designed for lay audiences and can be rented or purchased. A second resource is the useful booklet published by Budlong Press entitled, *A Doctor's Marital Guide* (1984) by Bernard R. Greenblat. This book, and others by Budlong Press, are often available at pharmacies. Useful books for use with very young couples are Gary Kelly's *Learning About Sex: The Contemporary Guide for Young Adults* (1977) and *Masters and Johnson on Sex and Human Loving* (1986).

Couples are sometimes surprised and intrigued when they learn that there are remarkable similarities in female and male anatomy and physiology. Frank Netter's *Reproductive Systems* (1974) graphically indicates anatomical and endocrine considerations.

Sexual Response and Interaction

The second portion of this unit should include material related to the basic sexual response cycle and sexual interaction. Kolodny's and McCary's books cited previously are valuable resources for the counselor.

An excellent resource for use with couples is part III of the audiovisual mentioned in the preceding anatomy section. The audiovisual on male and female physiology demonstrates the Masters and Johnson four-stage model describing the sexual response cycle and the refractory period. Like the anatomy portion of the audiovisual, this audiovisual is available in a filmstrip or slide format, and can be rented or purchased. The taped lecture accompanying the material is designed for lay audiences and discusses the sexual response process.

Booklets that the premarital counselor may wish to provide clients would include Greenblat's previously mentioned booklet, as well as his *A Doctor's Sex Guide,* published in 1980 by Budlong Press. In addition, clergy may wish to use several of the books that have recently been marketed for the Christian audience but which also contain good, factual sexual information, such as Michael and Joyce Grace's *A Joyful Meeting* (1980) and Clifford and Joyce Penner's *The Gift of Sex* (1981). The Grace book reflects the Marriage Encounter movement but presents a rather remarkable integration of spirituality and sexuality. It also, however, contains a sense of humor and uses rich and earthy metaphors. The Penner book is the most useful of the so-called Christian sexual manuals. It is very complete, straightforward, and factual in its presentation style. It also contains many diagrams, graphs, and pictures, all of which are excellent.

Family Planning

Third, basic information on family planning and contraception should be discussed with the couple. Kolodny, Masters and Johnson, cited previously, and Bradshaw et al.'s *Counseling on Family Planning and Human Sexuality* (1977) provide good information for the counselor.

Useful resources for couples again include the two Greenblat books cited previously, as well as the 1984 publication by Budlong Press, *A Doctor Discusses a Man's Sexual Health*. Although no companion volume to *Man's Sexual Health* for women exists in the current publications by Budlong Press, the booklet by Paul G. Neimark, *A Doctor Discusses Female Surgery,* is an excellent volume on other aspects of reproductive and sexual issues for women. Counselors should also not forget to examine the many brochures and pamphlets Planned Parenthood has available including their *Basic Birth Control* (No. 1253) and *A Guide to Birth Control: Seven Accepted Methods of Contraception* (No. 1218). Planned Parenthood not only has many of its publications available in Spanish but also provides a complete directory of all of its publications, which can be secured from Planned Parenthood, 810 Seventh Avenue, New York, New York 10019.

Summary

In premarital counseling, the sexual education unit is not designed to be sexual therapy. Rather, the premarital sexual education session is designed to provide pertinent sexual information via education. The task is that of helping the couple transmute their sexual education into fulfilling and socially responsible sexual behavior. All premarital counseling providers, whether they be clergy, counselors, or physicians, are expected to have the latest information in the area and (from the clients' point of view) to be able to deal with most all concerns and problems that are brought to them. The counselor, regardless of discipline, needs to be well informed about sexual matters.

We believe that the pertinent facts of anatomy and physiology, the sexual response cycle, fertility, and family planning should be understood by all adults. This is not privileged information for counselors. Some newly married couples especially need the unit on sexual education.

14
Marital Resource Management

Much of the thought that goes into planning for marriage focuses on the emotional and psychological nature of the premarital relationship. Courtship is an experience that emphasizes the social and emotional aspects of the relationship. Our concept of psychological marriage stresses the emotional building and bonding of the relationship. However, counselors and those in the prewedding process themselves often overlook the fact that the couple is in the process of uniting significant material and economic resources. As the marriage begins, it is also necessary for the couple to have appropriate decision-making skills and realistic expectations related to their material resources.

Developmental Tasks for the Couple

The premarital counselor is a catalyst and facilitator in helping the couple evaluate their present relationship and look to the future. This is particularly true when the counselor raises questions or brings up issues that the couple is not aware of or had not discussed openly at an earlier time.

Tasks for the New Husband

The newly married male has all of the expectations thrust upon him that are given to an adult male of his age, social status, and new role as a married person (Duvall and Miller 1985). Typically, society assigns such responsibilities to him as maintaining gainful employment and holding up his part of the family financial responsibility. Other public roles that are generally expected are such things as being an appropriate marital companion, in-law and family member, community citizen, and friend. The new wife also has expectations for him. She assumes that the new husband will be an adequate provider, companion, confidant, decision maker, sex partner, friend, and fulfill numerous similar expectations. When he meets his and others' expectations of his role as husband, he is evaluated as a good husband.

Tasks for the New Wife

Similarly, a new wife has expectations put on her that are to be met. She has in her mind an idea of what it is to be a wife in general and how she will function as the wife in her new marriage. She may have expectations placed upon her that are similar to those placed upon her husband. Yet, there are often some specific expectations for the wife. Being the couple's social secretary and planner and taking the lead in homemaking responsibilities frequently seem to be expected of the wife regardless of whether or not she is gainfully employed outside the home.

Marital Roles and Expectations

We believe that the premarital counselor needs to raise issues related to marital expectations and roles with the couple. As Duvall and Miller (1985) have pointed out, there are numerous complementary and conflicting developmental tasks that face the newly married couple. As an example, we will look at a rather straightforward situation that many inexperienced premarital counselors might think would not be an issue in modern society. Our experience has shown that the issue of the amount of the husband's time and attention given to his employment and the wife's time and attention devoted to household responsibilities are basic ones that all couples must work out.

For example, the new husband will likely be involved in becoming established in an occupation and the new wife will be working hard to establish the couple's home and manage the household and related responsibilities, whether or not she is employed outside the home. Here the marital roles can be complementary or conflicting depending upon the couple's expectations and actions. Things will go well (complementary) if the couple has similar expectations and corresponding behaviors. If both share an interest and responsibility in the home-making, there will likely be little conflict related to these issues and behaviors. On the other hand, if expectations and behaviors are dis-crepant, conflict is likely. If, for example, the husband is engrossed in his work and devotes greater amounts of time and attention to it than his wife expects, a problem can arise. In this example, if the well-meaning or insensitive husband shows little or no interest or involvement toward the household issues, conflict can arise. This is particularly true in the early months of marriage, as this is when the home and household are being established by the couple as physical and psychological entities.

The reader can create similar scenarios based upon personal ex-perience and reading. Such issues and topics as the spouses' dealing with expectations and behaviors related to family financial support, social activities, and sexual interaction and fulfillment are but a few of those to be considered and perhaps raised with the couple in counseling.

Origin of Value Exercise

An exercise that we have found to be helpful in raising such devel-opmental and role expectation issues with couples is built upon the value clarification work of Sidney B. Simon (1974). The purpose of this exercise is to help the couple see who may have influenced their values and behaviors on a specific issue or topic. Once the couple understand more clearly the roots of their values and behaviors, they are in a good position to negotiate and clarify their expectations and behaviors with their future spouse. Also, we have found that once a couple has been through this exercise on one issue or topic, they can readily use it to clarify others as they come up. We often build a homework assignment to apply the exercise to another issue before the next counseling session.

We begin this exercise with a piece of paper, usually on a clip-board, for each of the partners. At the top of the page we have printed the heading or ask the clients to write "Who influences my values and how much?" Below that we write the word "Issue:" and leave a space so that the clients can write in the specific issue that will be the focus. First, an issue related to marital role or value is determined with the couple. For our example here we will use the issue of "role of husband as breadwinner in the marriage." Each of the fiances are instructed to write that issue at the top of the page in the space indicated. See figure 14–1.

Next, and a core part of the exercise, is to answer the following questions: Who are eight (or six or ten) significant others in your life? What would they expect of you related to a specific issue? Each partner is instructed to identify significant others in categories such as mother, father, guardian, brother, sister, grandmother, grandfather, aunt, uncle, cousin, best friend, peer leader, religious leader, teacher, neighbor, famous person that you may not actually know, lover, person who dislikes you. By having the partners identify specific categories of persons and then identify actual persons in each of the categories, the exercise will come alive. We suggest that the couple write the name or initials of the person after the category so that the identity with the real person is strengthened. This can be done after the category, in parentheses as we have done in figure 14–1. They

Who influences my values and how much?

Issue: Role of husband as breadwinner in the marriage

Mother (M.Y.K.)
- Husband is the sole support.
- Wife only works outside the home in an emergency.
- Marry someone rich.

Best Friend (G.O.)
- Wife works to help get couple established.

Brother (H.K.)
- Husband = $!

Fiance (D.T.)
- Both will work while we finish school.
- Husband is wage earner.
- Wants to be home when the kids are young.

Father (W.R.K.)
- Support your wife.

Religious leader (B.N.)

Boss at work (H.U.)
- You two do whatever you must.

Grandfather (W.C.)

Figure 14–1. Origin of Values Exercise

are instructed to leave the center of the page blank and to write the categories and names of the persons at the top, bottom, and around the edge of the page.

The partner is then instructed to list three to five values or ideas that each of these persons would want that person to live by. As we say to the couple, "If I were to talk with each of the people that you have identified on your paper, what values or ideas would they have for you related to the role of the husband as breadwinner in your marriage? What key ideas would they have you live by related to that issue?" Each partner is then given time to complete the page. They are instructed to complete the page alone without consulting their partner. The counselor may be interested in observing their nonverbal behavior during this time.

The example in figure 14–1 shows a partially completed page from a person. After both partners have completed their separate page, the counselor instructs each person to look at his or her page and consider the variety and the similarities and/or differences among the values and expectations that these significant people would have for them. Then, each partner is to circle each item that he or she also accepts and wants for himself or herself. The clients are instructed to label the blank center of the page *ME* and to draw lines from the various values and expectations to the center *ME* area. Thus, as in our example (figure 14–1), the statements listed should represent much of the person's values and expectations on the role of husband as breadwinner in the marriage.

At this point, we instruct the couple to take a single piece of paper and write *US* at the top center. They also write the statement "Some of our values and expectations related to the role of husband as breadwinner in our marriage." As the reader might expect, this is the interactional part of the exercise. The couple is told to discuss together their two pages and to write the items which they want to or will accept as part of their new marital relationship. Once the couple have begun this process and the counselor has determined that they understand it and can follow the process, it can become an exercise to be completed outside the counseling session. If this is done, it should be followed up at the next meeting with the couple.

This exercise has also created other useful information for the individual partners and the couple. Specifically, the items listed on each page that were not circled are presumably those values and/or expectations, coming from a significant person in their life, that the person is rejecting. Such information may not have been previously so graphically brought to the person's awareness. This information may be significant for the individuals and the couple to be aware of and discuss as they plan for their marriage. Will their future spouse be supportive on the particular issue? Is it a major or minor issue for the couple to face? The premarital counselor may find an opportunity to help the couple as they anticipate dealing with their families or significant others on this or other values and expectations examined by the exercise.

Financial Resources of the Couple

We are not financial counselors nor are most persons who do premarital counseling. However, our practice of premarital counseling and marital therapy leads us to believe that the premarital process should raise financial questions and the financial awareness of the couple. Specific information is available to counselors (Mason 1985) and to couples from a variety of textbooks, as well as self-help budget and family financial planning books, at most book stores and libraries.

At a minimum, it would seem useful for the premarital counselor to provide an outline for a simple net worth statement for the couple to fill out. The information provided then can be used by the couple outside the counseling process, or in the counseling process, as communication skills or decision-making skills are taught, refined, or reviewed. In the net worth statement assets are listed at their current market value (what each could be sold for today) whereas liabilities are listed as the balances currently owed to creditors (Mason 1985). The net worth is the dollar amount obtained when total liabilities are subtracted from total assets. A basic net worth statement format is found in figure 14–2. We suggest that each partner complete his or her own net worth statement so that it describes his or her current status. The counselor should encourage them to list small but important items in all areas. For example, in personal property do not forget things such as furniture, kitchen items, tools, and recreational and sports equipment. After each partner has completed his or her personal statement, the couple can compare and discuss the statements and make one up that reflects the information for them as a couple.

Name of Individual or Couple _____

Assets

Cash $_____

Checking accounts   _____

Investments   _____

Personal property   _____

Home   _____

Automobile   _____

Business   _____

Other   _____

Total assets $_____

Liabilities

Rent (past due) $ _____

Utilities (past due)   _____

Charge accounts   _____

Credit cards   _____

Taxes   _____

Loan balances   _____

Auto loan   _____

Mortgage   _____

Other   _____

Total liabilities $_____

Net worth = Total assets – Total liabilities $_____

Figure 14–2. Net Worth Statement

Our experience is that such an exercise introduces an awareness and bonding that often was not previously present in the relationship.

Couples would often find it useful to project a budget or cash flow statement for their marriage. Looking to the time when they will be married, the couple are to project *income* from wages, interest, dividends, and other sources, and *expenditures* on items such as food, shelter, insurance, recreation, personal items, transportation, and loans. Again, our goal is to have the couple begin or continue a process of gaining information about their material resources so that they can maximize them in their upcoming marital relationship. When a couple enter marriage without both partners having similar knowledge of their financial assets and liabilities, problems related to expectations and trust often develop that have major negative impact on the relationship.

An often-used homework assignment is for the counselor to have the couple project a budget for the first six months or year of their marriage.

Decision Making

As we discussed earlier when presenting the dynamic relationship history (DRH), the premarital counselor is interested in how the couple have made decisions throughout the history of their relationship. Patterns in decision making are important for the couple to understand and can be the basis for strengths and weaknesses in the marriage. Here we wish to consider a different approach to understanding the couple's decision making than we presented in the DRH, an emphasis on expectations and the future rather than the past.

We are interested in the couple's expectations as to who will make various types of decisions in the marriage. The goal is developing a clear understanding for what is equitable for both partners. The equity of the decisions and the decision-making process is an important issue for the couple to work out. An appropriate function of premarital counseling is to provide the couple with a framework for understanding and communicating decision making. Richard Stuart's work with marital couples has provided us with a model which we have adapted for premarital couples (Stuart 1980).

The core question is, Who will make the various kinds of decisions in this marriage? Many decisions, large and small, face the couple daily. How decisions are made will either build or break the marriage. Following Stuart's model, there are five categories in decision making: (1) Wife only decides = W, (2) Wife decides after consulting husband = Wh, (3) Wife and Husband decide together = WH, (4) Husband decides after consulting wife = Hw, and (5) Husband only decides = H.

We begin this exercise by generating with the couple, on paper or the chalkboard, a written listing of a few decisions that they have made related to their marriage. Such things as deciding when to get married, whether to have an engagement ring, what type of a ring, how much time to spend together, and what activities to participate in together are sample items. We then change the focus and present decisions that they are likely to face when married. Such items as what employment the husband or wife takes, where the couple lives, division of household responsibilities, whether or not to have children, when to have children, how to spend leisure time, how much money to donate to church or charity, time spent in community service, and how to spend vacation time are examples. By this time the couple can generate further items in the list and we have them brainstorm additional items, leaving space on the page or chalkboard to add items. For example, a partial listing, leaving space on the right column for ratings, might look like this:

W, Wh, WH, Hw, H

1. When to get married
2. How much time to spend together now
3. Where to live
4. Purchase of major (costly) items
5. Division of household responsibilities
6. How to spend leisure time
7. When to get pregnant
8. Number of children to have
9. etc.

By having each partner copy the item numbers, a separate list for each partner can quickly be generated. Each person can then rate each item on his or her page by placing a check under the category (W, Wh, WH, Hw, H) based upon his or her perception of who should (will) make the decisions in the couple's marriage. As they compare and discuss their ratings, clarifications of expectations are made, and opportunities for compromise and adaptability may also arise. Thus, a model for clarifying decision making that can serve the couple throughout their marriage has been presented to them. In a dysfunctional relationship, the counselor would need to spend additional time developing basic decision-making skills, such as those discussed in Beebe and Masterson (1986).

It is important to note that many married couples (Barlow 1986) and premarital couples have the expectation that the ideal is to operate out of the category WH, wife and husband decide together. Not necessarily so! As Barlow pointed out, it is likely that the wife and husband have differing areas of expertise and interest. To believe and require that both spouses should together decide on all things would "overload our marriage with the trivia of the day (Barlow, p. 100)." The premarital counselor will serve the couple well if this expectation is addressed and the absurdity of it discussed.

15
Instrumentation in Premarital Counseling

I n this chapter, we wish to consider the various forms of instruments and assessment devices that can be used by both clergy and nonclergy counselors as aides to the premarital counseling process. The specific goals of the chapter are to present and discuss the issues related to the appropriate use of instruments and assessment devices, to present an in-depth discussion of two instruments which we believe are particularly appropriate to premarital counseling, and to present a broader list of typical instruments and assessment devices that can be used. The instruments and assessment devices which are discussed can appropriately be used in either conjoint couple or group premarital counseling.

The Nature of Instrumentation

In our discussion of *assessment devices* and *instruments* we have chosen deliberately to use those more broadly based terms, rather than the frequently used word *test*. Our purpose in selecting the broader terms is to underline the fact that the various approaches to assessment that can appropriately be used in premarital counseling over a broad range of devices, including specific forms such as questionnaires, personality inventories, psychological tests, rating scales, personal data forms, and other types of published material. Our point is that there is a wide variety of instruments available for use by the premarital counselor. We wish to be expansive and inclusive of many forms, rather than to limit the forms.

Though our approach to the presentation of various assessment forms is broad-based, we do not wish to be understood as endorsing all forms of assessment. Rather, we wish to allow the maximum flexibility possible to the counselor as he or she considers the appropriate use of the various instruments in a specific premarital context. It is the responsibility of each counselor to determine whether or not a specific instrument is appropriate for use with a particular couple or group, as well as to determine whether or not the chosen instrument seems to be constructed so that it provides accurate and meaningful data both to the couple and to the counselor. Often the counselor makes the erroneous assumption that just because an instrument or assessment device has been published or made available for use, it is appropriate. We have all, perhaps, been acquainted with instances in which persons have been provided with erroneous or misleading information based upon a supposedly accurate assessment device, when in fact the assessment device was really a gimmick rather than a systematic and accurate appraisal. Thus, we call for the judicious use of assessment devices in premarital counseling. We believe that if such devices are appropriately developed and appropriately used, both the couple and the counselor will benefit from their inclusion in the counseling process.

Counselor Considerations in Assessment

In addition to the rather obvious consideration of whether or not assessment devices of any type are compatible with the goals and procedures that a counselor is using in the premarital counseling process, a number of other considerations are important for the counselor.

Training and Background

Those persons with a master's degree in counseling will probably have had a course in assessment as part of their graduate work. We believe that such a course is a necessary prerequisite for the appropriate use of assessment devices in counseling. Clergy premarital counselors, who may not have had graduate study in assessment, can easily complete such a course at a nearby college or university. In addition, workshops and seminars are available on some of the instruments we recommend.

It is our experience that counselors will need to have specific practice and experience in using assessment devices that are primarily focused on relationship processes, such as premarital counseling. The typical assessment course does not cover such instruments in any detail. Once a counselor has been trained in appropriate methods for and resources in evaluating assessment devices, he or she can usually become familiar with the assessment devices that we will discuss.

Assuming that the premarital counselor has some formal background and training in assessment, we suggest that he or she should take the following steps when evaluating and considering a specific device for potential use in premarital counseling. These steps are necessary when the counselor is not familiar with the particular instrument.

1. Obtain a specimen set of the instrument from the publisher. The specimen set typically contains a copy of the instrument manual, the instrument answer sheets, scoring keys, and profile sheets if appropriate.
2. Take the device himself or herself.
3. Since the counselor will use the device in a couple context, he or she should administer it to another person whom he or she knows well: a spouse, a close friend of the opposite sex, or someone else significant to the counselor.
4. Read the manual to score and profile the instrument.
5. Read the manual so that the counselor can appropriately interpret the instrument. Interpret the results of the instrument for himself or herself and the other person.
6. Discuss the results of the instrument and the process of taking the instrument with the other person. Evaluate whether the instrument was obtrusive or upsetting to take. Evaluate the ease and clarity of scoring and interpreting the results of the instrument.
7. Evaluate whether the results of the instrument make sense to both people. Do the results support or contradict what the counselor knows about him- or herself and the other person?

8. Assuming that the instrument looks appropriate up to this point, administer it to several other sets of persons whom the counselor knows well, in an attempt to get their reactions to the process and to validate or document the accuracy of the information that the instrument yields.

9. Readminister the instrument to the counselor and the first other person about two weeks after the initial administration. Score and interpret the results. Compare the earlier results with the current results and note any changes that have occurred. Of course, we realize that any counselor's particular results are likely to be somewhat biased because most counselors are very familiar with the construction and process of the instrument. However, we are attempting to look at the reliability or stability of the assessment over a short period of time, to see what factors might affect the results of the device.

10. Assuming that the instrument has satisfactorily passed the judgments which the counselor has been making, the counselor then can begin to carefully use it in the premarital counseling process. Since the information gained from the assessment device will be used in combination with other information, the counselor will be in a safe position continually to monitor and validate the data that it provides in the counseling process.

It is apparent that the process just described will need to be modified a bit depending upon the specific nature of the instrument. For example, in evaluating an open-ended questionnaire or personal data blank, the counselor would not follow all of the steps as outlined. However, the point cannot be stressed too strongly: a counselor should always take an instrument or assessment device or complete a questionnaire before asking a couple to do so.

Advantages and Disadvantages of Using Assessment Devices

It is important to acknowledge that there are advantages and disadvantages to the use of assessment devices in premarital counseling. Generally, the use of paper-and-pencil assessment devices is warranted and justified; however, there will be times when the counselor will appropriately choose not to use such aids. Our idea here is really to determine whether or not the counselor will use paper-and-pencil assessment devices. We believe that it is safe to assume that even though counselors may choose to exclude such devices from the counseling process, they will be using informal and subjective clinical assessment as part of the process.

There are many advantages to using instruments in premarital counseling. The first is that instrumentation will promote a higher level of couple involvement in the premarital counseling process. By adequately explaining the rationale for the use of assessment devices by pointing out in general terms what information will be obtained, the counselor enlists a strong commitment from the couple to use the assessment process and to look for understanding. This commitment can further enhance the counseling process and outcome.

The second advantage to using assessment devices is that they can often help to obtain through simple means information that would take hours to obtain through interviewing. This is particularly true of the various questionnaires and personal data blanks that are available. The couple can complete the assessment device outside the counseling session and save precious counseling time.

The third advantage of using assessment devices is that they can ensure that the counselor will obtain information from the couple and for the couple on the multidimensional aspects of premarital information. For example, there are assessment devices of various types that can assist in obtaining information on knowledge, attitudes, personality dynamics, life values, and specific behaviors.

Another advantage of instrumentation is that depending upon the assessment device used, instruments can provide the counselor and couple with useful normative information. It is useful to have accurate data on some aspects of personal and interpersonal behavior in order to compare the couple with other groups that are included in the normative samples reported in test manuals. It has been established that a valid assessment device will provide the counselor with a more accurate basis for such comparisons than subjective clinical judgment can.

A final advantage of using assessment devices in premarital counseling is often overlooked: the possibility and potential of providing the counselor and couple with longitudinal data about themselves. Assessment data gathered at one time can be compared with data gathered at another time. Inventories can be taken twice during premarital counseling in order to document any change, or inventories can be taken during the premarital counseling and then at a later time in the marriage for purposes of comparison. Many couples have found it useful to go back to the premarital inventories and questionnaires to look at how they responded then and compare that to the way they would respond or score on the inventories now. Such an examination of the changes in the relationship are helpful, whether the couple is looking at changes in relation to marital problems or in terms of marital enrichment.

Among the disadvantages of using assessment devices in premarital counseling is that it is possible for couples to misunderstand the intent of using the assessment device. Assessment devices may instill in the couple the fear that they have something wrong with them or that they are troubled in their relationship. Because many premarital counselors do not regularly use standardized assessment devices, couples may not expect such use. This disadvantage can easily be overcome through a careful explanation by the counselor as to the reasons for and the potential information to be gained from the use of assessment devices.

The second disadvantage of the use of assessment devices could be that the counselor would tend to label or categorize the couple. Certainly, many instruments do yield information that leads to scales that have specific names, and therefore could lead to labeling or categorization. However, such a result is the fault of the counselor and not of the instrument. The use of information is solely the responsibility of the counselor. The skillful counselor will not use the information from an assessment device for labeling and categorization. The trained premarital counselor will interpret the information with the couple so that they can come to a better understanding of themselves and their premarital relationship.

The third disadvantage is the potential problem that the counselor will use the assessment results as the primary or only information that is conveyed to the couple about their relationship and themselves. In other words, the counselor can become "test-tied" and thereby use the test or assessment device as a crutch, sticking closely to the interpretation of the data as the primary focus of counseling. To do so is obviously inappropriate, because test interpretation is not counseling.

The instrument is a supplement to counseling and does not replace the counseling process.

Counselors can likely find additional advantages and disadvantages of instrumentation in the premarital counseling process. Our purpose is to highlight the major pros and cons so that the counselor might begin to evaluate the potentiality of instruments or assessment methods that will strengthen the premarital counseling process.

Guidelines for Using Instrumentation with Clients

A number of relevant guidelines for the appropriate use of instruments in human relations training have been suggested (Pfieffer, Heslin, and Jones 1976). These suggestions have been modified and are presented here as relevant to the process of using assessment devices in premarital counseling.

First, it is the responsibility of the counselor to justify the use of the assessment device or instrument to the couple. The couple need to understand the reason they are being asked to complete the instrument. By explaining to the couple that the instrument will yield information that will serve as an adjunct or supplement to the interview, or provide information from another frame of reference, the counselor will be responding to the couple's question, "Why should we take this instrument?" The counselor must also be sensitive to the clients' possible anxieties about the assessment device and attempt to assist the couple in dealing with those anxieties if they should arise.

Another very important guideline for the counselor is to assure the couple that they have control over their own test data. The counselor must describe carefully and in concrete terms his or her policies and practices regarding confidentiality of assessment data. This also applies to the confidentiality of the overall counseling process and any other counseling records which may be kept. The counselor must underscore the point that *all* information concerning the counseling, including assessment devices, will be reported to anyone only with the written permission of the client.

The counselor needs to make a conscious effort to uncover any mystery surrounding the assessment devices. This can be done by briefly discussing the real limits of what the assessment device can and cannot provide with the couple before they complete it. In the session following administration of the assessment device, the counselor should ask the couple about their reactions to taking or completing the instrument and deal with their feelings about the assessment device. We feel that the counselor should discuss the idea that even though the tests are generally reliable over time—meaning that the same approximate scores or answers will be obtained with the same device at different times—the scores or data are not absolute and are therefore subject to some change.

Depending upon how the instrument is used in the counseling process and the nature of the assessment device, the counselor needs to be sure that sufficient time is provided to process and understand completely the assessment results that are discussed.

Desirable Traits in Instruments

There are a number of traits or characteristics of assessment instruments that help counselors decide whether the devices are appropriate for use in premarital counseling. These are offered here in an attempt to help the premarital counselor determine whether or not a specific instrument is appropriate.

An important question to ask when considering using a specific assessment device in counseling is whether or not the information derived from it is necessary and appropriate for the counseling goals and purposes. For example, there are many personality tests that do not lend themselves to premarital counseling because they are designed to measure certain personality traits and diagnose various types of mental illness. If we assume that the typical premarital couple or group is not similar to hospitalized psychiatric patients, the use of such devices and the information obtained from them is not useful in the premarital counseling process.

The second consideration regarding the use of instruments in premarital counseling is whether they are nonobtrusive or whether they interfere with the counseling process. Our goal is to select and use instruments that blend with the counseling process and thus are a part of it. For example, the FIRO-B is an instrument that can be administered and scored during the counseling session with great ease, and it aids achievement of the interactional premarital counseling goals. Thus, an instrument can be considered obtrusive if it does not relate to the goals and outcomes, as discussed here.

The third criterion for the inclusion of an assessment device is that it must be compatible with the orientation of the counseling. The design of the assessment device, the manner in which it is administered, and the tasks and questions it raises, from the standpoint of the couple, are all important considerations. For example, if the primary goal and theoretical orientation of the counselor is for the couple to interact between themselves rather than for them to focus on their individual traits and characteristics, assessment devices that focus on the individual rather than the relationship would be inappropriate.

Another criterion for the selection of assessment devices is that the instruments must be easily understood by the couple. The couple must understand both the purpose of their investment of time in completing the instruments and the data and information that is yielded from the use of the instruments. Many questionnaires are self-explanatory, and the information is usually understood. In other psychometric instruments, a profile of scores will be generated. The question is, are the scores meaningful and understandable from the couple's point of view? Although it is important for information to be conveyed by the assessment devices, it is crucial for this information not to be misunderstood or threatening.

As mentioned previously, an important criterion for the use of assessment devices in premarital counseling is for them to have an interactional focus. Because the couple is the focus in premarital counseling, information that can help them assess their interactional dynamics and their relationship must be provided. Relatively few instruments or devices have this interactional dimension, and it is necessary in most cases for the counselor to extrapolate relationship and interactional information from traditional instruments.

Another consideration in the use of assessment devices is for the instruments to be economical. The devices must be reasonable from a monetary cost standpoint. They must also be economical in the sense of the time commitment involved both in completing and in scoring them to obtain the data.

Specific Assessment Devices

A discussion with premarital counselors regarding the use of instruments and assessment devices would likely reveal two categories of instruments. In the first category would be questionnaires, checklists, rating scales, and similar devices which counselors themselves have written and printed. Such devices are often developed after much clinical experience and are generally appropriately used to enhance the premarital counseling process. Although we encourage their use, we will not include them in our discussion here because of their limited availability. The second type of instrument or assessment device used by counselors is that which is more widely distributed and readily available from standard publishing sources. Another identifying quality of such devices is that they are referenced in the standard resource for assessment devices, *The Eighth Mental Measurement Yearbook* (MMY) (Buros 1978).

Taylor-Johnson Temperament Analysis

The Taylor-Johnson Temperament Analysis (T-JTA) is a 180-question instrument designed to measure nine bipolar personality characteristics. It requires approximately thirty to forty minutes to complete, and approximately fifteen minutes to score and profile the four answer sheets obtained. The T-JTA is appropriately used with individuals, couples, or families. As stated in the test manual, the T-JTA "is designed primarily to provide an evaluation in visual form showing a person's feelings about himself at the time when he answered the questions (Taylor and Morrison 1984)." Although the T-JTA is not designed to measure mental abnormalities in psychiatric terms, it does provide measures of temperament and personality patterns with sufficient validity and reliability for emotionally normal couples in a developmental-educational premarital counseling context. It also has the sensitivity to assist in identifying persons who might benefit from more individual or couple therapy.

The T-JTA yields nine bipolar scales which are used to assess the personality or temperament of individuals: nervous vs. composed, depressive vs. lighthearted, active/social vs. quiet, expressive/responsive vs. inhibited, sympathetic vs. indifferent, subjective vs. objective, dominant vs. submissive, hostile vs. tolerant, and self-disciplined vs. impulsive. In addition, there is an attitude scale which indicates to the counselor the attitude of the person taking the test and how he or she wishes to be seen. Thus, a high score on the attitude scale suggests that the person taking the test has described himself or herself as wanting to appear more admirable than he or she may actually be, whereas a low score suggests that the person has been overly critical of himself or herself.

A feature that is uniquely a part of the T-JTA and that makes it particularly appropriate for use in premarital counseling is the criss-cross testing. In the criss-cross testing, a spouse takes the test to describe him- or herself and then, on a separate answer sheet, completes the test again to describe the partner. Very useful information and test profiles are generated when one person's scores are plotted along with the scores of the partner's view. Thus, five profiles are generated in the criss-cross testing for a premarital couple: (1) Robert as he describes himself; (2) Joan as she describes herself; (3) a combination profile showing how Robert described himself and Joan described herself; (4) Robert as described by Joan; and (5) Joan as described by Robert. Samples of these five profiles are shown in figures 15–1 through 15–5.

The T-JTA manual is a model of thoroughness and completeness. The instrument itself is available in two levels of difficulty, the regular edition, at the eighth-grade reading level, and the secondary edition, at the fifth-grade reading level. It is also available in a Braille edition for blind persons and is currently published in a number of foreign languages (Spanish, German, French) with appropriate norms. T-JTA appears to be very adequately developed statistically. It is being used in a wide variety of research projects, and thus an ever-expanding body of literature is being generated regarding it. A variety of normative groups are available, all of which appear to be representative of the general adolescent and adult American population.

Probably the strongest feature in favor of the T-JTA for use in premarital counseling is the availability of well-validated criss-cross norms. These norms enable the counselor to compare each couple's responses to a well-validated sample of persons representative of the general population. The criss-cross profiles yield interactional information, which allows a couple to look at similarities and differences in perception between themselves. It is an excellent tool in assisting the couple to know and experience themselves as they truly are. As mentioned previously, the attitude scale gives an indication as to whether the person taking the test is disparaging, balanced, or overly positive in describing the person being rated (himself or herself or the other person). Such information can be helpful in assessing how re-

Husband

TAYLOR-JOHNSON TEMPERAMENT ANALYSIS PROFILE
Profile Revision of 1967

Name **White, Robert P.** Age **39** Sex **M** Date **6-27-68**

School **U. of Calif.** Grade **14** Degree _____ Major **Bus. adm** Occupation **Salesman** Counselor **R.T.**

Single _____ Years Married **18** Years Divorced _____ Years Widowed _____ Children: M **1** Ages **16** F _____ Ages _____

Answers made by: **SELF** and/or husband, wife, father, mother, son, daughter, brother, sister, or _____ of the person described

Norm(s): **1967-8 GEN. POP.**	A	B	C	D	E	F	G	H	I	Attitude (Sten) Score: **7**
Mids		**1**			**2**	**3**	**1**	**2**	**1**	Total Mids: **10**
Raw score	**10**	**3**	**36**	**32**	**28**	**17**	**35**	**28**	**33**	Raw score
Percentile	**50**	**27**	**91**	**65**	**28**	**81**	**95**	**96**	**84**	Percentile
TRAIT	Nervous	Depressive	Active-Social	Expressive-Responsive	Sympathetic	Subjective	Dominant	Hostile	Self-disciplined	TRAIT

| TRAIT OPPOSITE | Composed | Light-hearted | Quiet | Inhibited | Indifferent | Objective | Submissive | Tolerant | Impulsive | TRAIT OPPOSITE |

Excellent Acceptable Improvement desirable Improvement urgent

Definitions

TRAITS

Nervous—Tense, high-strung, apprehensive.
Depressive—Pessimistic, discouraged, dejected.
Active-Social—Energetic, enthusiastic, socially involved.
Expressive-Responsive—Spontaneous, affectionate, demonstrative.
Sympathetic—Kind, understanding, compassionate.
Subjective—Emotional, illogical, self-absorbed.
Dominant—Confident, assertive, competitive.
Hostile—Crical, argumentative, punitive.
Self-disciplined—Controlled, methodical, persevering.

OPPOSITES

Composed—Calm, relaxed, tranquil.
Light-hearted—Happy, cheerful, optimistic.
Quiet—Socially inactive, lethargic, withdrawn.
Inhibited—Restrained, unresponsive, repressed.
Indifferent—Unsympathetic, insensitive, unfeeling.
Objective—Fair-minded, reasonable, logical.
Submissive—Passive, compliant, dependent.
Tolerant—Accepting, patient, humane.
Impulsive—Uncontrolled, disorganized, changeable.

Source: Taylor, R.M., and Morrison, L.P. 1966–1977. *Taylor-Johnson Temperament Analysis* (T-JTA). Los Angeles, Calif.: Psychological Publications, Inc. Reprinted by permission.

Figure 15–1. Robert's T-JTA Profile

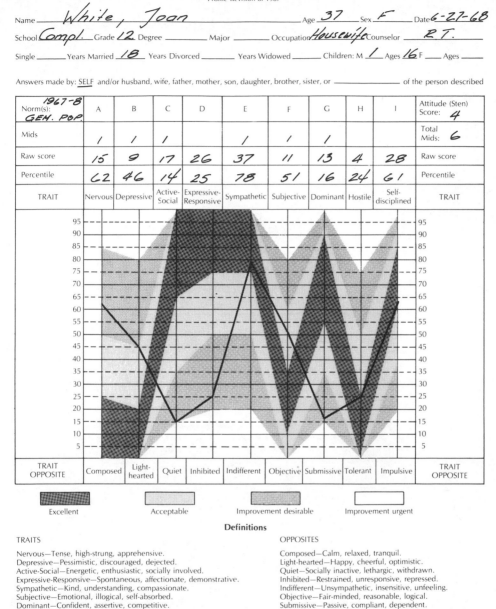

WIFE

TAYLOR-JOHNSON TEMPERAMENT ANALYSIS PROFILE
Profile Revision of 1967

Name *White, Joan*   Age *37*   Sex *F*   Date *6-27-68*

School *Compl.* Grade *12* Degree _____ Major _____ Occupation *Housewife* Counselor *R.T.*

Single _____ Years Married *18* Years Divorced _____ Years Widowed _____ Children: M *1* Ages *16* F ___ Ages ___

Answers made by: <u>SELF</u> and/or husband, wife, father, mother, son, daughter, brother, sister, or _____ of the person described

1967-8 Norm(s): *GEN. POP.*	A	B	C	D	E	F	G	H	I	Attitude (Sten) Score: *4*
Mids	/	/	/		/	/	/			Total Mids: *6*
Raw score	*15*	*9*	*17*	*26*	*37*	*11*	*13*	*4*	*28*	Raw score
Percentile	*62*	*46*	*14*	*25*	*78*	*51*	*16*	*24*	*61*	Percentile
TRAIT	Nervous	Depressive	Active-Social	Expressive-Responsive	Sympathetic	Subjective	Dominant	Hostile	Self-disciplined	TRAIT

| TRAIT OPPOSITE | Composed | Light-hearted | Quiet | Inhibited | Indifferent | Objective | Submissive | Tolerant | Impulsive | TRAIT OPPOSITE |

▨ Excellent   ▨ Acceptable   ▨ Improvement desirable   ☐ Improvement urgent

Definitions

TRAITS

Nervous—Tense, high-strung, apprehensive.
Depressive—Pessimistic, discouraged, dejected.
Active-Social—Energetic, enthusiastic, socially involved.
Expressive-Responsive—Spontaneous, affectionate, demonstrative.
Sympathetic—Kind, understanding, compassionate.
Subjective—Emotional, illogical, self-absorbed.
Dominant—Confident, assertive, competitive.
Hostile—Critical, argumentative, punitive.
Self-disciplined—Controlled, methodical, persevering.

OPPOSITES

Composed—Calm, relaxed, tranquil.
Light-hearted—Happy, cheerful, optimistic.
Quiet—Socially inactive, lethargic, withdrawn.
Inhibited—Restrained, unresponsive, repressed.
Indifferent—Unsympathetic, insensitive, unfeeling.
Objective—Fair-minded, reasonable, logical.
Submissive—Passive, compliant, dependent.
Tolerant—Accepting, patient, humane.
Impulsive—Uncontrolled, disorganized, changeable.

Source: Taylor, R.M., and Morrison, L.P. 1966–1977. *Taylor-Johnson Temperament Analysis (T-JTA).* Los Angeles, Calif.: Psychological Publications, Inc. Reprinted by permission.

Figure 15–2. Joan's T-JTA Profile

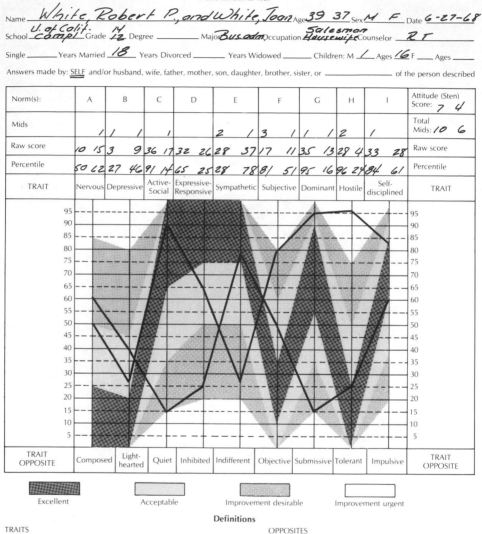

Couple
Husband and wife

TAYLOR-JOHNSON TEMPERAMENT ANALYSIS PROFILE
Profile Revision of 1967

Name **White, Robert P., and White, Joan** Age **39 37** Sex M F Date **6-27-68**

School **U. of Calif. compl** Grade **14 12** Degree _____ Major **Bus. adm** Occupation **Salesman Housewife** Counselor **R T**

Single _____ Years Married **18** Years Divorced _____ Years Widowed _____ Children: M **1** Ages **16** F _____ Ages _____

Answers made by: SELF and/or husband, wife, father, mother, son, daughter, brother, sister, or _____ of the person described

Norm(s):	A	B	C	D	E	F	G	H	I	Attitude (Sten) Score: **7 4**
Mids		/	/	/	/	2	/ 3	/	/ 2	/	Total Mids: **10 6**
Raw score	10 15	3 9	36 17	32 26	28 37	17 11	35 13	28 4	33 28	Raw score
Percentile	50 62	27 46	91 14	65 25	28 78	81 51	95 16	96 24	84 61	Percentile
TRAIT	Nervous	Depressive	Active-Social	Expressive-Responsive	Sympathetic	Subjective	Dominant	Hostile	Self-disciplined	TRAIT

	Composed	Light-hearted	Quiet	Inhibited	Indifferent	Objective	Submissive	Tolerant	Impulsive	
TRAIT OPPOSITE										TRAIT OPPOSITE

Excellent   Acceptable   Improvement desirable   Improvement urgent

Definitions

TRAITS
Nervous—Tense, high-strung, apprehensive.
Depressive—Pessimistic, discouraged, dejected.
Active-Social—Energetic, enthusiastic, socially involved.
Expressive-Responsive—Spontaneous, affectionate, demonstrative.
Sympathetic—Kind, understanding, compassionate.
Subjective—Emotional, illogical, self-absorbed.
Dominant—Confident, assertive, competitive.
Hostile—Critical, argumentative, punitive.
Self-disciplined—Controlled, methodical, persevering.

OPPOSITES
Composed—Calm, relaxed, tranquil.
Light-hearted—Happy, cheerful, optimistic.
Quiet—Socially inactive, lethargic, withdrawn.
Inhibited—Restrained, unresponsive, repressed.
Indifferent—Unsympathetic, insensitive, unfeeling.
Objective—Fair-minded, reasonable, logical.
Submissive—Passive, compliant, dependent.
Tolerant—Accepting, patient, humane.
Impulsive—Uncontrolled, disorganized, changeable.

Source: Taylor, R.M., and Morrison, L.P. 1966–1977. *Taylor-Johnson Temperament Analysis*
(T-JTA). Los Angeles, Calif.: Psychological Publications, Inc. Reprinted by permission.

Figure 15–3. Robert and Joan's T-JTA Profile

Husband by Wife
Criss-Cross

TAYLOR-JOHNSON TEMPERAMENT ANALYSIS PROFILE
Profile Revision of 1967

Name **White, Robert P.** Age **39** Sex **M** Date **6-27-68**

School **U. of Calif.** Grade **14** Degree _____ Major **Bus. Adm.** Occupation **Salesman** Counselor **R.T.**

Single _____ Years Married **18** Years Divorced _____ Years Widowed _____ Children: M **1** Ages **16** F _____ Ages _____

Answers made by: SELF and/or husband, wife, father, mother, son, daughter, brother, sister, or _____ of the person described

Norm(s): **1967-8** **G.P. C.C.**	A	B	C	D	E	F	G	H	I	Attitude (Sten) Score: **7 4**
Mids		**/**		**/**	**2**	**/ 3**	**2 /**	**2 2**	**2 /**	Total Mids: **10 8**
Raw score	**10 16**	**3 8**	**36 37**	**32 28**	**28 9**	**17 28**	**35 58**	**38 38**	**33 36**	Raw score
Percentile	**50 59**	**27 39**	**91 94**	**65 49**	**28 6**	**81 92**	**95 99**	**96 99**	**84 56**	Percentile
TRAIT	Nervous	Depressive	Active-Social	Expressive-Responsive	Sympathetic	Subjective	Dominant	Hostile	Self-disciplined	TRAIT

| TRAIT OPPOSITE | Composed | Light-hearted | Quiet | Inhibited | Indifferent | Objective | Submissive | Tolerant | Impulsive | TRAIT OPPOSITE |

Excellent   Acceptable   Improvement desirable   Improvement urgent

Definitions

TRAITS
Nervous—Tense, high-strung, apprehensive.
Depressive—Pessimistic, discouraged, dejected.
Active-Social—Energetic, enthusiastic, socially involved.
Expressive-Responsive—Spontaneous, affectionate, demonstrative.
Sympathetic—Kind, understanding, compassionate.
Subjective—Emotional, illogical, self-absorbed.
Dominant—Confident, assertive, competitive.
Hostile—Critical, argumentative, punitive.
Self-disciplined—Controlled, methodical, persevering.

OPPOSITES
Composed—Calm, relaxed, tranquil.
Light-hearted—Happy, cheerful, optimistic.
Quiet—Socially inactive, lethargic, withdrawn.
Inhibited—Restrained, unresponsive, repressed.
Indifferent—Unsympathetic, insensitive, unfeeling.
Objective—Fair-minded, reasonable, logical.
Submissive—Passive, compliant, dependent.
Tolerant—Accepting, patient, humane.
Impulsive—Uncontrolled, disorganized, changeable.

Source: Taylor, R.M., and Morrison, L.P. 1966–1977. *Taylor-Johnson Temperament Analysis (T-JTA)*. Los Angeles, Calif.: Psychological Publications, Inc. Reprinted by permission.

Figure 15–4. Robert's Criss-Cross T-JTA Profile

Wife by Husband
Criss — Cross

TAYLOR-JOHNSON TEMPERAMENT ANALYSIS PROFILE
Profile Revision of 1967

Name **White, Joan**   Age **37**   Sex **F**   Date **6-27-68**

School **Completed** Grade **12** Degree _____ Major _____ Occupation **Housewife** Counselor **R.T.**

Single _____ Years Married **18** Years Divorced _____ Years Widowed _____ Children: M **1** Ages **16** F ___ Ages ___

Answers made by: <u>SELF</u> and/or <u>husband</u>, wife, father, mother, son, daughter, brother, sister, or _____ of the person described

1967-8 Norm(s): G.P. C.C.	A	B	C	D	E	F	G	H	I	Attitude (Sten) Score: 4 3
Mids	1 2 1		1 1	3 1		1 4 1	2			Total Mids: 6 12
Raw score	15 20 9	8 17 11	26 17	37 34 11	18 13	18 4	6 28 28			Raw score
Percentile	62 71 46	39 14 11	25 16	78 74 51	66 16	30 24 26	61 64			Percentile
TRAIT	Nervous	Depressive	Active-Social	Expressive-Responsive	Sympathetic	Subjective	Dominant	Hostile	Self-disciplined	TRAIT

TRAIT OPPOSITE	Composed	Light-hearted	Quiet	Inhibited	Indifferent	Objective	Submissive	Tolerant	Impulsive	TRAIT OPPOSITE

▨ Excellent   ▢ Acceptable   ▨ Improvement desirable   ▢ Improvement urgent

Definitions

TRAITS
Nervous—Tense, high-strung, apprehensive.
Depressive—Pessimistic, discouraged, dejected.
Active-Social—Energetic, enthusiastic, socially involved.
Expressive-Responsive—Spontaneous, affectionate, demonstrative.
Sympathetic—Kind, understanding, compassionate.
Subjective—Emotional, illogical, self-absorbed.
Dominant—Confident, assertive, competitive.
Hostile—Critical, argumentative, punitive.
Self-disciplined—Controlled, methodical, persevering.

OPPOSITES
Composed—Calm, relaxed, tranquil.
Light-hearted—Happy, cheerful, optimistic.
Quiet—Socially inactive, lethargic, withdrawn.
Inhibited—Restrained, unresponsive, repressed.
Indifferent—Unsympathetic, insensitive, unfeeling.
Objective—Fair-minded, reasonable, logical.
Submissive—Passive, compliant, dependent.
Tolerant—Accepting, patient, humane.
Impulsive—Uncontrolled, disorganized, changeable.

Source: Taylor, R.M., and Morrison, L.P. 1966–1977. *Taylor-Johnson Temperament Analysis (T-JTA)*. Los Angeles, Calif.: Psychological Publications, Inc. Reprinted by permission.

Figure 15–5. Joan's Criss-Cross T-JTA Profile

alistic the partner's perceptions of each other are at this point in their premarital relationship.

T-JTA is a comprehensive instrument that is relatively straight-forward and easy for couples to understand. The available profiles offer direct and concrete explanations of the significant personal traits that are measured and focus them in an interpersonal context through the criss-cross procedure.

We recommend that the counselor go over the test results with each person individually, in the presence of the other partner, and then with both partners together. This can most effectively be done by introducing the couple conjointly to the blank test profile, which can then be explained in detail in relation to the scales and infor-mation that will be provided when it is completed. Then the counselor can give each person his and her individual profile. While one partner is silently examining this, the counselor can go over the results of the other person's individual and criss-cross profiles. Following that, the counselor reviews the first person's individual and criss-cross profiles and then goes over all five profiles conjointly.

The T-JTA manual presents a number of excellent guidelines for using the criss-cross tests in courtship analysis, premarital counseling, and marital counseling. Much of the discussion that follows relies heavily upon that section of the manual. Refer to the five sample profiles of a T-JTA administration shown in figures 15–1 through 15–5.

After the use of the T-JTA criss-cross in premarital counseling, the typical response of couples is to report that they have gained some, and in many instances a great deal of new information regard-ing themselves and their partner. As can be seen from an examination of the profiles, the scales are comprehensive, yet easily understood and quite descriptive in their presentation of information. The shaded areas on the profile are designed to provide immediate information to clients about traits that relate to successful and unsuccessful rela-tionships. As a rule of thumb, the more closely a person's scores follow the darker shaded areas on the profile, the better the indica-tions for both individual and marital adjustment. (This is a broad generalization, and the sensitive premarital counselor will accept it as such.)

An example of the need for individual interpretation is found in the profiles for Robert and Joan in figure 15–3. It will be noted that both Robert and Joan are moderately lighthearted, scoring relatively close together toward the lighthearted rather than the depressive direction on that scale. It could be said that this is a more desirable scoring range for the couple than if both had scored close together near the the depressive end or if one had been at the depressive end and the other at the lighthearted end of the scale. A similar comment could be made for Robert and Joan's scores on the self-disciplined versus impulsive scale.

Overall, in the self-descriptions of Robert and Joan, they reveal two basically divergent profiles which might indicate differences in temperament. The differences may or may not indicate a lack of compatibility in a marital relationship. We would want to explore with Joan and Robert what the divergence in their profiles means for their relationship. Does the divergence mean incompatibility? Are the two going separate ways? Are they competing in the relationship? On the other hand, the divergent profile may indicate compatibility in that the couple may in fact complement each other very well. Remember, the mate selection process is not accidental. The question is, why did each of them search out a partner who was temperamentally much more opposite than similar to himself or herself? The possible conflicts identified in Joan and Robert's profiles are discussed in detail in chapter 12, on counseling the seriously conflicted couple.

Although we do not have such a pattern with Robert and Joan, another fairly common set of profiles results when couples are nearly identical or much more similar than different. It would be a temptation with such a set of profiles to assume that the couple might be called a perfect match. Although it is true that the people are very similar in temperament, this does not necessarily mean that they are compatible. Compatibility depends upon the specific nature and interaction of the profile patterns. For example, two highly subjective and hostile people, or two persons who are very inhibited and indifferent, are not likely to build a well-functioning marriage simply because they are alike in temperament. The subjective and hostile persons might angrily compete with each other and escalate conflict in their marital relationship. The indifferent and inhibited persons would likely have a hard time in making decisions and in accomplishing the tasks required for a successful relationship or family functioning.

The criss-cross profiles are very useful in revealing the accuracy with which one person sees the other. As stated in the manual, the information obtained in criss-cross administration may be more important to the relationship and to the counseling process than the individual profile patterns. If the potential spouses see each other with clarity and accuracy, their relationship will probably be far better than if their marriage were based upon unrealistic expectations about each other. It can be seen in figures 15–4 and 15–5 that Robert and Joan have quite accurate perceptions about each other's temperamental patterns.

The T-JTA is published by Psychological Publications, Inc., 5300 Hollywood Boulevard, Los Angeles, California 90027.

PREPARE Inventory

The PREPARE Inventory (from PREmarital Personal and Relationship Evaluation) is a 125-question inventory designed to identify and measure premarital "relationship strengths" and "work areas" in eleven categories. The instrument also contains an Idealistic Distortion scale which serves as a correction score for idealism or the tendency for the respondent to answer the items in an idealistic way (Olson, Fournier, and Druckman 1986). It requires approximately thirty minutes to complete the inventory. PREPARE must be computer scored which provides a very useful couple profile. In addition to the standard form, there is available PREPARE-MC (Marriage with Children), which was developed to be used where one or both of the premarital partners have children.

The eleven relationship areas reported on PREPARE are: realistic expectations, personality issues, communication, conflict resolution, financial management, leisure activities, sexual relationship, children and parenting, family and friends, equalitarian roles, and religious orientation. There is also very useful background information reported, including age, education, monthly income, the number of months that each person has known his or her partner, the number of months before marriage that the inventory was taken, the parents' reaction to the marriage, friends' reaction to the marriage, parents' marital status, birth position or birth order, number of siblings, and population of the place of current residence and of residence during childhood.

The authors' stated purpose for PREPARE is as a tool to be used for assessment of the relationship strengths and work areas for engaged couples (Olson, Fournier, and Druckman 1986). It is designed for use in counseling, to promote couple dialogue, and to assist in promoting greater relationship enhancement. PREPARE is widely used by clergy and premarital counselors in a variety of settings. In addition to these purposes of PREPARE, we believe that a significant strength of PREPARE and contribution to premarital counseling is the ongoing research being done by the authors based upon the expanding data collected as the inventories are sent for scoring and profiling (Fowers and Olson 1986; Nickols, Fournier, and Nickols 1986).

The definitions of the PREPARE categories (scales) are summarized as follows (Olson, Fournier, and Druckman 1986).

Idealistic distortion. This is a scale designed to measure the tendency of persons to answer questions in a socially desirable direction. (This is a validity scale to measure test taking attitude, and thus is not interpreted with the following scales as directly relating to the relationship.)

Realistic expectations. This scale assesses a person's expectations about love, commitment, and conflict in the relationship. As the scale name implies, the goal is to assess the degree to which expectations about marriage are realistic and based on objective reflection.

Personality issues. This scale assesses a person's perception of his or her satisfaction with his or her partner in regard to such traits as tardiness, temper, moodiness, stubbornness, jealousy, and possessiveness. Also, personal behaviors related to public demonstration of affection and smoking and drinking habits are assessed.

Communication. This scale assesses the individual's feelings, beliefs, and attitudes toward the role of communication in the maintenance of the relationship. The items in this scale focus on the level of comfort felt by the couple in being able to share emotions and beliefs, the perception of the partner's way of giving and receiving information, and perception of adequacy of communication in the relationship.

Conflict resolution. This scale assesses the partner's attitudes, feelings, and beliefs about the existence and resolution of conflict in the relationship. As with other scales, specific behaviors are assessed which can be useful for feedback to the couple in the counseling process.

Financial management. This scale assesses the attitudes and concerns about the handling of money and related economic issues in the relationship.

Leisure activities. This scale assesses attitudes and preferences for spending leisure time actively or passively with or without the partner.

Sexual relationship. This scale assesses both sexual and affectional aspects of the relationship. Items get at questions related to affection, sexual behavior, family planning, and the ability to discuss such topics.

Children and parenting. This scale assesses attitudes and feelings about having and raising children, including issues such as family size and the impact of children on the marital relationship.

Family and friends. This scale assesses each partner's feelings and perceptions about relationships with friends, in-laws, and relatives, focusing on the roles that such persons may have in the marriage.

Equalitarian roles. This scale assesses beliefs, feelings, and attitudes related to certain occupational, household, parental, and sex roles in marriage.

Religious orientation. This scale assesses the partner's attitudes, feelings, and beliefs in regard to religious activity and values in the marriage context.

There are two additional scales on PREPARE which assess information from the partner's family of origin. These scales are provided on the Couple Profile and can be plotted on an attached graph of the Circumplex Model. The first scale, *family adaptability,* assesses each partner's perception of adaptability, change, and flexibility in his or her family of origin. The second scale, *family cohesion,* assesses the concepts of closeness and togetherness, and how these were balanced in the partner's family of origin. The Circumplex Model is discussed in chapter six in relation to the family-of-origin (FOE) exploration and is shown in figure 15–6.

For each of the above thirteen categories, the PREPARE Couple Profile graphically and numerically presents the score for the male and female partners and indicates the meaning of the score. Also, the profile contains two interpretive statements for each category, which assist in understanding the meaning of the scores. For example, the following two statements are made on the profile for the *realistic expectations* category: "High Scorers—(60 or more) are realistic about the challenges and demands of marriage. Low Scorers—(30 or less) are idealistic and unaware of the challenges of marriage." See figure 15–7.

The PREPARE profile lists each of the 125 items grouped according to eleven categories. See figure 15–8. For each of the eleven cat-

Family of Origin
Based on the Circumplex Model

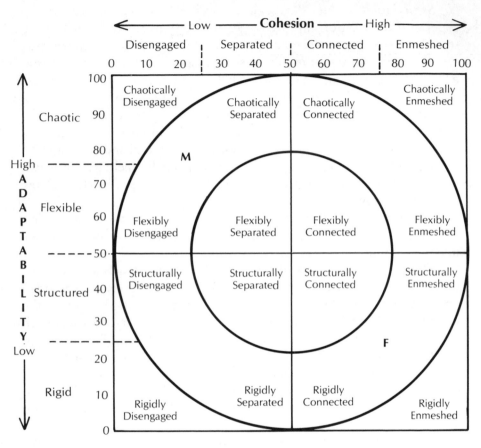

$\textcircled{M}$ = Male's Family of Origin $\textcircled{F}$ = Female's Family of Origin

REFER TO THE FAMILY OF ORIGIN HANDOUT FOR HOW TO SHARE THIS

INFORMATION WITH A COUPLE

Source: Olson, D.H., Fournier, D.G., and Druckman, J.M. 1986. *PREPARE/ENRICH Coun-selor's Manual.* Minneapolis, Minn.: Prepare-Enrich, Inc. Reprinted by permission.

Figure 15–6. Circumplex Model or Family Map

PREPARE COUPLE PROFILE

prepare	This Couple Profile is designed to help you complete your Counselor's Feedback Form. This is a summary of the couple's **relationship strengths** and **work areas** on PREPARE. *Both the Male and Female in each category have been revised (corrected) based on their score on the Idealistic Distortion scale.	prepare

MALE AND FEMALE REVISED SCORES* IDEALISTIC DISTORTION	POSITIVE COUPLE AGREEMENT
MALE MMMMMMMMMMMMMMMMMMMMMMMMMMMMMM 78 FEMALE FFFFFFF 13	A Positive Couple Agreement score computed for Idealistic Distortion. The Male and Female scores are used to correct NOT APPLICABLE and produce the Revised Scores for the other categories.

HIGH SCORERS-(60 or more) are idealistic about their relationships and tend to deny or minimize any problems.
LOW SCORERS-(30 or less) are more open to admitting limitations or problems in their relationship.

REALISTIC EXPECTATIONS		
MALE MMMMMMMM 22 FEMALE FFFFFFFFFFFFFFFFFFFFFFFFFFFFFFFF 80	10%	WORK AREA

HIGH SCORERS-(60 or more) are realistic about the challenges and demands of marriage.
LOW SCORERS-(30 or less) are idealistic and unaware of the challenges of marriage.

PERSONALITY ISSUES		
MALE MMMMMMMMMMMMMMMMMMMMMMM 61 FEMALE FFFFF 10	20%	WORK AREA

HIGH SCORERS-(60 or more) like the personality, behavior and habits of their partner.
LOW SCORERS-(30 or less) are concerned about several personality traits or behaviors of their partner.

COMMUNICATION		
MALE MMMMMMMMMMMMMMMMMMMMM 52 FEMALE FFFFFFFFFFFFF 30	50%	STRENGTH AND WORK AREA

HIGH SCORERS-(60 or more) feel they are understood by their partner and are able to easily resolve difference with their partner.
LOW SCORERS-(30 or less) are concerned about their communication and feel unable to share their feelings with their partner.

CONFLICT RESOLUTION		
MALE MMMMMMMMMMMMMMMMMMMMMMMMMMMM 67 FEMALE FFFFFFFFFFFFFFFFFF 39	50%	STRENGTH AND WORK AREA

HIGH SCORERS-(60 or more) feel they are able to discuss and easily resolve differences with their partner.
LOW SCORERS-(30 or less) feel that arguments are difficult to resolve, avoid disagreements, and feel they must give in to their partner.

FINANCIAL MANAGEMENT		
MALE MMMMMMMM 21 FEMALE FFFFFFF 17	20%	WORK AREA

HIGH SCORERS-(60 or more) have realistic plans and attitudes about their budget and agree on financial matters.
LOW SCORERS-(30 or less) have not yet decided how to handle their finances and/or are concerned about their financial situation.

Source: Olson, D.H., Fournier, D.G., and Druckman, J.M. 1986. *PREPARE/ENRICH Counselor's Manual*. Minneapolis, Minn.: Prepare-Enrich, Inc. Reprinted by permission.

Figure 15–7. Partial PREPARE Couple Profile

egories, one of four "Relationship Strengths" or "Work Areas" are designated. The four messages and their definitions are: (1) Relationship Strength—"You and your partner are *very satisfied* with this aspect of your relationship and you agree on *most issues* in this area." (2) Possible Relationship Strength—"You and your partner are *somewhat satisfied* with this aspect of your relationship and *agree on many issues* in this area." (3) Possible Work Area—"You and/or your partner are *somewhat dissatisfied* with this aspect of your relationship and disagree on some issues in this area." (4) Work Area—"You and/ or your partner are *generally dissatisfied* with this aspect of your relationship and *disagree on several issues* in this area." See figure 15–8.

A recent study supported the predictive and discriminate validity for the instrument (Fowers and Olson 1986). In this study, 164 couples who took PREPARE before marriage were followed up approximately three years later. The researchers found that couples who were satisfied with their marriage scored significantly higher on PREPARE than couples who were dissatisfied, divorced, or who cancelled their marriage. In relation to discriminate validity, the study reported that the instrument predicted, with 80 to 90 percent accuracy, which couples were happily married from those who were separated or divorced three years later. Thus, the authors of the study point to the usefulness of PREPARE as a means to assist in identifying premarital couples who may be high risk for marriage and could likely benefit from thorough premarital counseling. We agree. Because this study analyzed group data in descriptive and predictive ways, the use of the conclusions from the study and the use of PREPARE data with specific couples must be done with caution. The authors stated that PREPARE "should *not* be used for predicting marital success rates for individual couples (Fowers and Olson 1986, p. 412).

The PREPARE manual is clearly written and contains excellent guidelines and instructions for the administration and interpretation of the instrument. The sections on administration and research have particular information addressed to clergy and church settings, as well as to other uses. The *PREPARE Counselor Feedback Form* is an outstanding aid, designed to assist the counselor in summarizing and organizing the information to go over with the couple in a feedback session. As stated on the form, the goals of the feedback session are: (1) To help the couple explore their *relationship strengths* and *growth areas,* (2) to help the couple discuss their own *family of origin* with each other, (3) to have the couple resolve some issues using the *Ten Steps for Conflict Resolution* (see *Building a Strong Marriage* [Olson 1987]), and (4) to motivate the couple to invest time, energy, and resources to improve their marriage over time (Olson, Fournier, and Druckman 1986)." See figure 15–9.

Building a Strong Marriage (Olson 1987) is a brief (28-page)

Figure 15–8.
Partial PREPARE Couple Profile

Source: Olson, D.H., Fournier, D.G., and Druckman, J.M. 1986. *PREPARE/ENRICH Counselor's Manual.* Minneapolis, Minn.: Prepare-Enrich, Inc. Reprinted by permission.

1-STRONGLY AGREE 2-AGREE 3-INDECISION 4-DISAGREE 5-STRONGLY DISAGREE

REALISTIC EXPECTATIONS

prepare

MALE %	FEMALE %	POSITIVE COUPLE %	RELATIONSHIP STRENGTH OR WORK AREA
22	80	10	WORK AREA

MALE	FEMALE	Agreement	Indecision	Disagreement	Special Focus	+/-	Item
4	4	A				(+)	14. There are probably many people in the world with whom I could have a happy marriage.
3	4		–			(–)	19. I think we will never have problems in our marriage.
3	3		–			(–)	32. Time will resolve most of the problems that we have as a couple.
2	3			D		(–)	36. Increasing the amount of time together will automatically improve our relationship.
4	1		I			(+)	52. Some of my needs for security, support and companionship will be met by persons other than my partner.
2	3				S	(–)	53. There is nothing that could happen that would cause me to question my love for my partner.
2	2			D		(–)	82. After marriage, it will be easier to change those things about my partner I don't like.
2	5			D		(–)	88. I believe that I have already learned everything there is to know about my partner.
3	5			D		(+)	99. I expect that some romantic love will fade in my marriage.
2	5			D		(–)	113. I believe that most difficulties experienced before marriage will fade once we are married.

PERSONALITY ISSUES

prepare

MALE %	FEMALE %	POSITIVE COUPLE %	RELATIONSHIP STRENGTH OR WORK AREA
61	10	20	WORK AREA

MALE	FEMALE	Agreement	Indecision	Disagreement	Special Focus	+/-	Item
5	1			D		(–)	8. There are times when I am bothered by my partner's jealousy.
4	2			D		(–)	13. Sometimes I am concerned about my partner's temper.
5	3			D		(–)	24. At times, I am concerned that my partner appears to be unhappy and withdrawn.
2	1				S	(–)	30. My partner should smoke, drink or use drugs less often.
3	3		I			(–)	37. At times, my partner is not dependable or does not always follow through on things.
5	2				S	(–)	44. When we are with others, I am sometimes upset with my partner's behavior.
5	2			D		(–)	63. Sometimes my partner is too stubborn.
4	4					(–)	78. My partner is often critical or has a negative outlook.
4	4	A				(–)	95. Sometimes I have difficulty dealing with my partner's moodiness.
5	2	A				(–)	115. At times I think my partner is too domineering.

COMMUNICATION

prepare

MALE %	FEMALE %	POSITIVE COUPLE %	RELATIONSHIP STRENGTH OR WORK AREA
52	30	50	STRENGTH AND WORK AREA

MALE	FEMALE	Agreement	Indecision	Disagreement	Special Focus	+/-	Item
2	4					(+)	2. It is very easy for me to express all my true feelings to my partner.
4	2			D		(–)	6. When we are having a problem, my partner often gives me the silent treatment.
4	2			D		(–)	40. My partner sometimes makes comments which put me down.
4	4			D		(–)	54. I am sometimes afraid to ask my partner for what I want.
3	3		I			(–)	66. I wish my partner was more willing to share his/her feelings with me.
4	4	A				(–)	73. Sometimes I have trouble believing everything my partner tells me.
5	3	A				(–)	81. Sometimes my partner does not understand how I feel.
2	1	A				(+)	91. I am very satisfied with how my partner and I talk with each other.
4	5	A				(–)	98. I do not always share negative feelings with my partner because I am afraid she/he will get angry.
1	2	A				(+)	109. My partner is always a good listener.

POSITIVE COUPLE AGREEMENT: Couple agrees with each other in a positive way.
DISAGREEMENT: Couple disagrees by 2 or more points on an item.

INDECISION: One or both individuals have not yet made a clear decision on this item.
SPECIAL FOCUS: Both individuals have some concern about the issues.

PREPARE-ENRICH, INC. © Copyright, 1979 (Rev. 1986)

PREPARE Counselor Feedback Form

Couple Number: _____ Couple Name: _____

Date PREPARE Administered: _____ Date of Feedback Session: _____

The *Building a Strong Marriage* booklet is designed to be used in the feedback sessions. A couple should be given the booklet at the beginning of the session so they can follow along as you work with them on the various components of the feedback process. Couples should be encouraged to read and use this booklet when future issues arise.

Goals of Feedback with the couple:

1. To help the couple explore their relationship strength and growth areas.
2. To help the couple discuss their own Family of Origin with each other.
3. To have the couple resolve some issues using the Ten Steps for Conflict Resolution (See the *Building a Strong Marriage* booklet).
4. To motivate the couple to invest time, energy and resources to improve their marriage over time.

Instructions for Completing Box Below

(Use Couple Profile Section of Computer Report, pages 3–4).

1. Select three (3) areas of Relationship Strengths and put a plus sign (+) next to the PREPARE Categories.
2. Select three (3) areas that are Growth Areas and put a minus sign (−) next to the PREPARE Categories.
3. The space to record the Individual Revised Scores and % Positive Agreement is only for your reference.
   Do not give Positive Agreement or Individual Scores to the couple.

Instructions for Selecting Discussion Items

(Use Items for Discussion of Computer Report, pages 6–9).

1. For each Relationship Strength you selected, choose 2–3 agreement items to share with couple.
2. For each Growth Area you selected, choose 2–3 items that are Special Focus, Disagreement and Indecision to share with the couple.
3. Review Family of Origin scales: Family Cohesion and Family Adaptability (pages 10–11).

Idealistic Distortion Scores:

Male: _____

Female: _____

PREPARE Categories:

	PREPARE Computer Results		
(Select 3 of each) Relationship Strengths (+) and Growth Area (−)	Individual Revised Scores Male% Female%	Positive Couple Agreement Percentage	
Realistic expectations	_____ _____	_____	
Personality issues	_____ _____	_____	
Communication	_____ _____	_____	
Conflict resolution	_____ _____	_____	
Financial management	_____ _____	_____	
Leisure activities	_____ _____	_____	
Sexual relationship	_____ _____	_____	
Children and marriage	_____ _____	_____	
Family and friends	_____ _____	_____	
Equalitarian roles	_____ _____	_____	
Religious orientation	_____ _____	_____	

Family of Origin:

Family adaptability

Family cohesion

Couple's Responses on Couple Feedback Form

Relationship Strengths		*Growth Areas*	
Male	Female	Male	Female
_____	_____	_____	_____
_____	_____	_____	_____
_____	_____	_____	_____
_____	_____	_____	_____
_____	_____	_____	_____
_____	_____	_____	_____

Procedures for Giving Feedback to a Couple

1. Re-establish rapport with the couple.
2. Ask the couple how they felt about taking PREPARE.
3. Have the couple complete the Couple Feedback Form. Have couple tear out pages 13 and 15 in their *Building a Strong Marriage*.
4. Ask the couple to discuss their Relationship Strengths. Then you present them with the PREPARE results.
5. Ask the couple to discuss their Growth Areas. Then you present them with the PREPARE results.
6. Discuss their Family of Origin, based on the Circumplex Model.
7. Follow the steps described in "Feedback on Family of Origin" (Right box). Help the couple discuss and begin resolving some relevant issues. Select items to discuss giving priority to focus on the Growth Areas. Special Focus items, then Disagreement items, then Indecision items.
   Use the "Ten Steps for Resolving Couple Differences" below. Have couple follow along in their *Building a Strong Marriage* booklet (Page 23).
8. Ask the couple the value of PREPARE feedback and your feedback with them.
9. Encourage them to keep their marriage a priority and to seek out marriage enrichment, and go to marriage counseling early if problems persist.
10. Discuss and schedule future sessions together.

Ten Steps for Resolving Couple Differences

Have couple follow along in *Building a Strong Marriage* (page 23).

1. Set a time and place for discussion.
2. Define the problem or issue of disagreement.
3. Define how you each contribute to the problem.
4. List things you have done in the past which have not been successful.
5. Brainstorm and list all possible solutions.
6. Discuss each of these solutions.
7. Agree on one solution to try.
8. Agree how each person will work toward the solution.
9. Set a time for another meeting to review your progress.
10. Reward each other as each of you contributes toward the solution.

Feedback on Family of Origin

Refer to the *Building a Strong Marriage* booklet, pages 17–22 for leading the couple through this discussion.

1. Given an overview of Family Cohesion, Family Adaptability and the Circumplex Model.
2. Locate on the Family Map how each person described their Family of Origin.
   The computer report indicates how each person sees their Family of Origin. It is important how much closeness (cohesion) and adaptability (flexibility) each perceived in their Family of Origin, and how satisfied each was with their family's cohesion and adaptability.
   The following are useful questions you can use in helping them discuss their Families of Origin.
3. Discuss what it is like to live in that type of family (for example, a Flexible Connected" one).
   It is important to review the level of adaptability in the families of origin. That is, how adaptable the family system was in terms of its roles, its rules, the way discipline was handled, decisions made, etc.
   Then review the level of cohesion or emotional closeness in the families of origin. How close were the parents to each other; the children with their parents, and with each other. How much did the family do together compared with how much they did separately.
4. In what ways was your type of family satisfying and how was it frustrating to you?
5. How would you like your family to be different on cohesion and adaptability if you could have changed it?
6. Did your family change on cohesion and adaptability when it encountered stress?
7. Explore the similarities and differences between your two types of families.
8. What levels of cohesion (togetherness) and adaptability (flexibility) do you currently have in your relationship?
9. What level of cohesion and adaptability do you want in your marriage?

Source: Olson, D.H., Fournier, D.G., and Druckman, J.M. 1986. *PREPARE/ENRICH Counselor's Manual.* Minneapolis, Minn.: Prepare-Enrich, Inc. Reprinted by permission.

Figure 15–9. PREPARE Counselor Feedback Form

booklet designed for use in the feedback session and for the couple to take home for later use. The booklet provides the couple with helpful ideas about marriage and the information from their PRE-PARE inventory. Also included is a communication exercise and worksheet focusing on "ten steps for resolving couple conflict (pp. 23–25)." The counselor who uses the PREPARE inventory and related materials will find that they do encompass what the Prepare-Enrich developers have termed the "PREPARE Program" (Olson 1987, p. 4).

PREPARE is published by Prepare-Enrich, Inc., P.O. Box 190, Minneapolis, Minnesota 55440.

Fundamental Interpersonal Relationship Orientation-Behavior (FIRO-B)

The FIRO-B is a fifty-four item questionnaire that measures three fundamental dimensions of interpersonal relationships: inclusion, control, and affection. Each of the three dimensions is measured by two scores, the person's *expressed* or manifested behavior and the person's *wanted* or desired behavior. Thus, the scales on the FIRO-B are expressed inclusion, expressed control, expressed affection, wanted inclusion, wanted control, and wanted affection.

The FIRO-B scales are shown in figure 15–10. "Inclusion" indicates the degree to which a person associates or wants to be associated with other people. Ryan (1977) has indicated that the poles of inclusion are similar to Karen Horney's concept of moving toward people or moving away from people and the Jungian concept of introversion

	Inclusion	Control	Affection
Expressed (toward others)	I join other people and I include others.	I take charge; I influence people.	I get close to people
Wanted (from others)	I want people to include me.	I want people to lead me.	I want people to get close and personal with me.

Figure 15–10. FIRO-B Dimensions

and extroversion. "Control" assesses the extent to which a person assumes control and responsibility or, on the other hand, wants people to assume responsibility, dominate, or make decisions for him or her. "Affection" indicates the degree to which a person becomes emotionally close to others or wants other persons to become emotionally close to her or him.

In spite of its brevity, the FIRO-B has a clinically sound base and yields valid information. It is an excellent choice for use in premarital counseling. It can assist couples in becoming aware of the dimensions of their interpersonal relations, with which they will be dealing during their married life. In the FIRO-B, it is not the normative group that is important for couple comparisons. Rather, it is the specific score values of the couple being assessed that are important. A brief but thorough clinical manual is available for the instrument and provides rich clinical information for use in premarital counseling (Ryan 1977).

A primary feature of the instrument is that it makes a meaningful distinction between what people want from others and what they express toward others. A second positive feature is that the dimensions are also relevant for understanding how a person relates to others outside of the premarital relationship. These dimensions are tied to Will Schutz's theory of group development and interpersonal relations (Schutz 1976).

Another positive feature of the FIRO-B for use in premarital counseling is that the items and scales have no assumed social desirability. Both extremes of these scales represent styles of living that people use with relative comfort. Also, the instrument is brief and unobtrusive. Third, the scales are reliable. Fourth, the FIRO-B is a nonthreatening instrument to take, specifically because it does not suggest possible interpretations of psychological abnormalities. Fifth, the scores are easy to interpret because all scales have the same number of items and use a common reference system. And last, it is possible to look at score combinations for understanding both individual behavior and the behavior between two people in a relationship.

One concern with the instrument is that some of the items are repeated. Test-takers often report a feeling of annoyance because of this repetition. Because the FIRO-B is a self-report instrument, it is open to lying and self-deception on the part of the test-taker. However, since the statements and subscales are relatively free from overtones of psychological abnormality, the person usually does not feel a need to be defensive. Additionally, a person's response style—for instance, the tendency to be cautious and use only moderate response choices in completing the inventory—will affect that person's score on all scales. Depending upon how the person responded to the inventory, an inflation or a depression of all scores could occur. Of course, the discovery of a responsive bias can give insight into the personality of the person and can provide material for discussion and interpretation in its own right.

In the FIRO-B, each scale is assigned a score of 0 through 9. Low scores (0 through 3) indicate that a person expresses or wants very little of the need area. For example, a low expressed-inclusion score would indicate that the person is uncomfortable around people and would tend to move away from them. Scores of 4 to 5 are middle or borderline scores and indicate an average or typical expression or desire. For example, a score of 5 on expressed control would mean that a person sometimes likes to take charge and influence people and at other times does not need to express control by being in charge. A high score (6 through 9) indicates that the trait is a characteristic of the person. For example, an expressed-affection score of 8 would indicate that a person readily expresses affection and emotion and establishes close relationships with people.

As an illustration of the FIRO-B data for a couple, we have obtained FIRO-B scores for Robert and Joan, who were previously discussed regarding the T-JTA (see figures 15–1 through 15–5). The FIRO-B scores for Robert and Joan are shown in figure 15–11.

Robert's expressed-inclusion score of 8 indicates that he is highly sociable and has a strong tendency to join with other people. His score of 7 in wanted inclusion means that he has a compatible high need for people to include him in various activities. There is no discrepancy between the high scores on both expressed and wanted inclusion, and therefore we get an accurate picture of a social person who seeks and becomes involved in social activity.

Robert's extremely high expressed-control score of 8 means that he wants to take charge of most interpersonal situations and directly influence and control people. Conversely, his wanted-control score of 1 indicates that he does not want to be controlled and would probably not stand for any suppressing manner in other people.

His average or moderate expressed-affection score of 4 would indicate that he has typical desires to get close to people, but they are not abnormally high or low. Similarly, his wanted-affection score of 5, which is moderate also, indicates that he has average needs for people to be close and personal with him.

Figure 15–11 shows that Joan is relatively low on expressed inclusion and thereby moves away from people. She tends to be exclusive and not to join with other people and include others in her activities. Her wanted-inclusion score of 2 is compatible with this and indicates that she generally does not want other people to include her in their activities.

Joan's expressed-control score of 2 would indicate that she is not a leader and does not take charge or attempt to influence other persons. However, her wanted-control score of 7 indicates that she is a good follower and she wants other people to lead her.

Her expressed-affection score of 4 indicates a moderate degree of expressed affection; she does get close to people, at least as close as is generally acceptable in interpersonal relationships. Her wanted-affection score of 6 would indicate a moderately strong desire for people to get close to her. This might imply that she is a good listener,

Robert

	Inclusion	Control	Affection
Expressed	8	8	4
Wanted	7	1	5

Joan

	Inclusion	Control	Affection
Expressed	3	2	4
Wanted	2	7	6

Figure 15–11. FIRO-B Scores for Robert and Joan

although because of her other scores, we would assume that she does not offer much advice or give much leadership after listening.

Although it is not a standard practice, and to our knowledge is not included in the literature on the FIRO-B, using the FIRO-B in a criss-cross manner has proved worthwhile for us. The test can be taken twice, once to describe oneself and the other time to describe the partner, as with the T-JTA. Another manner in which the criss-cross can be done is for the person to take the FIRO-B once; then, prior to the scoring or interpretation of the results, the person is given an explanation of the FIRO-B dimensions. The person is then instructed to rate his or her partner as low, average, or high on each of the six scales. The counselor can translate these ratings to numerical scores corresponding to 2, 5, and 8, respectively. Thus, in our example, since we have learned in the criss-cross for Robert and Joan in the T-JTA (figures 15–4 and 15–5) that their perceptions are quite accurate, we surmise that if Joan had been instructed to rate Robert as described on the FIRO dimensions, she would have given him a high rating on expressed inclusion.

Other Assessment Devices

This section presents a number of assessment devices that have been demonstrated to be useful in premarital counseling. Each of these is referenced in the *Eighth Mental Measurement Yearbook* (Buros 1978). As the counselor considers the possibility of using these instruments, he or she should refer to the *MMY* as a first step. No evaluation of the instruments is made here. Actual information regarding these scales and/or the nature of each instrument is presented along with the name and address of the publisher, so that the counselor may obtain additional information.

California Marriage Readiness Evaluation. Premarital counselees. Three general categories and eight areas: personality (character structure, emotional maturity, marriage readiness), preparation for marriage (family experiences, dealing with money, planning ability), interpersonal compatibility (marriage motivation, compatibility). Published by Western Psychological Services, 12031 Wilshire Boulevard, Los Angeles, California 90025.

California Psychological Inventory. Ages thirteen and over. Eighteen scores: dominance, capacity for status, sociability, social pressure, self-acceptance, sense of well-being, responsibility, socialization, self-control, tolerance, good impression, communality, achievement via conformance, achievement via independence, intellectual efficiency, psychological-mindedness, flexibility, femininity. Published by Consulting Psychologist Press, 577 College Avenue, Palo Alto, California 94306.

Caring Relationship Inventory. Premarital and marital counselees. Seven scores: affection, friendship, eros, empathy, self-love, being love, deficiency love. Published by Educational and Industrial Testing Service, P.O. Box 7234, San Diego, California 92107.

The El Senoussi Multiphasic Marital Inventory. Premarital and marital counselees. Ten scores: frustration and chronic projection, cumulative ego strain, adolescent hangover or immaturity, revolt against femininity, flight into rejection, early conditioning against marriage, will-o-the-wisp, sex dysfunction, sex dissatisfaction and projection, total. Published by Western Psychological Services, 12031 Wilshire Boulevard, Los Angeles, California 90025.

Edwards Personal Preference Schedule. College students and adults. Fifteen scores: achievement, difference, order, exhibition, autonomy, affiliation, intraception, succorance, dominance, abasement, nurturance, change, endurance, heterosexuality, aggression. Published by the Psychological Corporation, 757 3rd Ave., New York, New York 10017.

Family Adaptability and Cohesion Evaluation Scales. (FACES III). Married adults. Couple Form for those without children and Family Form for couples with children. Provides information on person's perception as to current and ideal family functioning on adaptability (rigid, structured, flexible, chaotic) and cohesion (disengaged, separated, connected, enmeshed). Published by Family Social Science, 290 McNeal Hall, University of Minnesota, St. Paul, Minnesota 55108.

Fundamental Interpersonal Relationship Orientation-Behavior (FIRO-B). See discussion earlier in this chapter.

The Marital Communication Inventory (MCI). Adults. Total score. Published by Family Life Publications, Incorporated, P.O. Box 427, Saluda, North Carolina 28773.

The Marital Expectation Inventories. Form I for engaged couples and Form II for married couples. Seven area scores: love, sex, communication, children, money, in-laws, religion. Published by Family Life Publications, Inc., P.O. Box 427, Saluda, North Carolina 28773.

Marital Inventories (MI). Premarital and married couples. Computer scored. Assesses values, unity or agreement, couple and personal readiness for marriage, future marital success, and social desirability. Sub-scales and total score are reported. Published by Department of Family Sciences, 1000 SWKT, Brigham Young University, Provo, Utah 84602.

The Marriage Counseling Report (MCR). Premarital and married couples. Computer scored report based upon the *16 Personality Factor Questionnaire (16PF)*, provides information about each partner and the couple in profile and narrative format. Published by Institute for Personality and Ability Testing, Inc. (IPAT), P.O. Box 188, Champaign, Illinois 61820.

Marriage Scale (for Measuring Compatibility of Interests). Premarital and marital counselees. Attitudes toward twenty-one major factors in a happy marriage, item forms only. Published by Psychologists and Educators Incorporated, Suite 212, W. Slate St., Jacksonville, Illinois 62650.

The Marriage Skills Analysis. Marital counselees. Sixteen scale scores: physical, sex, loving, togetherness, talking, listening, adapting and conforming, money management, learning, family goal-setting, reconciliation, creating, helping, sense of humor, aggression, total. Published by Personal Growth Press, Incorporated, Box M, Berea, Ohio 44017.

Otto Premarital Counseling Schedules. Premarital counselees. Three sections: premarital survey, family finance, sexual adjustment. Published by Consulting Psychologists Press, Inc. 577 College Avenue, P.O. Box 60070, Palo Alto, California 94306.

Pair Attraction Inventory. College age and adults. Seven scores: mother-son, daddy-doll, bitch-nice guy, master-servant, hawks, doves, person-person. Published by Educational and Industrial Testing Service, P.O. Box 4234, San Diego, California 92107.

Premarital Counseling Inventory. Premarital couples. No scores, six areas: family background, past marital history, history of present relationship, agreement on marital roles, 20-year marital contract agreement, looking at marriage with the other person. Published by Research Press Company, 2612 North Mattis Ave., Champaign, Illinois 61820.

Premarital Counseling Kit. Premarital couples. Six forms: background compatibility, communication, incomplete sentences, relationship strengths and problem areas, counselor's summary, marriage preparation. Published by Family Life Publications, Inc., Box 427, Saluda, North Carolina 28773.

PREmarital Personal and Relationship Evaluation (PREPARE). See discussion earlier in this chapter.

Sex Knowledge and Attitude Test (Second Edition). College age and adults. Five scores: attitude (heterosexual relations, sexual myths, autoeroticism, abortion), knowledge. Published by The Center for the Study of Sex Education in Medicine, University of Pennsylvania, 4025 Chestnut Street, Suite 210, Philadelphia, Pennsylvania 19104.

Sex Knowledge Inventory. Form Y. Premarital and Marital Couples. Published by Family Life Publications, Inc., P.O. Box 427, Saluda, North Carolina 28773.

Taylor-Johnson Temperament Analysis (T-JTA). See discussion earlier in this chapter.

References

Ackerman, N.W. 1938. "The Unity of the Family." *Archives of Pediatrics*.

Ackerman, N.W., Beatman, F.L., and Sherman, S.N., eds. 1961. *Exploring the Base for Family Therapy*. Papers from the M. Robert Gomberg Memorial Conference. New York: Family Service Association of America.

Adams, B.N. 1979. "Mate Selection in the United States: A Theoretical Summarization." In *Contemporary Theories About the Family*. Vol. 1. Edited by W.R. Burr, R. Hill, F.I. Nye, and I.L. Reiss. New York: Macmillan.

Albrecht, S.L., Bahr, H.M., and Goodman, K.L. 1983. *Divorce and Remarriage: Problems, Adaptations, and Adjustments*. Westport, Conn.: Greenwood Press.

Allen, J.E. 1973. *The Early Years of Marriage*. Nashville: Graded Press.

Allred, G.H. 1976. *How to Improve Your Marriage and Family*. Provo, Utah: Brigham Young University Press.

Avery, A.W., Ridley, C.A., Leslie, L.A., and Mulholland, T. 1980. "Relationship Enhancement with Premarital Dyads: A Six-month Follow-up. *American Journal of Family Therapy* 8:23–30.

Bach, G., and Wyden, P. 1969. *The Intimate Enemy*. New York: Morrow.

Bader, E., Microys, G., Sinclair, C., Willett, E., and Conway, B. 1980. "Do Marriage Preparation Programs Really Work? Results of Recent Research in Canada." *Journal of Marital and Family Therapy* 6:171–79.

Barlow, B.A. 1986. *Twelve Traps in Today's Marriage*. Salt Lake City, Utah: Deseret Book.

Barnard, C.P., and Corrales, R.G. 1979. *The Theory and Techniques of Family Therapy*. Springfield, Ill.: Charles C. Thomas.

Beavers, R.W. 1985. *Successful Marriage: A Family Systems Approach to Couples Therapy*. New York: W.W. Norton.

Beebe, S.A., and Masterson, J.T. 1986. *Family Talk: Interpersonal Communication in the Family*. New York: Random House.

Bienvenu, M.J. 1975. "A Measurement of Premarital Communication." *Family Coordinator* 24:65–68.

Bioke, D.E. 1977. "The Impact of a Premarital Program on Communication Process, Communication, Facilitativeness, and Personality Trait Variables of Engaged Couples." Unpublished doctoral dissertation, Florida State University.

Bowman, H.A., and Spanier, G. 1978. *Modern Marriage.* New York: McGraw-Hill.

Bradshaw, B.R., Wolfe, W.M., Wood, T.J., and Tyler, L.S. 1977. *Counseling on Family Planning and Human Sexuality.* New York: Family Service Association of America.

Broderick, C.B. 1979. *Marriage and the Family.* Englewood Cliffs, N.J.: Prentice-Hall.

Buckner, L.P., and Salts, C.J. 1985. "A Premarital Assessment Program." *Family Relations* 34:513–20.

Burgum, M. 1942. "The Father Gets Worse: A Child Guidance Problem." *American Journal of Orthopsychiatry.*

Burkhart, R.A. 1950. "A Program of Premarital Counseling." *Pastoral Psychology* 1:24–33.

Buros, O.K. 1978. *The Eighth Mental Measurement Yearbook.* Highland Park, N.J.: The Gryphon Press.

Burr, W.R. 1973. "The Effects of Premarital Factors on Marriage." In *Theory Construction and the Sociology of the Family.* New York: Wiley.

Burr, W.R., Hill, R., Nye, I., and Reiss, I.L., eds. 1979. *Contemporary Theories About the Family.* New York: Macmillan.

Butterfield, O.M. 1956. *Planning for Marriage.* Princeton, N.J.: Van Nostrand.

Cannon, K.L. 1978. *Attaining Marital Satisfaction in a Secular World.* Provo, Utah: Brigham Young University Press.

Cannon, W.R. 1960. *History of Christianity in the Middle Ages.* New York: Abingdon.

Carter, B. 1986. "Success in Family Therapy." *The Family Networker* (July–August).

Christensen, H.T., ed. 1964. *Handbook of Marriage and the Family.* Chicago: Rand-McNally.

Clinebell, H.J., Jr. 1977. "Premarital Counseling: Religious Dimensions." In *Klemer's Counseling in Marital and Sexual Problems: A Clinician's Handbook* (2d ed.), edited by R.F. Stahmann and W.J. Hiebert. Baltimore: Williams and Wilkins.

———. 1975. *Growth Counseling for Marriage Enrichment.* Philadelphia: Fortress Press.

———. 1973, 1974. *Growth Counseling: New Tools for Clergy and Laity.* Nashville, Tenn.: Abingdon Press. Cassette tapes, pts. I and II.

———. 1972. *The Mental Health Ministry of the Church.* Nashville, Tenn.: Abingdon Press.

Cohn, F. 1974. *Understanding Human Sexuality.* Englewood Cliffs, N.J.: Prentice-Hall.

Curran, D. 1983. *Traits of a Healthy Family.* Minneapolis: Winston Press.

Curtis, J.J., and Miller, M.E. 1976. "An Argument for the Use of Paraprofessional Counselors in Premarital and Marital Counseling." *Family Coordinator* 25:47–50.

D'Angelli, A.R., Deyess, C.S., Gwerney, B.G., Hershenberg, B. and Sborofsky. 1974. "Interpersonal Skill Training for Dating Couples: An Evaluation of an Educational Mental Health Service." *Journal of Counseling Psychology.* 21:385–89.

DeBurger, J.E. 1977. *Marriage Today: Problems, Issues and Alternatives.* New York: John Wiley and Sons.

Dickenson, R.L. 1928. "Premarital Examination as Routine Preventive Gynecology." *American Journal of Obstetrics and Gynecology* 16:631–39.

Dicks, R.R. 1950. "Premarital Counseling: The Minister's Responsibility." *Pastoral Psychology* 1:41–53.

Duvall, E.M., and Miller, B.C. 1985. *Marriage and Family Development.* New York: Harper and Row.

Ehrentraut, G. 1975. "The Effects of Premarital Counseling of Juvenile Marriages on Marital Communication and Relationship Patterns." Unpublished doctoral dissertation, United States International University.

Elkin, M. 1977. "Premarital Counseling for Minors: The Los Angeles Experience." *Family Coordinator* 26:429–43.

Ellis, A. 1961. *Creative Marriage.* New York: Institute for Rational Living.

Fairchild, R.W. 1959. "Variety in Premarital Interviewing." *Pastoral Psychology* 10:9–13.

Foley, V. 1974. *An Introduction to Family Therapy.* New York: Grune and Stratton.

Foster, R.G., and Laidlaw, R.W. 1950. "Preparation for Marriage." *Pastoral Psychology* 1:38–40.

Fournier, D.G., and Olson, D.H. 1986. "Programs for Premarital and Newlywed Couples." In *Psychoeducational Approaches to Family Therapy and Counseling,* edited by R.F. Levant. New York: Springer.

Fowers, B.J., and Olson, D.H. 1986. "Predicting Marital Success with PREPARE: A Predictive Validity Study." *Journal of Marital and Family Therapy* 12:403–13.

Framo, J.L. 1982. *Explorations in Marital and Family Therapy*. New York: Springer.

Freud, S. 1959. "Psycho-analytic Notes Upon an Autobiographical Account of a Case of Paranoia." In *Collected Papers*. New York: Basic Books.

Fromm-Reichmann, F. 1948. "Notes on the Development of Schizophrenia by Psychoanalytic Psychotherapy." *Psychiatry*.

Gleason, J., and Prescott, M.R. 1977. "Group Techniques for Premarital Preparation." *Family Coordinator* 26:277–80.

Glendening, S.E., and Wilson, A.J. 1972. "Experiments in Group Premarital Counseling." *Social Casework* 53:551–62.

Glick, I.D. 1986. "Treating the New American Couple." *Journal of Sex and Marital Therapy,* 12:297–306.

Glick, I.D., and Kessler, D.R. 1974. *Marital and Family Therapy*. New York: Grune and Stratton.

Grace, M., and Grace, J. 1980. *A Joyful Meeting*. Minneapolis, Mn.: National Marriage Encounter.

Grover, K.J., Russell, C.S., Schumm, W.R., and Paff-Bergen, L.A. 1985. "Mate Selection Processes and Marital Satisfaction." *Family Relations* 34:383–86.

Guldner, C.A. 1971. "The Post-Marital: An Alternative to Premarital Counseling." *Family Coordinator* 20:115–19.

Gurman, A.S. 1985. *Casebook of Marital Therapy*. New York: Guilford Press.

Gurman, A.S., and Kniskern, D.P. 1977. "Enriching Research on Marital Enrichment Programs." *Journal of Marriage and Family Counseling* 3:3–11.

Greenblat, B.R. 1984. *A Doctor Discusses a Man's Sexual Health*. Chicago: Budlong Press.

———. 1984. *A Doctor's Marital Guide*. Chicago: Budlong Press.

———. 1980. *A Doctor's Sex Guide*. Chicago: Budlong Press.

Gurney, B.G., Jr., ed. 1977. *Relationship Enhancement*. San Francisco: Jossey-Bass.

Hancock, L. 1984. "A Pilot Evaluation of Engaged and Newly-wed Couples in a Marital Preparation Program Using Dyadic Relationship Measures." Unpublished Doctoral Dissertation. Provo, Utah: Brigham Young University.

Harper, J.M. 1984. "The Use of Sibling Position in Marital Therapy." In *Counseling in Marital and Sexual Problems: A Clinician's Handbook* (3rd ed.), edited by R.F. Stahmann and W.J. Hiebert. Lexington, Mass.: Lexington Books.

Hiebert, W.J., and Gillespie, J. 1984. "The Initial Interview." In *Klemer's Counseling in Marital and Sexual Problems: A Clinician's Handbook*

(3d ed.), edited by R.F. Stahmann and W.J. Hiebert. Lexington, Mass.: Lexington Books.

Hinkle, J.E., and Moore, M. 1971. "A Student Couples Program." *Family Coordinator* 20:153–58.

Hoopes, M.H., Fisher, B.L., and Barlow, S.H. 1984. *Structured Family Facilitation Programs*. Rockville: Aspen.

Horejsi, C.R. 1974. "Small-Group Sex Education for Engaged Couples." *Journal of Family Counseling* 2:23–27.

Hoult, T.F., Henze, L.F., and Hudson, J.W. 1978. *Courtship and Marriage in America*. Boston: Little, Brown.

Hubbard, C.W. 1973. *Family Planning Education*. St. Louis, Mo.: C.V. Mosby.

Humphrey, F.G. 1983. *Marital Therapy*. Englewood Cliffs, N.J. Prentice-Hall.

Jackson, D.D., ed. 1973. *Therapy, Communication, and Change*. Palo Alto, Calif.: Science and Behavior Books.

Jacobson, N., and Gurman, A. 1986. *Marital Therapy*. New York: Guilford Press.

James, M. 1973. *Born to Love*. Reading, Mass.: Addison-Wesley.

Johnson, P.E. 1953. *Psychology of Pastoral Care*. New York: Abingdon Press.

Jones, S.M. 1978. "Divorce and Remarriage: A New Beginning, A New Set of Problems." *Journal of Divorce* 2, no. 2:217–27.

Josimovich, J.B. 1977. "Medical Aspects of Contraception and Family Planning." In *Klemer's Counseling in Marital and Sexual Problems: A Clinician's Handbook* (2nd ed.), edited by R.F. Stahmann and W.J. Hiebert. Baltimore: Williams and Wilkins.

Kardiner, A. 1939. *The Individual and His Family*. New York: Columbia University Press.

Kasanin, J., Knight, E., and Sage, P. 1934. "The Parent-Child Relationship in Schizophrenia." *Journal of Nervous and Mental Disease*.

Kelly, G. 1977. *Learning About Sex: The Contemporary Guide for Young Adults*. Woodbury, N.Y.: Barron's.

Kilgo, R.D. 1975. "Counseling Couples in Groups: Rationale and Methodology." *Family Coordinator* 24, no. 3:337–62.

Knox, D. 1979. *Exploring Marriage and the Family*. Glenview, Ill.: Scott, Foresman.

———. 1972. *Marital Happiness: A Behavioral Approach to Counseling*. Champaign, Ill.: Research Press.

Kolodny, R.C., Masters, W.H., and Johnson, V.E. 1979. *Textbook of Sexual Medicine*. New York: Little, Brown.

L'Abate, L., and McHenry, S. 1983. *Handbook of Marital Interventions.* New York: Grune and Stratton.

Landau, E.D., Egan, M.W., and Rhode, G. 1978. "The Reconstituted Family." *Family Perspective* 12:65–74.

Lasch, C. 1977. *Haven in a Heartless World.* New York: Basic Books.

Lederer, W.J., and Jackson, D.D. 1968. *The Mirages of Marriage.* New York: W.W. Norton.

Lewis, R.A., and Spanier, G.B. 1979. "Theorizing About the Quality and Stability of Marriage." In *Contemporary Theories About the Family.* Vol. 1. Edited by W.R. Burr, R. Hill, F.I. Nye, and I.L. Reiss. New York: Macmillan.

Lidz, T., Cornelison, A., Terry, D., and Fleck, S. 1958. "Intrafamilial Environment of the Schizophrenic Patient." *Archives of Neurology and Psychiatry.*

Lidz, R., and Lidz, T. 1949. "The Family Environment of Schizophrenic Patients." *American Journal of Psychiatry.*

Mace, D.R. 1985. *Getting Ready for Marriage.* Nashville, Tenn.: Abingdon Press.

Mace, D.R. 1952. "The Minister's Role in Marriage Preparation." *Pastoral Psychology* 2:45–48.

Mace, D.R., and Mace, V. 1984. *How to Have a Happy Marriage.* Nashville, Tenn.: Abingdon Press.

———. 1976. *Marriage Enrichment in the Church.* Nashville, Tenn.: Broadman Press.

———. 1974. *We Can Have Better Marriages If We Really Want Them.* Nashville, Tenn.: Abingdon Press.

Marks, S.R. 1986. *Three Corners: Exploring Marriage and the Self.* Lexington, Mass.: Lexington Books.

Martin, D., and Martin, M. 1985. *Families in Transition: Divorce, Remarriage and the Stepfamily.* Salem, Wis.: Sheffield Publishing Co.

Mason, J.M. 1985. "Financial Counseling." In *Counseling: A Guide to Helping Others.* Vol. 2. Edited by R.L. Britsch and T.D. Olson. Salt Lake City, Utah: Deseret Book.

Masters, W.H., Johnson, V.E., and Kolodny, R.C. 1986. *Masters and Johnson on Sex and Human Loving.* Boston: Little, Brown.

Matheson, K.W. 1976. "Education for Premarital Counseling." Unpublished doctoral dissertation, University of Utah.

McCary, J.L. 1978. *Human Sexuality* (3d. ed.). New York: Van Nostrand Reinhold.

McGoldrick, M., and Gerson, R. *Genograms in Family Assessment.* 1985. New York: W.W. Norton.

McRae, B.C. 1975. "A Comparison of a Behavioral and a Lecture/Discussion Approach to Premarital Counseling." Unpublished doctoral dissertation, University of British Columbia.

Meadows, M.E., and Taplin, J.F. 1970. "Premarital Counseling with College Students: A Promising Triad." *Journal of Counseling Psychology* 17:516–18.

Messinger, L. 1976. "Remarriage Between Divorced People With Children From Previous Marriages: A Proposal for Preparation for Remarriage." *Journal of Marriage and Family Counseling* 2, no. 2:193–200.

Miller, S., Nunnally, E.W., and Wackman, D.B. 1975. *Alive and Aware: Improving Communication in Relationships*. Minneapolis: Interpersonal Communication Programs.

Moreno, J.L. 1957. *The First Book on Group Psychotherapy*. New York: Beacon House.

Morrison, E.S., and Price, M.U. 1974. *Values in Sexuality, a New Approach to Sex Education*. New York: Hart.

Mudd, E.H. 1957. "Premarital Counseling." In *Understanding Your Patient*, edited by S. Liebman. Philadelphia: Lippincott.

Neimark, P.G. *A Doctor Discusses Female Surgery*. Chicago: Budlong Press.

Netter, F. 1974. *Illustrated Atlas of Human Reproductive Systems*.

———. 1974. *Reproductive Systems*. New York: Ciba.

Nichols, J.H. 1956. *History of Christianity 1650–1950*. New York: Ronald Press.

Nickols, S.A., Fournier, D.G., and Nickols, S.Y. 1986. "Evaluation of a Preparation for Marriage Workshop." *Family Relations* 36:563–71.

Olsen, M.G. 1975. "Premarriage Counseling: A New Program for Marriage Preparation." Paper presented at the annual meeting of the American Association of Marriage and Family Counselors, Toronto.

Olson, D.H. 1987. *Building a Strong Marriage*. Minneapolis: Prepare-Enrich, Inc.

———. 1983. "How Effective is Marriage Preparation?" In *Prevention in Family Services*, edited by D.G. Mace. Beverly Hills: Sage.

Olson, D.H., ed. 1976. *Treating Relationships*. Lake Mills, Iowa: Graphic.

Olson, D.H., Fournier, D.G., and Druckman, J.M. 1986. *Prepare/Enrich Counselor's Manual*. Minneapolis: Prepare-Enrich, Inc.

———. 1978. "Counselor's Manual: Inventory of Premarital Conflict (IPMC)." University of Minnesota, St. Paul, Family Social Science.

———. 1978. "Counselor's Manual: Premarital Personal and Relationship Evaluation (PREPARE)." *Family Social Science*.

Olson, D.H., and Norem, R. 1977. "Evaluation of Five Premarital Programs." Unpublished report, Department of Family Social Sciences, University of Minnesota.

Paolino, T.J., and McCrady, B.S., eds. 1978. *Marriage and Marital Therapy.* New York: Brunner/Mazel.

Peck, B.B., and Swarts, E. 1975. "The Premarital Impasse." *Family Therapy* 2:1–10.

Penner, C., and Penner, J. 1981. *The Gift of Sex.* Dallas: Word Books.

Pfeiffer, W., Heslin, R., and Jones, J. 1976. *Instrumentation in Human Relation Training* (2nd ed.). San Diego: University Association.

Plumb, J.H. 1971. *The Great Change in Children.* New York: American Heritage.

Ransom, J.W., Schlesinger, S., and Derdeyn, A.P. 1979. "A Step Family in Formation." *American Journal of Orthopsychology* 49, no. 2:46–53.

Rappaport, A.S. 1976. "Conjugal Relationship Enhancement Program." In *Treating Relationships,* edited by D.H. Olson. Lake Mills, Iowa: Graphic.

Richardson, H.B. 1945. *Patients Have Families.* New York: Commonwealth Fund.

Robbins, G., and Tommer, J. 1976. "Innovative Uses of the FIRO-B in Marriage Counseling." *Journal of Marriage and Family Counseling* 3:24–28.

Rolfe, D.J. 1977a. "Premarriage Contracts: An Aid to Couples Living Together with Parents." *Family Coordinator* 26:281–85.

———. 1977b. "Techniques with Premarriage Groups." *British Journal of Guidance and Counseling* 5:89–97.

———. 1976. "Premarriage Assessment of Teenage Couples." *Journal of Family Counseling* 4:32–39.

Ross, J.H. 1977. "The Development and Evaluation of a Group Premarital Counseling Workshop." Unpublished doctoral dissertation, University of Northern Colorado.

Rudin, E. 1916. "Vererbung und Enstehung Geistigen Storungen, I. Zur Vererbung und Neuentstehung der Dementia Praecos." *Monographien aus dem Gesamt-Gabiete der Neurologie und Psychiatrie.* Berlin: Springer.

Rutledge, A.L. 1966. *Premarital Counseling.* Cambridge, Mass.: Schenkman.

Ryan, L.R. 1977. *Clinical Interpretation of the FIRO-B.* Palo Alto, Calif.: Consulting Psychologists Press.

Satir, V. 1972. *Peoplemaking.* Palo Alto, Calif.: Science and Behavior Books.

Schlesinger, B. 1978. "Premarital and Marital Counseling: Implications for the School Guidance Counselor." *School Guidance Worker* 33, no. 5:30–33.

Schonick, H. 1975. "Premarital Counseling: Three Years' Experience of a Unique Service." *Family Coordinator* 24:321–324.

Schumm, W.R., and Denton, W. 1979. "Trends in Premarital Counseling." *Journal of Marital and Family Therapy* 5, no. 4:23–32.

Schutz, W.C. 1976. *The FIRO scales.* Palo Alto, Calif.: Consulting Psychologists Press.

Scoresby, A.L. 1977. *The Marriage Dialogue.* Reading, Mass.: Addison-Wesley.

Sherman, I.C., and Kraines, S.S. 1943. "Environmental and Personality Factors in Psychoses." *Journal of Nervous and Mental Disease.*

Shostrom, E.L. 1976. *Actualizing Therapy.* San Diego, EDITS/Educational and Industrial Testing Service.

Shostrom, E.L. 1966. *Caring Relationship Inventory.* San Diego: EDITS/Educational and Industrial Testing Service.

Simon, S. 1972. *Values Clarification.* New York: Hart.

Simon, S.B. 1974. *Meeting Yourself Halfway.* Niles, Ill.: Argus.

Smith, E.L. 1950. "The Lord's Prayer in Premarital Counseling." *Pastoral Psychology* 1:34–37.

Spencer, M.J., Stahmann, R.F., and Hiebert, W.J. 1977. "Premarital Counseling: Sexuality." In *Klemer's Counseling in Marital and Sexual Problems: A Clinician's Handbook* (2d ed.), edited by R.F. Stahmann and W.J. Hiebert. Baltimore: Williams and Wilkins.

Stahmann, R.F., and Barclay-Cope, A. 1977. "Premarital Counseling: An Overview." In *Klemer's Counseling in Marital and Sexual Problems: A Clinician's Handbook* (2d ed.), edited by R.F. Stahmann and W.J. Hiebert. Baltimore: Williams and Wilkins.

Stahmann, R.F., and Hiebert, W.J., eds. 1984. *Counseling in Marital and Sexual Problems: A Clinician's Handbook* (3d ed.). Lexington, Mass.: Lexington Books.

Stahmann, R.F., and Hiebert, W.J. 1984. "Process and Content in Prewedding Counseling." In *Counseling in Marital and Sexual Problems: A Clinician's Handbook* (3d ed.), edited by R.F. Stahmann and W.J. Hiebert. Lexington, Mass.: Lexington Books.

Stahmann, R.F., and Hiebert, W.J. 1980. *Premarital Counseling.* Lexington, Mass.: Lexington Books.

Stahmann, R.F., and Hiebert, W.J., eds. 1977a. *Klemer's Counseling in Marital and Sexual Problems: A Clinician's Handbook* (2d ed.). Baltimore: Williams and Wilkins.

Stahmann, R.F., and Hiebert, W.J. 1977b. "Premarital Counseling: Process and Content." In *Klemer's Counseling in Marital and Sexual Problems: A Clinician's Handbook* (2d ed.). Baltimore: Williams and Wilkins.

Stewart, C.W. 1970. *The Minister as Marriage Counselor.* Nashville, Tenn.: Abingdon Press.

Stone, A., and Levine, L. 1956. *The Premarital Consultation.* New York: Grune.

Stroup, M.R., Harper, J.M., Steele, W.R., and Hoopes, M.H. 1984. "Helping Stepfamilies Get in Step." In *Structured Family Facilitation Programs,* edited by M.H. Hoopes, B.L. Fisher, and S.H. Barlow. Rockville, MD: Aspen.

Stuart, R.B. 1980. *Helping Couples Change: A Social Learning Approach to Marital Therapy.* New York: The Guilford Press.

Stuart, R.B., and Stuart, F. 1975. *Premarital Counseling Inventory.* Champaign, Ill.: Research Press.

Stuckey, F., Eggeman, K., Eggeman, B.S., Moxley, V., and Schumm, W.R. 1986. "Premarital Counseling as Perceived by Newlywed Couples: An Exploratory Study." *Journal of Sex and Marital Therapy* 12:221–28.

Sullivan, H.S. 1927. "The Onset of Schizophrenia." *American Journal of Psychiatry.*

Taylor, R.M., and Morrison, L.P. 1984. *Taylor-Johnson Temperament Analysis Manual.* Los Angeles: Psychological Publications, Inc.

Thomas, E.J. 1977. *Marital Communication and Decision Making.* New York: Free Press.

Tinque, A. 1958. "The Minister's Role in Marriage Preparation and Premarital Counseling." *Marriage and Family Living* 20:11–16.

Toman, W. 1976. *Family Constellation* (3rd ed.). New York: Springer.

Trainer, J.B. 1979. "Premarital Counseling and Examination." *Journal of Marital and Family Therapy* 5, no. 2:61–78.

Van Zoost, B. 1973. "Premarital Communication Skills Education with University Students." *Family Coordinator* 22:187–91.

Visher, E.B., and Visher, J.S. 1978. "Common Problems of Stepparents and Their Spouses." *American Journal of Orthopsychiatry* 48, no. 2:252–62.

Walker, W. 1959. *A History of the Christian Church.* New York: Charles Scribner's Sons.

Watzlawick, P., Beavin, J.H., and Jackson, D.D. 1967. *Pragmatics of Human Communication.* New York: W.W. Norton.

Whitaker, C.A. 1973. Audiotape (No. 3). Instructional Dynamics, Inc.

Whitaker, C.A., and Keith, D.V. 1977. "Counseling the Desolving Marriage." In *Klemer's Counseling in Marital and Sexual Problems: A Clinician's Handbook* (2d. ed.), edited by R.F. Stahmann and W.J. Hiebert. Baltimore: Williams and Wilkins.

Wiser, W. 1959. "Launching a Program of Premarital Counseling." *Pastoral Psychology* 10:14–17.

Wright, H.N. 1983. *Premarital Counseling.* Chicago: Moody Press.

Index

About the Authors

Robert F. Stahmann is a professor and chairman of the Department of Family Sciences at Brigham Young University. He is a fellow and approved supervisor in the American Association for Marriage and Family Therapy, and a Certified Sex Therapist in the American Association of Sex Educators, Counselors, and Therapists. In addition, he is a member of the American Psychological Association, the National Council on Family Relations, and President-elect of the Utah Council on Family Relations. Dr. Stahmann is author of numerous professional articles and reviews.

William J. Hiebert is director of educational services at the Marriage and Family Counseling Service in Rock Island, Illinois, and an adjunct professor of pastoral theology at the University of Dubuque Theological Seminary. An approved supervisor and fellow in the American Association for Marriage and Family Therapy, he is also past president of the Illinois Association for Marriage and Family Counselors. He is a former editor-in-chief of *Family Therapy News* and is co-editor, with Dr. Stahmann, of *Counseling in Marital and Sexual Problems: A Clinician's Handbook*.